DICKSONIA

Rare Plants Manual

STEPHEN RYAN

Illustrations by Craig Lidgerwood

Cantua buxifolia

HYLAND HOUSE PUBLISHING

First published in Australia in 2008 by
Hyland House Publishing Pty Ltd
PO Box 122
Flemington, Victoria 3031

National Library of Australia Cataloguing-in-publication entry

Author: Ryan, Stephen Godfrey.
Title: Dicksonia rare plants manual / Stephen Ryan.
ISBN: 9781864471113 (hbk.)
Subjects: Ferns.
Ferns – Identification.
Dewey Number: 635.9373

Edited by Jeannie Campbell
Layout and design by Rob Cowpe Design
Printed by Everbest, China

Contents

Botanical names
Botanical names have been verified as far as is possible. Sometimes the most recent publication does not necessarily have the most recently established name.

Measurements
The ultimate maximum size of any plant will depend on a number of factors, including soil, span of hours of sunlight, orientation, atmospheric humidity, water and nutrients.
The sizes given in this manual are for plants grown under average to good conditions and will obviously vary for each; so will the size of leaves and flowers.

My other books
Throughout this manual, I refer to 'my first book' and 'my second book'. These are, respectively, *Exceptional Plants* and *More Exceptional Plants* – see the back jacket flap of this book.

Preface

This book started life (many more years back than I like to think about) as a humble nursery catalogue and in many ways still functions as one. It is, after all, a list of plants that can be obtained from Dicksonia Rare Plants at Mt Macedon in their proper seasons (and when crop failures don't happen). It has, however, taken on something of a life of its own.

When I realised that the number of entries was going to exceed 2000, and that it was going to become unwieldy as a stapled piece of ephemera, I had to sit back and work out how to deal with it in a different way.

Thus it has been reborn as a manual which basically means that a complete rewrite was needed as in most cases a lot of additional information on each plant was required to make it a useful reference work for collectors and home gardeners alike. After all, just saying it grows to 2 metres and has white flowers isn't enough to satisfy those doing some research, but may well have been enough to sell the plant to those already in the know and only looking for a source of the plant they wish to purchase.

To my knowledge, this is the first time in Australia that such an enterprise has been attempted, and I do hope that all my customers and anyone else in possession of a copy will find it a useful, opinionated and entertaining read. Those that have read my two previous books will know how opinionated I can get, and I at least find my humour entertaining!

Finally, I would like to thank those that have had the faith in this project that was needed to bring it off.

Firstly, my partner Craig for his stunning botanical art that I'm sure you will all agree gives this book a special look. I also have to thank Jeannie Campbell for editing the manuscript. (I must also point out that any inaccuracies will be my fault!) She has been thorough and enthusiastic about the project from the moment I mentioned it to her. I must also thank my publisher Michael Schoo from Hyland House for having the faith in the project to even go as far as to suggest a hard cover with dust jacket which I'm sure you will all agree makes any book a pleasure to hold and to own.

Stephen Ryan,
2008

Trees and Shrubs

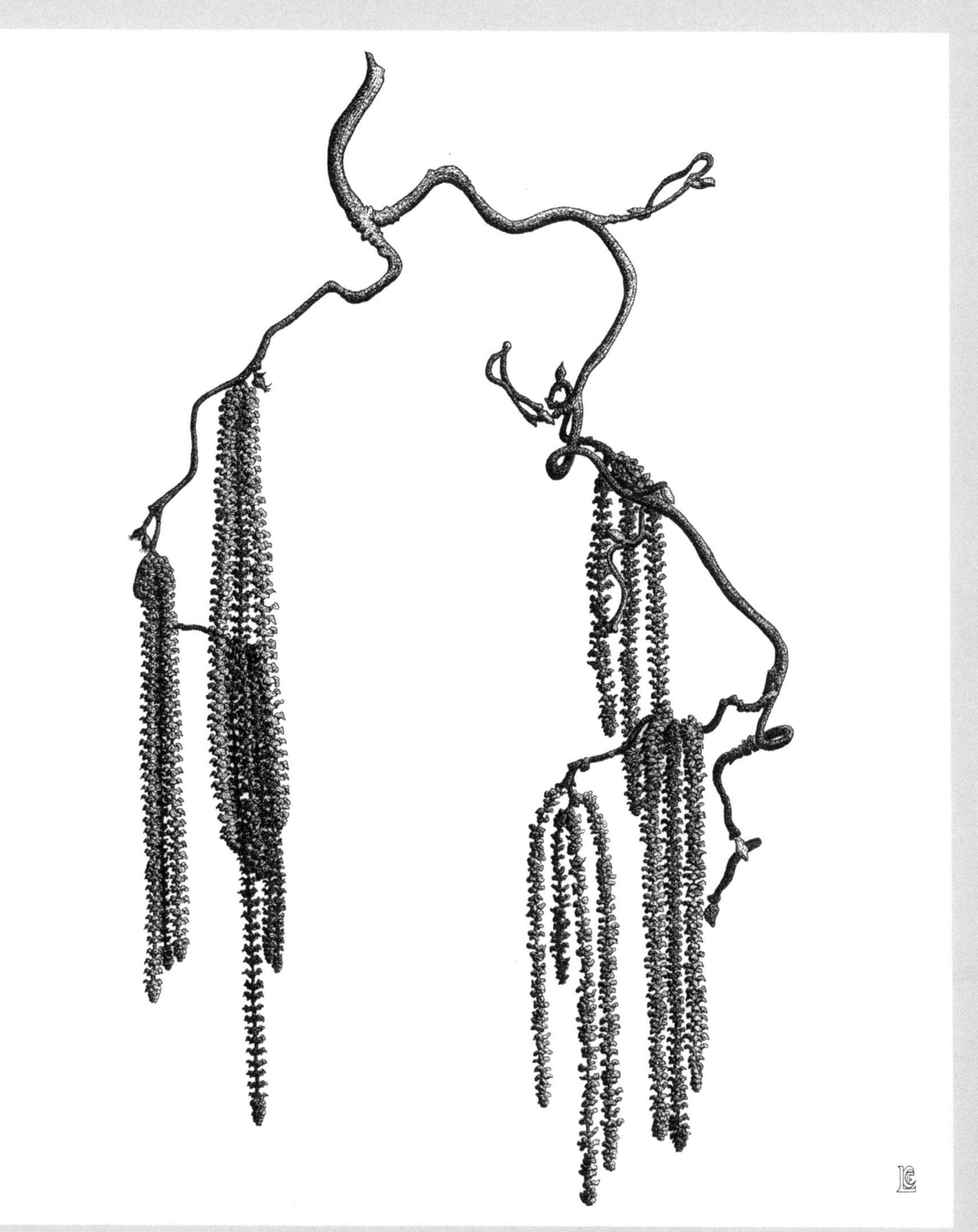

Corylus avellana 'Contorta'

Abelia floribunda

A very hardy evergreen arching shrub to 2 metres, from Mexico, that likes it sunny. It has long tubular cherry-pink flowers in late spring and early summer set off by its glossy foliage. A good gap filler or wall shrub, where it can be trained up to 3 metres or even more. The most spectacular species in the genus. It features in my first book *Exceptional Plants*, so it must be good!

A. triflora A charming if subtle, arching (more or less), evergreen shrub to 3 metres from the Himalayas. It produces highly scented tubular white flowers in summer with attractive furry calyx lobes. This is an underused shrub so don't continue the tradition. It will grow almost anywhere as one would expect from an Abelia.

Abeliophyllum distichum

A deciduous, arching shrub to 2 metres from Korea. It has white scented Forsythia-like flowers in late winter, from almost black flower buds. It will grow well in sun or semi-shade and is a charming cut flower.

***A. d.* 'Roseum'** One of my own importations that differs only in having soft pink flowers. This is for the Barbara Cartland types amongst you.

Abutilon 'Goblin'

A hardy, arching, evergreen shrub to 2 metres that makes a lovely espalier or standard. It produces its drooping flowers all year round and these consist of red petals and an inflated red calyx. This whole genus will attract lots of honeyeaters, as many as any Grevillea!

A. 'Halo' Similar to the above but has larger flowers with a coppery calyx and soft apricot petals.

A. megapotamicum Hardy evergreen arching shrub from Brazil that is best trained as a climber. Masses of red and yellow Chinese lantern-like flowers most of the year. Unsupported, will grow 1 metre tall but much wider.

***A. m.* 'Variegatum'** This form differs from the above in having leaves boldly mottled with yellow just to add to the show, which almost seems overkill!

A. 'Milleri' This lovely hybrid has the same sized flowers as *A.* 'Goblin' but with rich apricot petals and a red calyx.

A. 'Souvenir de Bonn' This is an upright and bushy form to 1.5 metres with boldly white-edged leaves that are the main feature of this cultivar even though it has lovely, and quite large, soft orange drooping lanterns. Although it will grow almost anywhere, its bold foliage will light up the shade.

Acanthus pubescens

A rare, shrubby plant in a normally herbaceous genus from Central Africa. It has tall, sparsely-branched stems to 3 metres that will form a suckering clump. The shiny, large, evergreen holly-like leaves cluster towards the tips of the branches and at the very tip it produces spikes of deep pink flowers in summer that give away its relationship to the better-known species. Likes a sunny to semi-shaded site, is fairly drought-tolerant but frost-tender in really cold areas where it could even become herbaceous.

Acer campestre (Field Maple)

A 'tough-as-they-come' maple from Europe and western Asia that will make a picturesque rounded crown to 10 metres or so making it a good choice as a lawn specimen in moderate to smallish gardens. The leaves are mid-green turning a good clear yellow in autumn with rather rounded lobes.

***A. capillipes* (Snake Barked Maple)** A small spreading deciduous tree to 6 metres or so from Japan with green and white-striped trunks, red twigs and shallowly lobed lanceolate leaves that turn brilliantly in autumn. This is, in my humble opinion, one of the loveliest of its group.

***A. cappadocicum* 'Aureum'** A medium tree to 10 metres with large bright yellow leaves that have burgundy tips in spring fading later to straight yellow. In autumn its leaves turn a rich luminous yellow.

A.'Esk Flamingo' This hybrid of uncertain parentage was raised in New Zealand by Peter Cave and is of the snake bark group and has bright pink twigs that in time develop green and white-striped bark. The leaves are spearhead-shaped with mottled pink and white variegation that turn all sorts of colours in autumn. Will probably reach 4 metres or more and has a quite pendulous form.

***A. griseum* (Paperbark Maple)** Magnificent small tree to 8 metres from China with brilliant red autumn foliage and peeling cinnamon-coloured bark. Very rare and hard to propagate, yet fairly hardy and heat-tolerant for a maple. A must in every connoisseur's garden as long as we don't end up with too many connoisseurs!

***A. japonicum* 'Aconitifolium'** A small spreading open-framed tree to 5 metres with large deeply cut leaves, brilliant orange and scarlet in autumn. One of the most elegant of maples and, like most forms of this species, a good doer.

***A. j.* 'Fairy Lights'** This charming dwarf selection was made by Yamina Rare Plants in Victoria's Dandenong Ranges. It makes an elegantly layered shrub to 1 metre with exceedingly finely cut green foliage that turns brilliantly in autumn. Fabulous as a tub specimen or instant bonsai.

***A. j.* 'Green Cascade'** A horizontal form with deeply cut leaves and good autumn colour. Available on standards of 1 to 1.5 metres it will spread up to 3 metres across so allow it oodles of room, as a butchered specimen is a nightmare. Would be ideal with its branches sweeping out over a pond.

***A. j.* 'Vitifolium'** This bold and beautiful form is a small spreading tree to 7 metres with almost Liquidambar-sized, mid-green leaves with 10 to 12 lobes. Brilliant autumnal colour.

A. laxiflorum A rarely seen tree to 10 metres with a fan-shaped habit, from China. It has green and white streaked bark and its long tapered leaves turn rich autumn colours.

***A. macrophyllum* (Oregon Maple)** This maple has the largest leaves of all species up to 30 cm across and somewhat Liquidambar-shaped. A lovely soft green in summer, then bright orange and yellow in autumn. This is a large spreading tree of 15 metres or more.

***A. palmatum* 'Aureum'** This old form has the classic fan-shaped habit that one would expect of a maple to 5 metres or so with soft yellow foliage in spring that greens somewhat in summer and then turns soft yellows again in autumn.

***A. p.* 'Bloodgood'** A fan-shaped small tree to 7 metres with rich burgundy leaves right from spring to autumn when it turns bright scarlet. Probably the best burgundy maple as it doesn't fade brownish-green in the summer as many others do. It also produces drooping clusters of red-winged seeds to boot!

***A. p. dissectum* 'Atropurpureum'** A weeping form usually available on 1 to 2 metres standards as are all my Dissectum maples. This one has very fine foliage that starts burgundy in spring, turns green in summer and finally goes yellow and orange in autumn.

***A. p. d.* 'Beni Shidare Variegated'** Attractive fine-leafed weeping form with bronze-green foliage splashed with pink and white variegation during spring and summer. The foliage turns gold in autumn.

***A. p. d.* 'Crimson Queen'** A form with very persistent burgundy-coloured foliage through summer, turning scarlet in autumn.

***A. p. d.* 'Ever Red'** A form with deep burgundy foliage through spring and summer, turning scarlet in autumn.

***A. p. d.* 'Filigree'** A form with fine green foliage with cream veins in spring, and turning bright gold in autumn.

***A. p. d.* 'Garnet'** A rich garnet-red form with a particularly strong growth habit.

***A. p. d.* 'Inaba Shidare'** This form has rich burgundy foliage from spring until autumn when it turns brilliant red. Its main point of difference with other similar coloured forms is that in time it will build up quite a bit of height above its graft.

***A. p. d.* 'Orangeola'** This remarkable form (with a slightly silly name) has finely cut leaves that start bronze in spring, turn greenish in summer and then bright orange in autumn. Its main claim to fame however is the fact that the branches cascade almost straight down so it takes up far less space than most selections.

***A. p. d.* 'Red Filigree Lace'** A form with such fine deep burgundy foliage that it looks skeletal. This is probably one of the slowest growing forms which, for some people, also makes it one of the most desirable.

***A. p. d.* 'Seiryu'** A small upright tree to 7 metres with very finely cut leaves, turning bright scarlet in autumn. This is the only upright Dissectum and is surprisingly hardy to sun and wind unless you live in the Little Desert! As it isn't a weeper, it isn't grafted onto standards as the others in this group are.

***A. p. d.* 'Viridis'** A lovely, soft-green-leafed weeper, that turns bright orange yellow in autumn. This is probably a name encompassing almost any green weeping form and as such should probably not have the cultivar name of 'Viridis' but as everyone seems to use it, what am I to do?

***A. p. d.* 'Waterfall'** A very pendulous green-leafed form with rich orange and yellow autumn foliage.

***A. p.* 'Fjellheim'** This is a witches' broom of *A. p.* 'Sango kaku' so is a smaller plant to 3 metres or so, with the same red stems but more of them, and the same soft green leaves that turn yellow in autumn. This form is thus a good subject for a tub or smaller garden space.

***A. p.* 'Herbstfeuer'** This large-leafed and vigorous form may be a hybrid with *A. circinatum* and grows into a small spreading tree to 7 metres with rich green foliage that turns brilliant scarlet in autumn. Its German name means 'autumn fire'.

***A. p.* 'Horizontalis'** This unusual form is normally grafted onto standards and has classical green Japanese maple leaves that turn brilliantly in autumn. Its claim to fame is that its branches grow almost flat making a large open umbrella-shape. Good next to a pond or in a tub. This cultivar name doesn't appear in any reference books I have and so could be wrong or even an unregistered Australian selection.

***A. p.* 'Ichigyo-ji'** This form has good-sized leaves of a rich green in summer turning yellow and gold in autumn making it a good companion to *A. p.* 'Osakazuki' which looks similar until it turns brilliant red.

***A. p.* 'Kagiri Nishiki' (syn. *A. p.* 'Roseo-Marginatum')** A charming small upright tree to 3 metres with typical Japanese Maple-shaped leaves attractively margined with pink-white. Its autumn colour is usually orange with pink edges.

***A. p.* 'Kashima'** This form has typical Japanese Maple foliage that is however smaller than usual on a slow-growing, spreading bush that isn't likely to exceed 1.5 metres in the lifetime of most people! It in fact looks like a large bonsai and is ideal in tubs or as a centre-piece in a semi-shaded rock garden.

***A. p.* 'Lutescens'** This cultivar makes a small spreading tree to 3 metres or so with soft yellow foliage in spring that turns green in summer and bright yellow in autumn.

***A. p.* 'Okushimo'** This interesting clone has a quite narrow habit to 7 metres tall by about 1 metre wide with tiny green leaves that have rolled-in edges that give the foliage an interesting three dimensional quality. Can colour richly in autumn.

***A. p.* 'Omurayama'** This distinct form of Japanese Maple is usually grafted onto 1.5 metre standards. It produces stems that weep over as well as ascending slightly so that it will build up into a small weeping tree. The foliage is deeply divided and soft green in spring turning scarlet in autumn.

***A. p.* 'Osakazuki'** This cultivar has comparatively large bright green leaves and turns one of the most brilliant reds imaginable in autumn. It is also a lovely small fan-shaped tree that will grow to about 7 metres.

***A. p.* 'Red Pygmy'** Dwarf upright fan-shaped maple to 2 metres with fine finger-type leaf lobes, burgundy in spring, greening somewhat in summer and turning orange in autumn.

***A. p.* 'Sango Kaku' (Coral Stemmed Maple)** A small fan-shaped tree to 7 metres with pale green leaves turning light yellow in autumn and coral-red twigs during the winter.

***A. p.* 'Shaina'** This form arose as a witches' broom (apparently on *A. p.* 'Bloodgood') and probably won't grow more than 1.5 metres. It has rich burgundy foliage that can turn brilliant scarlet in autumn. This form would be good as a tub or rock garden subject. I also have it grafted on standards that would look a whole lot better outside your neo-Georgian than the usual standards!

***A. p.* 'Shindeshojo'** This cultivar makes a spreading shrub to 3 metres that in spring has bright cherry-red foliage that fades greenish in summer, then turns orange and yellow in autumn. Ideal in areas where autumn colour is unreliable as the spring tones are stunning and will develop anywhere a maple will grow.

***A. p.* 'Shishi Gashira'** Dense bushy upright dwarf to 2 metres with bright green, parsley-crinkled leaves; the poodle of the maple world. It turns bright orange-red in autumn.

***A. p.* 'Trompenburg'** A lovely deep burgundy form of Japanese Maple with fine finger-type lobes that roll under at the edges. It will turn rich deep reds in autumn and has an upright habit to about 5 metres.

***A. p.* 'Villa Taranto'** A charming dwarf maple to 2 metres is similar to *A. p.* 'Red Pigmy' but the foliage in spring is bronze-coloured, going green in summer and turning gold in autumn.

A. pentaphyllum Fine finger-type leaflets giving a bamboo-like effect, this fast-growing medium tree with a vase-shaped habit to 7 metres is one of the rarest species in the wild state, and the least maple-like of trees. If you don't believe me, look in my first book.

***A. platanoides* 'Crimson King' (Purple Norway Maple)** A hardy medium to large deciduous tree to 10 metres with large, rich, deep purple leaves from spring till autumn, and clusters of tiny yellow flowers as the leaves unfold.

***A. p.* 'Crimson Sentry'** This newer selection has foliage just like the above but grows as a quite narrow, almost pencil-type tree, so is ideal for the space-challenged!

***A. p.* 'Drummondii'** A lovely form of Norway maple with white-edged green leaves, that will grow to 10 metres.

***A. p.* 'Laciniatum' (Eagles Claw Maple)** This strangely attractive form makes an upright narrow vase-shaped tree to 8 metres with drooping cut leaves with lobes that end in curved claws. A striking cultivar rarely offered in Australia.

***A. p.* 'Lorbergii'** A most unusual form to 10 metres with heavily cut foliage. The tips of the lobes tend to stick up making it very sculptural.

***A. pseudoplatanus* 'Prinz Handjery'** A strange and slow-growing form of Sycamore that will eventually grow to 5 metres or so. Its large leaves start out in spring a creamy-pink that fades to a whitish-green and then to green with a purple reverse. In autumn it will often turn a respectable shade of apricot.

***A. shirasawanum* 'Aureum' (Golden Half Moon Maple)** This lovely form has long been grown incorrectly as *A. japonicum* 'Aureum'. It makes a slow-growing shrub or small tree if you live long enough! The leaves are comparatively large and a soft yellow, from spring till autumn, when they turn yellow and orange. A great tub specimen for a sheltered site.

A. sikkimense This is a striking species from the Himalayas, long grown as *A. hookeri*. It is an upright vase-shaped tree to 7 metres or so with large spearhead-shaped leaves that start ruby-red in spring, turn green then red, orange and yellow in late autumn. The bark is handsomely striped with white.

Acradenia frankliniae

Evergreen Tasmanian shrub to 3 metres with attractive deep green foliage and clusters of small pure white flowers in late spring; shade-tolerant and reasonably drought proof once established.

Aesculus californica (Californian Buckeye)

A spreading, small deciduous tree to 6 metres each way, with large compound leaves and candles of white scented flowers in summer. The bark is silvery and will entertain you throughout winter. Sun-loving and drought-tolerant to the extent that in extra dry weather it will shed its leaves.

***A. × carnea* (Red Horse Chestnut)** Large-growing deciduous tree to 13 metres or so with handsome foliage and spikes of deep pink flowers in spring, followed by its large glossy conkers which may be a mixed blessing.

A. × c. 'Briotii' A smaller-growing form with extra deep pink flowers. This is the most appropriate Horse Chestnut for smaller gardens if you are one of those that worry about how big a tree will be in 50 years!

***A. hippocastanum* (Common Horse Chestnut)** A truly impressive large deciduous tree to 20 metres or so with candles of white flowers blotched with yellow in spring.These are followed by the large, rich brown nuts used by English children to make 'conkers'.The huge handsome leaves turn yellow in autumn.

***A. indica* (Indian Horse Chestnut)** A majestic tree to 15 metres or more with large light green leaves and candles of white-flushed pink flowers in late spring. The foliage is attractively bronze-tinged when young. Produces the classic large seeds just like the European species.

***A. × neglecta* 'Erythroblastos'** This remarkable small tree to 7 metres or so has hand-shaped leaves that start a brilliant coppery-pink and turn slowly to a soft pale green later in the season. It has soft yellow flowers in upright spikes in early summer just to gild the lily!

***A. parvifolia* (Bottlebrush Buckeye)** A truly remarkable, but rarely seen, suckering deciduous shrub – to 3 metres tall by at least as wide. It has large hand-shaped leaves, as one would expect of this genus, and spikes of white flowers with long red anthers in slender panicles in summer followed by rich yellow autumn leaves. It is native to south-eastern parts of the U.S.A. Should grow well if sheltered from hot summer winds and given some half-reasonable soil.

Aetoxicon punctatum

This rare Chilean tree makes an upright evergreen specimen to 10 metres or more and is grown for its habit and its rich green foliage that starts out a lovely coppery colour. It produces small yellow flowers followed by black berries. It prefers a moist soil in a cool sheltered site.

Agapetes buxifolia

A bushy arching evergreen shrub to 60 cm from Bhutan with bright green leaves and slightly flared drooping red flowers tipped with a fine green edge followed by white berries spotted with purple.All Agapetes like a cool aspect with acid soil and grow well in tubs and hanging baskets.

A. flava A rare form that makes an open lax shrub to 60 cm with comparatively large heavily-veined leaves that are copper when young. It produces yellow waxy trumpets with a reddish calyx.

A.'Ludgvans Hybrid' Evergreen arching shrub to 1 metre with attractive bronze new growth and pink pendulous trumpet flowers with red horizontal stripes.

A. meiniana Species from Queensland that can be a climber or trailer. I have one that for years has grown in a 1-metre length of tree fern, and another in the ground that is 7 metres up a gum tree. Brilliant, deep cerise-pink flowers in spring, and bright salmon-red new growth.

A. moorei An upright shrub to 2 metres with quite large foliage by the standards of this genus that start out coppery-pink then green, and its red flowers are formed in clusters and are flared out (this also being an unusual character in this group).

A. serpens Western Chinese species with small leaves and red flowers with darker bands and brightly coloured new growth. This species has long arching branches and is a good basket subject or can be trained as a lovely weeping standard. Free standing, it usually grows to about 2 metres.

A. 'Red Elf' A bushy, slightly arching shrub up to 1 metre with green-tipped red flowers in spring and summer, followed by quite large white berries dotted with red. This isn't the true name as this is probably a species but it will all be revealed in the end. It is certainly worth growing in the meantime.

A. smithiana This species is much like *A. serpens* but with even more arching stems so that it can't support itself. Grow it as a climber or trail it over a wall or out of a basket. It has small bright green leaves and bright yellow trumpets.

Alangium platanifolium

Handsome, large deciduous shrub to 5 metres or so, with large maple-like leaves and pendulous white flowers in summer. The petals curl back as the flowers open like little springs. This East Asian prefers a spot sheltered from hot winds, and an acid soil.

***Albizia julibrissin* (Pink Siris or Silk Tree)**
Hardy, extremely quick-growing small deciduous tree to 7 metres tall, with as wide a spread, from Asia to the Middle East. Soft, feathery, rich green foliage and masses of fluffy pink flowers in summer. Ideal specimen tree for small gardens, it loves an open, sunny well-drained site. This tree usually has a short but merry life, rarely lasting past its 21st birthday!

Alniphyllum fortunei
Rare Chinese deciduous conical-shaped tree to 7 metres. Richly coloured autumn foliage and clusters of white to pale pink bell-shaped flowers in outward-facing spikes in spring. Give it a spot sheltered from strong winds much like one would for a Rhododendron. (Perhaps even replace a Rhododendron with an Alniphyllum!)

***Alnus glutinosa* 'Imperialis' (Cut Leafed Alder)**
Good cut-leafed form to 10 metres with a birch-like habit. The main trunk usually has a slight lean making this a picturesque and elegant tree nothing like its notorious evergreen relative. Like the rest of the genus it is fast-growing and is happy in moist to wet soil.
***A. g.* 'Laciniata'** Similar to *A. g.* 'Imperialis' but with larger leaves that are not so deeply lobed. This form doesn't usually lean (so is better for anal gardeners).
***A. incana* 'Aurea'** This forms an upright deciduous tree to 8 metres and has rounded pale yellow leaves and lovely red-tinted catkins in late winter. The stems also have an orange colour in winter, which is most effective.

***Amelanchier canadensis* (Shad Bush)**
Deciduous multi-stemmed shrub to 5 metres with masses of pure white flowers in spring and brilliant orange to red autumn leaves. It also produces edible red berries that turn black with age.
A. laevis A more tree-like species to 6 metres, otherwise similar in flower, fruit and foliage.

***Anopterus glandulosus* (Tasmanian Mountain Laurel)**
Handsome, evergreen native shrub that grows slowly to 2 metres for a cool aspect. Spikes of white flowers in the spring, and very attractive, deep glossy green foliage. If you have a copy of my first book you will already know all about it!
***A. g.* 'Woodbank Pink'** A lovely form with soft pink flowers and burgundy flower and growth buds. You can tell this form even out of bloom by these buds.

***Aralia elata* (Japanese Angelica Tree)**
This handsome Japanese plant is usually seen as a sparsely-branched suckering shrub or small tree to 5 metres or so. Its huge compound leaves are gathered at the tops of the stems into a giant ruff. It produces large heads of tiny white flowers in summer followed by small black berries and good autumn foliage colour. It will grow in sun or shade.
***A. e.* 'Silver Umbrella'** A rare form with striking white-edged leaves that is difficult to obtain due to it being hard to graft. It is, however, worth spending hundreds of dollars (as you may well have to!) to get one.

Arbutus × andrachnoides
A hybrid strawberry tree to 10 metres with remarkable cinnamon-red bark, rich dark evergreen foliage and white flowers, rather like Lily-of-the-Valley, in autumn and winter. Its red-orange fruit are rarely produced. Like all of the following species this will grow well in full sun to part shade, will cope well with cold and drought and should be in every garden, however this would make them common, so, on the other hand …!
***A. canariensis* (Canary Islands Strawberry Tree)** A hardy, vigorous species to 13 metres with quite large, rich green foliage, white flowers and extra large orange-red fruit. The bark is deep rich brown and flakes to show light green patches. Native of the Canary Islands.

A. glandulosa **(Mexican Strawberry Tree)** A beautiful evergreen small tree to 7 metres with grey-green foliage and bark that is a mixture of rich orange-brown when mature which, when peeling off in large sheets, exposes green-white underbark. Flowers and fruit are similar to other species. This species is rarely offered in Australia but features in my first book, and it even has pride of place on the back cover as it's so impressive!

A. menziesii **(Madrona)** A very rare species from California with magnificent, smooth red-brown bark that peels off in sheets to expose the green underbark in summer. Its white flowers are followed by small, bright red fruit. It could eventually grow to 20 metres tall. This species needs to stay quite dry in summer once established. One of the world's truly spectacular bark-producing trees, but I only have it once in a while and you will pay for the privilege of owning one.

Arctostaphylos arbutoides

A hardy, evergreen shrub from southern North America, to 3 metres. It has leathery, rich green foliage and clusters of green-white flowers, similar to those of Lily-of-the-Valley, followed by black fruit. Once established, it is very drought-tolerant and with age will exhibit shaggy bronze bark.

A. manzanita **'St Helena'** This selection makes a grey-leafed free form evergreen shrub to 1.5 metres tall and has stunning copper bark and clusters of pretty little pale pink flowers of the usual shape in spring. Like most in this underused genus it is quite drought-tolerant.

A. uva-ursi **'Woods Red'** A trailing evergreen shrub to 15 cm tall and 1 metre or more across with rich deep green foliage. It produces clusters of urn-shaped pink flowers in spring followed by red berries. Makes a good ground cover in sun or semi-shade and a tea can be made from the leaves to flush your kidneys!

Argyrocytisus battandieri syn. *Cytisus battandieri* (Moroccan Broom)

A very hardy, quick-growing shrub to 5 metres or so with silky silvery foliage and tight clusters of yellow flowers with an apple fragrance. It prefers a sunny and well-drained aspect and can be pruned hard or grown as a wall shrub. Features in my first book. (Haven't you got a copy yet!)

Aristotelia chilensis (Chilean Wine Berry, Macqui)

Small evergreen tree to 7 metres that makes a good screen with rich green leaves some of which turn red in winter. Masses of tiny green flowers in spring are followed by small edible berries that must be an acquired taste. This tree will grow well in sun or light shade and is drought-tolerant to boot.

A. fruticosa **(Mountain Wine Berry)** A charming, evergreen, narrow growing shrub to 3 metres or so native to New Zealand. Its tiny bronze-tinged leaves set off its minute white flowers followed by white, pink-tinged berries in the form I grow.

A. serrata **(New Zealand Wine Berry)** Attractive evergreen tree with large serrated leaves that are green on the top and burgundy beneath. Clusters of small, deep rose-coloured flowers in spring followed by black berries. It grows quickly to about 7 metres and is a good, light, screening plant to hide that block of flats next door.

Aronia arbutifolia (Red Chokeberry)

Hardy deciduous shrub from North America with white flowers in spring followed by deep red, edible berries. Foliage is brilliant red in autumn. In fact, this and the following species are up there in my list of best autumn-coloured shrubs. Grows to about 3 metres and suckers slightly. Give it a sunny site that isn't too dry.

A. melanocarpa **(Black Chokeberry)** Similar to the above but with black berries and orange-coloured autumn foliage and not quite as tall, growing usually up to 2 metres.

Asimina triloba (North American Pawpaw)

A North American small deciduous tree to 7 metres or so, that is not related to the tropical Pawpaw. It has quite large drooping leaves that turn yellow in autumn, strange dark purple flowers in spring and bottle-shaped edible fruit. A sunny sheltered site with moist but well-drained soil.

Atherosperma moschatum (Southern Sassafras)

A striking, upright, evergreen native tree to 7 metres. It has dark green nutmeg-scented foliage and small white fragrant flowers in winter. It prefers a cool moist aspect.

Aucuba japonica 'Crotonifolia' (Japanese Stardust Laurel)

An almost indestructible evergreen shrub with large glossy leaves splotched and spotted with yellow that is sure to light up those dark and dry corners that all Aucubas handle with great aplomb. It will grow to about 2 metres and, if it has a boyfriend, will produce lots of scrumptious-looking red berries.

***A. j.* 'Longifolia'** I imported this form from Heronswood nursery in the U.S.A. and it is supposed to be a female form. It has long narrow straight green leaves quite unlike the better-known forms and is ideal for the gardener that is nervous and scared of the variegated forms.

***A. j.* 'Picturata'** For the truly fearless this form has brilliant yellow leaves with an uneven deep green edge. It won't light up a shaded corner it will ignite it. (Go on, you know you want to!) I believe this form comes as both male and female forms and, as I didn't get it in either a pink or a blue pot, I'm not sure which it is!

***A. j.* 'Sulphurea Marginata'** This female form has yellow margins to the leaves instead of the hectic blotching so may well be the choice of the timid gardener. It does need high levels of light as the foliage tends to fade to green in heavy shade.

***A. j.* 'Rozannie'** For the truly terrified, this form, which is also female, has straight glossy green leaves so has done away with that vulgar variegation altogether. Some authorities list this one as a hermaphrodite but I'm still not convinced about its sexuality.

Azara celestrina

A graceful, evergreen, fan-shaped small tree to 7 metres with very glossy, deep green leaves and clusters of gold stamens with an attractive scent in autumn. Like the rest of this genus it comes from Chile and will grow in most aspects.

A. integrifolia This handsome species has a lovely arching habit and can grow to 7 metres each way. Its yellow, perfumed flowers are produced in autumn.

***A. i.* 'Variegata'** A large evergreen shrub with handsome, gold, variegated leaves that become burgundy-tinted in winter. It has a somewhat arching to weeping habit. Rarely exceeds 3 metres. This one made it into my first book so look it up for more information.

A. lanceolata Small, fan-shaped tree to 7 metres with narrow glossy leaves and masses of yellow wattle-like flowers in spring. This one has virtually no scent but the flowers are showy.

A. microphylla Tiny dark green leaves and cream flowers with a very strong vanilla fragrance in early spring on a small, upright, elegant evergreen tree to 8 metres. One of my all-time favourite scented trees.

***A. m.* 'Variegata'** A lovely but slow-growing form that is unlikely to exceed 3 metres in a lifetime. It has beautiful tiny leaves heavily edged in creamy white and the same stunningly perfumed almost invisible flowers.

A. petiolaris This species has comparatively large deep green leaves and yellow-scented flowers and differs from the rest in having quite pendulous branches on its 3-metre frame.

A. serrata Similar to *A. lanceolata* with rounded leaves. This short description doesn't mean it's not a good thing!

Berberis chitria

This large arching evergreen shrub from the Himalayas is, sadly, rarely grown in Australia. It has for this genus quite large oblong leaves and the new stems are red. The flower clusters are also quite large, and the usual yellow shade is then followed by conspicuous, dark red bloomy berries. Hardy in sun or semi-shade and grows to about 3 metres.

B. darwinii Evergreen shrub to 3 metres from South America with small dark holly-like leaves and masses of bright yellow-orange flowers in late winter and spring followed by blue-black berries. It makes a good impenetrable hedge and will grow in most aspects and in cool climates; it is known to be spread by birds.

***B. julianae* 'Spring Glory'** This stunning arching evergreen shrub to 2 metres is one of my importations and has narrow deep green leaves that start out ruby-red. It has clusters of soft yellow flowers in spring and impressive long green thorns.

B. koreana Hardy deciduous thorny shrub to 2 metres from Korea that will make suckering colonies. Small yellow flowers in drooping spikes followed in autumn by coral-red berries. The quite large leaves colour brilliantly in autumn.

***B. × ottawensis* 'Silver Miles'** This deciduous form has almost black foliage that is irregularly blotched with silvery-grey. It also colours brilliantly in autumn and will make a 2-metre tall shrub. At the risk of being thought immodest I think it one of my best imports. As I didn't breed it, it probably is immodest!

***B. × o.* 'Superba'** This is possibly the best deep burgundy-leafed deciduous berberis that will grow to almost 2.5 metres tall with largish leaves of a rich colour turning glowing scarlet in autumn.

***B. stenophylla* 'Corallina Compacta'** A lovely dwarf evergreen shrub to 30 cm with small deep green leaves and clusters of tangerine flowers in spring. This form suckers lightly and is a good hardy rock garden shrub.

***B. thunbergii* 'Atropurpurea Nana'** Dwarf deciduous shrub to 30 cm with pale yellow flowers in spring and deep burgundy foliage from spring to autumn, when it turns bright scarlet before shedding. Good rock garden specimen.

***B. t.* 'Aurea'** A lovely form to 1 metre with bright yellow leaves that turn apricot-orange in autumn. It has the same pale yellow flowers and red fruit of the wild species and may scorch in the hottest sites, like many golden-leafed plants do.

***B. t.* 'Gold Ring'** This form has deep burgundy leaves edged with gold–green, a subtle but interesting look. It has brilliant autumn foliage and grows to 2 metres.

***B. t.* 'Helmond Pillar'** A rather bizarre narrow-growing form, to 2 metres tall with classic purple foliage. An ideal vertical accent shrub for tubs or rock gardens that isn't a conifer. It may need tying in with fishing line to keep it neat.

***B. t.* 'Rose Glow'** An unusual form with burgundy foliage and new growth that is marbled with pink and white variegation. Grows to 2 metres or so and turns rich red and deep pink in autumn.

B. wilsoniae Hardy deciduous shrub to 2 metres from China. The pale yellow flowers are followed by beautiful coral-pink to red berries in autumn. Spectacular autumn foliage and vicious child-proof thorns.

Betula albosinensis var. *septentrionalis* (Chinese Birch)

A lovely tree to 10 metres with shining bronze-pink, grey and white bark that sheds in large papery sheets. The leaves are larger than the usual silver birch and the tree is more upright. A truly lovely species that deserves to be used more.

***B. maximowicziana* (Monarch Birch)** An impressive birch native to Japan that can reach 30 metres tall. It possesses the largest leaves in the genus, being up to 12 cm long and more like a hazelnut's foliage than a birch's. The leaves turn clear butter-yellow in autumn. It also gets extra long catkins and the bark is an attractive grey.

***B. nana* (Dwarf Birch)** A dainty dwarf deciduous shrub from northern Europe with tiny round green leaves. Ideal for rock gardens and bonsai, it rarely exceeds 30 cm in height.

***B. nigra* (River Birch)** A very attractive North American species with deep brown-and-grey shaggy bark. As the name would suggest, this species will grow well in wet soils and grows into a bushy tree to 10 metres.

***B. pendula* 'Fastigiata' (Pencil Silver Birch)** An upright form of the European Silver Birch, with white bark. The branches have an unusual form growing back and forth as they go up, thus giving the tree a waving yet narrow look.

***B.* 'Royal Frost'** A stunning new hybrid birch with white bark and rich, deep burgundy leaves that turn orange-red in autumn. (Ideal for a Gothic copse!)

***B. p.* 'Tristis'** Lovely form with an extra white straight trunk and very pendulous side branches. Ideal where space is limited and extreme elegance is required. (Isn't that all the time!)

***B. p.* 'Trost's Dwarf'** A dainty little slow-growing birch with furry heavily cut foliage that is usually grafted onto a 1 metre standard. The head will grow to about 1 metre each way.

***B. utilis* (Himalayan Birch)** Attractive bushy upright tree that in the form I grow has pure white bark that peels off in large sheets exposing fawn underbark. It will grow to about 10 metres.

***B. u.* var. *jacquemontii* (Himalayan White Birch)** A rare birch with very white bark (the best bark in the genus most people will tell you – and who am I to argue) and large rounded leaves much bigger than *B. utilis* itself, so it looks quite different.

***B. u.* var. *j.* 'Jermyns'** This form was selected at Hilliers Nursery in England and if all is to be believed is even better in every way to that of the species.

Bowkeria verticillata syn. *B. gerrardiana*

An evergreen shrub to 3 metres or so from South Africa. It produces white-pouched flowers rather like those of a Calceolaria during summer and autumn (it is in the same family). The leaves are narrow, heavily veined and dark green. Grows quickly in sun or semi-shade as long as it doesn't dry right out. A good screening plant that is rarely used, so off you go!

Bosea amherstiana 'Variegata'

A rare, evergreen shrub to 2 metres from India, that is grown for its bold white-edged foliage (pink-tinged when young) and is drought-tolerant. It hasn't anything else to offer. (You greedy thing!)

Brachyglottis repanda (Bushman's Toilet Paper)

Handsome large shrub 3 metres from New Zealand with large soft leaves, bright green above and silvery-white and softly felted beneath. Flower heads of small scented white daisies in late spring, ideal in shade to sun and fairly drought-tolerant once established. The leaves are as soft as 'Sorbent'!

***B. r.* 'Purpurea'** A form of the above with rich, deep purple upper leaf surfaces and silvery reverse. Ideal if you have a mauve bathroom!

Brachyotum ledifolium

A rare upright evergreen shrub to 2 metres from South America. It has stunning, rich green foliage and drooping, soft yellow trumpets suspended from a shrimp-coloured calyx. A sunny, well-drained but moist aspect for this genus.

B lindleyi This species grows to much the same size as the above but has darker, shinier leaves, and the flowers are an almost black-purple hanging below shrimp-red calyxes.

Buddleja alternifolia

Large deciduous shrub to 3 metres with long weeping branches and fine grey very un-buddleja-like leaves. Scented mauve flowers run down the length of the previous years' stems in spring, so don't prune in winter as you may with some better-known species or you will loose your flowers. A very hardy and beautiful shrub from China that can be trained as a weeping standard.

B. colvilei Evergreen shrub to 4 metres from the Himalayas. Large, deep grey-green leaves and clusters of cherry-pink flowers in drooping terminal panicles in summer. Has the largest individual flowers of the genus. Only prune out twiggy, spent wood as heavy cutting isn't needed with this one.

B. crispa A large bushy semi-evergreen shrub to 3 metres from northern India, with huge white-felted leaves and masses of scented lilac flowers in early spring. Probably the best

foliage plant in this genus and happy in any well-drained spot in sun or semi-shade.
B. lindleyana A charming, lightly arching evergreen species from China to 3 metres. It produces drooping racemes of violet-purple bells all summer and autumn and will make a suckering clump.
B. madagascariensis A large spreading evergreen shrub with attractive silver foliage and stems. It produces panicles of deep yellow flowers in winter. Its rangy habit makes it a far better climber than a shrub and I have one in the home garden that is 10 metres up a gum tree. You could also use it as an espalier.
B. salvifolia A very large evergreen tree-like species from South Africa to 7 metres or so. It produces broad panicles of richly-scented mauve flowers throughout winter. It can be coppiced after flowering to restrict its size.
***B. × weyeriana* 'Moonlight'** A garden hybrid of rapid growth to 4 metres with panicles of soft lemon flowers with an orange centre. The flower buds have a mauve tinge.
***B. × w.* 'Sungold'** This form is a richer yellow sister seedling of the above.

Bupleurum fruticosum

A bushy evergreen shrub to 2 metres from southern Europe and northern Africa with handsome mid-green leaves and large heads of tiny yellow-green flowers in summer rather like parsley. They are related! Sun and drought-tolerant and showy to boot.

Bystropogon canariensis (Canary Island Smoke Bush)

Hardy evergreen shrub to 2 metres with pennyroyal-scented foliage and fluffy grey flower plumes in summer and autumn that look good in the garden or as cut flowers. Very drought-tolerant but should be cut hard after flowering each year to keep it bushy. This features, as it should, in my first book.

Callicarpa bodinieri 'Giraldii'

Deciduous shrub to 3 metres with small violet flowers followed by brilliant violet berries in clusters during the winter. The foliage often turns a strange purple and lemon before shedding. This native to China is hardy and happy in sun or semi-shade. The berries are lovely for picking, as they are from the next two plants.
C. dichotoma albifructa This Asian species to 2 metres tall has soft green leaves, tiny fluffy white flowers in summer and clusters of pearly white berries and soft yellow autumn foliage.
C. japonica A hardy deciduous shrub to 2 metres from Japan. It is an arching shrub and has beautiful rich mauve autumn foliage and purple berries.

Callicoma serratifolia (Black Wattle)

A tall evergreen native tree to 10 metres from shaded gullies in N.S.W. and southern Queensland, it was called 'Wattle' before the Acacias were. The rich green foliage sets off the fluffy cream flowers produced in spring.

Calycanthus floridus (Carolina Allspice)

A very hardy deciduous shrub to 3 metres each way that is known for its scented brown-red, narrow-petalled flowers in summer. The leaves are a pleasant bright green that turn bright yellow in autumn.

Camellia amplexicaulis

A new and stunning species from the forests of northern Vietnam that no-one will guess is a Camellia. It has huge heavily-veined leaves as big as the sole of my boot. These foliar wonders start rich reddish-purple and go bright green then deep green at maturity. The flowers are large single and mid-pink edged in white but I don't really give a damn! Give it an aspect with constant light shade and we assume it isn't completely frost-hardy considering its homeland although it is coping well with what Macedon can throw at it!
C. minutiflora Another new species from Vietnam that is at the other extreme from *C. amplexicaulis* with tiny deep green leaves that start off coppery-red and tiny little single white nodding flowers externally marked with pink. The leaders are fairly upright and the side branches weep in a most elegant fashion. This one will be perfect for those that are space-challenged.

C. tsaii This elegant species hails from western China, Burma and Vietnam and will grow into a small arching tree to 4 metres with bronze new growth and tiny nodding white scented flowers in spring. This one made it into my first book.

Cantua buxifolia

An arching open-growing evergreen shrub to 3 metres or so from the Andes that produces remarkable, brilliant cerise trumpets in spring that almost pull the branches to the ground. Its small leaves and lack of presence out of bloom will hardly prepare you for what is to come. A sunny aspect suits best and it is fairly drought-tolerant.

***C. b.* 'Tricolor'** This form has soft yellow trumpets with a white mouth and the whole is streaked with cerise. All in all a showy thing to say the least and no less so when it sends out reverted branches with the original cerise flowers on them.

C. pyrifolia This evergreen arching shrub from Bolivia, Peru and Ecuador looks very like the preceding species but it grows a metre or so taller and its stunning flowers are yellow trumpets with white around the mouth.

Carpenteria californica

Hardy evergreen shrub to 2 metres from California. It has grey-green leaves and large white fragrant flowers in summer. Quite rare in cultivation due to the difficulty of propagation but not due to any lack of quality. It is so good that it features in my tree and shrub book. But you already knew that!

Carpinus betulus (Hornbeam)

This large deciduous tree to 10 metres or so has soft green Elm-like leaves that turn yellow in autumn. It also has pleasant grey-fluted trunks with age. Often used to make hedges in England and it could well do so here in cooler areas and I could sell a lot more!

***C. b.* 'Fastigiata' (Pencil Hornbeam)** Handsome tall conical-shaped tree to 10 metres with bright green leaves turning bright yellow before they drop in autumn. A good feature tree that won't take up too much room.

***C. caroliniana* (American Hornbeam)** This is a lovely medium deciduous tree to 7 metres or so with a rustic outline and rich red-brown autumn foliage. Wind and drought-tolerant in all but the driest climates.

C. shensiensis A moderate-sized tree to 7 metres from China with foliage slightly smaller than the European Hornbeam that turns rich orange and red in autumn.

C. turczaninowii A lovely small to medium tree to 10 metres from China, Korea and Japan with a picturesque habit. Its foliage starts out copper, turns green and goes orange, gold and red in autumn.

Carpodetus serratus (New Zealand Marbleleaf)

Small evergreen tree to 5 metres from New Zealand for sun or semi-shade. Upright habit with branches that zigzag and lovely small bronze-tinged leaves as well as a mist of tiny pink-white blossom in spring. A good substitute for *Nothofagus* in climates not to their liking.

Caryopteris × *clandonensis*

Showy, deciduous small shrub to 40 cm with grey-green foliage and masses of lavender-blue flowers through summer and autumn that will attract every known pollinator. Prune hard each winter.

Castanea sativa 'Albomarginata' (Silver Variegated Sweet Chestnut)

A large, impressive deciduous tree to 17 metres laden with cream catkins in spring. The foliage has a silvery-white edge. Very rare.

Catalpa bignonioides (Indian Bean Tree)

A large and elegant spreading shade tree to 20 metres or so with big handsome leaves, spikes of white flowers marked with yellow and purple in summer and drooping bean-like pods later.

***C. b.* 'Aurea' (Golden Indian Bean Tree)** A truly outstanding small deciduous tree to 10 metres which has very large heart-shaped golden leaves to 25 cm across. The foliage is tinted copper when new and greens slightly by late summer. The flowers are formed in impressive panicles in summer and are white with purple and yellow markings. If coppiced every year it makes a wonderful tropical effect for the back of a border and will then rarely exceed 3 metres.

C. ovata A Chinese species to 13 metres with large rich green leaves and panicles of white flowers marked with red and yellow during summer.

C. speciosa A North American species that also makes a large shade tree and has purple-marked white flowers and burgundy young leaves later turning green.

Cavendishia acuminata

South American evergreen shrub to 2 metres with rich green leaves, bronze when young. The flowers are red tubes with white-green tips. Ideal in tubs and can be trained as a climber. It prefers a cool moist aspect and is a little frost-tender.

Ceanothus arboreus 'Trewithen Blue'

A vigorous and hardy upright evergreen shrub to 7 metres with glossy bright green foliage and fluffy clusters of slightly scented rich blue flowers in spring and summer. It likes a sunny and well-drained aspect and is so much better than 'Blue Pacific' that it features in my first book.

Cercidiphyllum japonicum

Medium-sized Japanese tree that could reach 17 metres or more with spreading fan-shaped branches. The lovely heart-shaped pale green leaves turn a lovely yellow (sometimes pink tinged) in the autumn. The leaves smell of toffee as they shed. This lovely tree likes a cool root run and shelter from hot winds as do the following.

C. magnificum Rare tree similar to *C. japonicum* that grows larger and has bigger foliage that starts out in early spring as a lovely rich burgundy, greening later.

***C. m.* 'Pendulum'** A lovely weeping form that requires staking to gain initial height then it will be off and away creating a charming and picturesque small tree that has none of the smugness of a weeping cherry.

Cercis canadensis 'Forest Pansy'

This is a small spreading tree to 4 metres or so with tiny magenta pea-flowers up the bare stems in late winter followed by handsome burgundy heart-shaped leaves. A sunny but not too hot and dry aspect should suit. (Who on earth thought to give this lovely thing such a naff name!)

***C. chinensis* (Chinese Redbud)** A lovely large shrub or small deciduous tree to 7 metres with attractive heart-shaped leaves that turn yellow in autumn and masses of small magenta pea-shaped flowers on the bare gnarled stems in late winter. This is a very good hardy sun-loving tree that should be used a lot more.

***C. siliquastrum* 'Alba' (White Judas Tree)** A lovely form with pure white to very pale pink pea flowers (as opposed to the strident magenta form) ideal for the timid gardener! It has the usual picturesque form of the genus.

Chaenomeles cathayensis

A rare but indestructible evergreen shrub or small tree to 5 metres or so from China. It has soft pink to white flowers in spring followed by very large yellow-green quinces (yes, you can use them if you can bear to pick them). This plant also has thorns that Jesus would have winced at! If freestanding it will grow as wide as tall but it is also a great plant for espalier work in sun or shade.

***C. speciosa* 'Falconnet Charlet'** This form of flowering quince will grow to about 2 metres and like all forms is a slightly spiny deciduous shrub that is ideal as an indestructible hedge and an indispensable cut flower in late winter. In this case the flowers are large double salmon-pink confections.

***C. s.* 'Moerloosei' syn. *C. s.* 'Apple Blossom'** This form also grows to about 2 metres and has single soft pink and white flowers in late winter.

***C. s.* 'Nivalis'** A pure white-flowered form of the above.

***Chimonanthus praecox* (Wintersweet or Allspice)** Hardy deciduous shrub to 3 metres or so from China. Masses of heavily scented pale yellow flowers in winter that will lift you off your feet. Sun or semi-shade in any old soil will do but be prepared for a wait of three years or so for flowers.

Chionanthus retusus (Chinese Fringe Tree)

Very rare hardy deciduous large shrub or small tree to 7 metres with masses of snow white flowers with strap-shaped petals in late spring and early summer. This is a surprisingly hardy plant that will tolerate quite a lot of heat and dry soil once established. It is a shame that both species are so hard to propagate, at least it is for those that don't own any.

***C. virginicus* (North American Fringe Tree)** This species has similar flowers to its Chinese counterpart and grows about the same height but has much larger leaves and will usually make a wider tree.

Choisya 'Aztec Pearl'

This hybrid between the following species and *C. ternata* has dark green foliage divided into narrow leaflets and masses of slightly scented flowers throughout the summer. It is tough-as-guts and makes a bushy shrub to 1.5 metres.

C. dumosa* var. *arizonica I imported this fabulous evergreen shrub from North America in 2003 and it is sure to be a winner. It will grow into a sun-loving drought-tolerant shrub to 1.5 metres with glandular warty narrow leaflets that are a lot prettier than they sound. In summer it produces masses of slightly scented pure white flowers.

***C. ternata* 'Sundance'** A hardy evergreen shrub to 1.5 metres with white scented flowers in summer and attractive gold foliage. Best planted out of the hottest afternoon sun but otherwise as tough as they come.

Cladrastis kentuckae (Yellow Wood)

A very handsome medium tree to 10 metres or so from the southern United States with soft green, ash-like leaves that turn yellow in autumn. It produces drooping clusters of white scented wisteria-like flowers in spring. It likes an open sunny well-drained aspect.

Clerodendrum bungei

A deciduous suckering shrub to 3 metres from China with large deep green leaves with a burgundy reverse. Its foliage stinks like burning rubber if rubbed (a great joke) however its large heads of pink flowers produced in summer are sweetly scented. Will grow well in sun or shade, is reasonably drought-tolerant and features in my first book.

C. chinense* var. *chinense This suckering shrub to 2 metres or so could be confused with the above until it flowers as its leaves are much the same to look at and to smell and it will sucker into goodly colonies in time. It flowers a little later and its pale pink buds open up to elegant full double white flowers with a lovely scent. This one has had more names than I've had hot breakfasts and they include *C. philippinum* and *C. fragrans* var. *pleniflorum*. Who knows, it could be different tomorrow!

C. trichotomum This small suckering tree to 5 metres from China and Japan has open heads of fragrant flowers in summer and when these drop the calyxes turn cerise-red and in the centre of each is a bright blue seed. It grows in both sun and shade.

***C. t.* 'Carnival'** I imported this form from England several years ago and it differs from the above in having grey-green leaves boldly edged with creamy-white. Considering everything else this species does could this be over kill? It will probably only grow to about half the size of the green-leafed form.

Clethra alnifolia (Sweet Pepper Bush)

A medium upright deciduous shrub to 2 metres form North America. It produces candle-like spikes of white scented flowers in late summer. It likes, as do the following, a moist aspect and a cool spot making them great companions for Rhododendrons, etc. In fact, you could pull out some to make room for a *Clethra*.

C. arborea A large upright evergreen shrub or small tree to 7 metres or so with rich, deep green foliage and long spikes of heavily musk-scented white flowers in summer. Native of Madeira.

***C. a.* 'Flora Plena'** A double-flowered form of the above that holds its flowers for longer but because of the small size isn't visually that different. It is, however, nice to say that you have the rare double form.

C. barbinervis Similar to *C. alnifolia* although a bit larger growing and with flower spikes that are not so upright. Native of China.

C. delavayi Large deciduous shrub with an upright habit to 4 metres from western China. Long spikes of scented white flowers in summer (like Lily-of-the-Valley). Good autumn foliage.

C. fargesii Similar to *C. delavayi* but a more spreading habit to 3 metres and more drooping flower spikes.

Cleyera japonica 'Tricolor'

Spreading evergreen shrub of great elegance with variegated leaves very like those of a camellia (not a real surprise as it is in the same family) that become pink-tinged in winter. The small white flowers hide under the leaves so aren't the reason for growing it. Ideal as a tub specimen in a shady aspect 1 to 2 metres each way.

Colquhounia coccinea

A hardy sun-loving evergreen shrub to 1.5 metres related to Salvias. It has downy grey-green scented leaves and tubular orange-scarlet flowers in autumn. Prune it back really hard in winter. Native to the Himalayas.

Coprosma 'Black Cloud'

A very tough evergreen shrub from New Zealand to 1 metre tall with spreading branches and small glossy leaves that turn a rich coppery-black with winter cold. A good tall ground cover in sun. It will tolerate some shade but at the expense of foliage colour.

***C.* 'Cappuccino'** An upright evergreen shrub to 3 metres, ideal as a feature plant or where space is limited. It is clothed with tiny rich chocolate leaves and will grow well in almost any well-drained sunny site.

Cornus alba 'Elegantissima'

A hardy shrubby dogwood to 2 metres with red winter canes and silver variegated foliage. It grows best in moist to wet soils and should be cut to the ground at the end of winter every second year or so to maintain the colour of the canes, as should the following varieties of the species.

***C. a.* 'Kesselringii'** This form has deep green foliage stained bronze whilst young and almost black stems in winter that contrast well with the other forms.

***C.a.*'Sibirica' (Red Stem Dogwood)** Deciduous shrub to 3 metres with burgundy autumn foliage and brilliant red winter canes.

***C. a.* 'Spaethii'** A golden variegated form of the above.

***C. alternifolia* 'Argentea'** A lovely silver variegated deciduous shrub to 3 metres with flat tiers of branches on the top of which it gets tiny white flowers in flattish heads in late spring. It is similar to the better-known *C. controversa* 'Variegata' but is smaller in all its parts.

C. angustata A recent introduction from China This evergreen small tree probably reaches 7 metres and produces lemon-coloured flowers in early summer. It also has attractive glossy leaves. This species is a good one for beginners with this genus as it is fairly forgiving.

***C.* 'Aurora'** This hybrid from Rutgers University in New Jersey is a cross between *C. florida* and *C. kousa* bred to combat a fungal decease effecting American Dogwoods. It is vigorous with an upright habit to 3 metres or so and large white overlapping bracts. A seriously good bloomer with the best foliage in its hybrid group and sold in Australia as the 'Stella' series.

C. bretschneideri A rare deciduous shrub to 3 metres from northern China with clusters of small white flowers followed by black berries. The leaves turn lovely autumnal tones and the bare twigs in winter are orange and yellow.

***C. capitata* (Evergreen Dogwood or Strawberry Tree)** Evergreen tree to 7 metres, with large cream-bracted flowers in late spring and red strawberry-like fruit in autumn and winter. This is probably the hardiest of the flowering tree species for our climate.

C. c. 'Rag Doll' This Australian selection has leaves edged in soft yellow.

C. 'Celestial' Another Rutger hybrid that has large white bracts that almost overlap. A lovely selection that is a bit smaller growing that *C.* 'Aurora'. Also a strong doer with layered branches that is resistant to the dreaded Anthracnose fungus.

C. 'Constellation' Yet another Rutger hybrid (can you see a theme here?) this time with long white bracts that don't overlap. This one is probably the most vigorous clone in the group.

***C. contraversa* (Tabletop Dogwood)** Elegant small tree to 10 metres from Japan and China with layers of horizontal branches and masses of tiny white flowers in clusters during spring. Good autumn colour.

C. c. 'June Snow' This is a new selection from North America that is just like the above but 'on steroids'! It grows taller and faster, has bigger leaves and larger heads of flowers. Definitely one for the size queen!

C. c. 'Variegata' (Variegated Tabletop Dogwood) Large shrub or small tree to 7 metres with branches in flat layers giving a tiered effect. The drooping silver variegated leaves almost hide the masses of tiny white flowers.

C. 'Eddies White Wonder' Huge white-bracted flowers in spring and brilliant red autumn leaves. Small tree with pendulous outer branches. This is a hybrid between *C. florida* and *C. nuttallii*. This one found its way into my first book.

C. 'Eric Genat' This hybrid between *C. kousa* and *C. capitata* was found in the Dandenong garden of the great plantsman it was named after. It has the same parentage as the better-known *C.* 'Norman Hadden' but has larger flowers that also start cream and flush pink as they age. Also has large attractive fruit.

***C. florida* (American Flowering Dogwood)** A small deciduous tree to 4 metres with white flowers in spring and rich autumn foliage. The classic dogwood to the mind of most. Elegant but requiring a site sheltered from hot winds as do all its cultivars.

C. f. 'Cherokee Chief' Deeper pink form of *C. f.* 'Rubra' with extra deep coloured autumn foliage.

C. f. 'First Lady' White flowers and lovely gold variegated leaves turning burgundy and apricot in autumn.

C. f. 'Pendula' Weeping form on 1 metre standards with white flowers. The branches hang close to the trunk with some going up which increases the trees height (albeit slowly) unlike most weeping standards.

C. f. 'Pleurobracteata' Double white form with odd green markings in the bracts.

C. f. 'Purple Glory' A small tree dogwood with deep purple-brown markings in the foliage from spring to autumn and pink flowers.

C. f. 'Pygmy' Dwarf shrub form of American dogwood to 2 metres with white bracted flowers.

C. f. 'Rubra' (Pink Dogwood) Pink form of Cornus florida.

C. f. 'Welches Junior Miss' Semi-evergreen form with clear pink blooms.

***C. kousa* var. *chinensis* (Chinese Dogwood)** Small tree to 4 metres or so with creamy white flowers along the tiers of flat branches in late spring and early summer, followed by red fruit and good autumn colour.

C. k. c. 'Milky Way' This heavy-flowered selection has creamy white flowers of exceptional size. This name was given to a group of seedlings and not a single clone so the name is probably invalid but the form we have here is a good thing well worth planting.

C. k. 'Miss Satomi' This Japanese selection has deep salmon pink flowers and rich autumn foliage on a spreading small tree to 3 metres.

C. k. 'National' Yet another large white-flowered selection with good vigour. How does one choose?

***C. mas* (Cornelian Cherry)** Small hardy deciduous tree to 7 metres with masses of tiny yellow flowers on the bare branches in winter. Its bright red edible fruit are supposed to make the best jelly to have when eating wild game! It also has good autumn colour. A picturesque little tree that should be used more. Its hard wood was even used to make rolling pins.

***C. m.* 'Variegata'** A silver variegated form of the above. The red berries with the silver foliage are most effective.

***C.* 'Norman Hadden'** A lovely semi-evergreen hybrid between *C. capitata* and *C. kousa* to 4 metres. Its flowers are cream and age to soft pink and it has attractive red strawberry-like fruit in autumn.

***C. nuttallii* (West American Dogwood)** Huge creamy white-bracted flowers in spring and sometimes in autumn, good autumn foliage on an upright tree to 9 metres.

C. officinalis This Asian species is very similar to *C. mas* but is a bit earlier flowering and possibly showier but having said this they are hard to tell apart.

C. paucinervis A small-growing deciduous shrub to 1 metre from China. It has narrow, light green leaves and because it produces its clusters of tiny white flowers in late summer, when flowering shrubs are rare (especially Cornus), this makes it a useful form. It is hardy in sun or shade but likes it moist.

C. pumila A hardy dwarf deciduous shrub to 1 metre tall by somewhat more than this in width with attractive autumn foliage and twigs in winter. It rarely flowers but with its nice rounded habit is worth a place in the garden. Its origin is unknown. It tolerates wet soil.

C. racemosa Deciduous shrub to 2 metres. Small white flowers and brilliant autumn foliage. This isn't the best of Dogwoods but adds to the ranks of autumn coloured shrubs with distinction. Tolerates wet soil.

***C.* 'Stella Pink'** Yet another Rutger hybrid. (Boy was Dr Elwin Orton busy!) This time we have a white that ages to soft pink. This is also quite a spreading clone that in time could reach 4 metres.

***C. stolonifera* 'Flaviramea' (Yellow Stem Dogwood)** Similar to *C. alba* 'Siberica' and requiring the same treatment. Autumn foliage is bright yellow, and the winter stems are yellow green. They look good if both species are planted together (and I will make two sales).

Corokia buddleioides

A charming and hardy evergreen New Zealand shrub to 3 metres or so with narrow bronze green leaves with a silvery reverse. It also has small, yellow star-shaped flowers followed by dark red berries. A good screen or hedging plant and (dare I say it) a real improvement on the 'James Stirling Pittosporum'.

***C. cotoneaster* (Wire Netting Bush)** A fascinating evergreen shrub from New Zealand to 3 metres with tiny sparse bronze leaves amongst its tortuous tracery of dark branches that are good for picking. It also produces tiny yellow starry flowers followed by orange berries. A sunny to semi-shaded spot will suit.

***C.* 'Little Prince'** Like the above but with a tighter branching arrangement and a more upright habit. A little bit smaller in fact in all aspects and rarely exceeds 1.5 metres. A good feature shrub or unusual tub specimen.

Corylopsis glabrescens

A large spreading deciduous shrub to 3 metres with grey-green foliage that turns yellow in autumn and drooping spikes of sweetly-scented lemon flowers in late winter. Sun or semi-shade in a moist acid soil out of the hot winds suits all this genus. All come from Asia.

C. sinensis Similar to the above but a bit more upright in habit to 4 metres and with smaller greener leaves.

***C. s.* var. *calvescens* (syn. *C. hypoglauca*)** Similar in flowers and habit to the species but with rounder larger leaves of a more grey-green colour.

***C. s.* var. *sinensis* 'Spring Purple'** This form has an arching habit to 3 metres and does much the same as the other types except that in spring its new growth is a lovely burgundy colour.

C. spicata The largest growing species to 5 metres with the largest leaves in the genus. The flowers are the usual drooping soft yellow.

Corylus avellana 'Aurea' (Golden Hazel)

This soft yellow-leafed form is an excellent contrast to the purple hazel. Always buy any

Filberts on their own roots and not grafted as these will sucker for the rest of your life and theirs! These are fairly hardy multi-stemmed small trees for sun or light shade and in this case will grow to 7 metres.

***C. a.* 'Contorta' (Contorted Hazel)** Medium shrub to 2 metres with weirdly curled and twisted branches that are strung with golden catkins in late winter. The leaves also twist and curl which is off-putting to the ignorant.

***C. maxima* 'Purpurea' (Purple Filbert)** Large shrub or small tree to 5 metres. The large leaves are rich burgundy in spring fading to green in summer. Its nuts, if they form, have large leafy bracts surrounding them which the Hazel doesn't have.

Corynabutilon × *suntense* (syn. *Abutilon* × *suntense*)

A very fast-growing evergreen shrub to 5 metres. It has grey-green, maple-like leaves and rich mauve-blue, hibiscus-like flowers off and on throughout the warmer months. A sunny well-drained aspect and shelter from wind is needed.

C. vitifolium One of the parents of the above differing only in its larger leaves and bigger, very pale mauve to white flowers.

Cotinus coggygria 'Flame' (Smoke Bush)

Hardy quick-growing European deciduous shrub to 5 metres. Bright green leaves that go brilliant orange red in autumn. Also has lovely soft fluffy pink to grey plumes in summer. Sun-loving and drought-tolerant.

***C. c.* 'Golden Spirit'** A brand-new selection with golden yellow leaves that is a true departure in this genus. It will grow to 3 metres or so, still produce lovely plumes and good autumn colour. Give it a little shelter from hot afternoon sun.

***C. c.* 'Grace'** This newish cultivar has rich almost chocolate-coloured leaves, good plumes and unlike the other purple clones has stunning autumn colour. If unpruned it will grow to 3 metres or so.

***C. c.* 'Royal Purple'** A smaller growing form to about 2 metres with the darkest and richest purple foliage of any form which, if looked at closely, usually has a very fine pink edge. Plumes only sparingly produced and autumn colour is patchy at best, but let's not get too greedy!

***C. c.* 'Rubrifolia Group'** This large-growing shrub to 4 metres has light purplish foliage and large fluffy plumes. The foliage forms like the one above and the one below are richer selections raised from this one.

***C. c.* 'Velvet Cloak'** This American selection is very like *C. c.* 'Royal Purple' and only seems to differ in the lack of the inconspicuous pink edge.

Cotoneaster atropurpureus 'Variegatus'

This is a lovely spreading deciduous ground cover shrub very like and often offered as a variegated *C. horizontalis.* It is smaller in all its parts however and has lovely silvery-white edges to the leaves and in the autumn its foliage turns red and pink dotted throughout with red berries.

C. dammeri This species is an evergreen ground cover from China with glossy green leaves, small white flowers and bright red berries. It will follow the contours of whereever it is grown and looks at its best hanging down a wall. Will grow almost anywhere.

***C. salicifolius* 'Rothschildianus'** A very hardy, grow-almost-anywhere, large evergreen shrub to 5 metres with a spreading habit. It produces clusters of tiny white flowers in spring followed in autumn by clusters of butter yellow berries.

Craibiodendron yunnanense

A very rare Chinese shrub to 3 metres in the Rhododendron family with dark green evergreen foliage that is bronze-red when young and clusters of small white (Lily-of-the-Valley) flowers in summer. Treat it like an Azalea with regard to position and soil. (In fact, rip out an Azalea to put one in!)

Crataegus azarolus (Azarole)

This lovely small deciduous tree to 6 metres or so comes from northern Africa and western Asia and is almost indestructible (as most Hawthorns are). It has grey-green cut foliage that turns yellow in autumn. Its small white flowers are born in clusters and these are followed by large yellow berries that taste like bruised apple. Yum! Ideal – as are all the following – as a screen, hedge or small lawn specimen tree, or for the makers of jelly.

***C. crus-galli* (Cockspur Thorn)** A hardy, small deciduous tree to 7 metres from North America. It has an attractive spreading habit with long woody thorns. It has white blossom in spring, good autumn foliage with clusters of rich red berries.

***C. c.* var. *pyracanthifolia* (Horizontal Thorn)** This form is usually grafted onto a standard and then grows out in flat layers like an open umbrella. The leaves are very narrow and colour well in autumn, the flowers are the usual white. The berries naturally red but in this form, no thorns.

***C. × lavallei* 'Carrieri' (French Thorn)** Hardy deciduous tree with large orange fruit in autumn and winter, good red autumn leaves and small white flowers in spring. It grows to about 7 metres and is a thornless Thorn!

C. orientalis A lovely spreading, small deciduous tree to 5 metres with furry grey cut leaves that turn yellow in autumn and fairly large orange-red berries. The open habit of this tree means that you can grow lots of lovelies under it. This one is usually incorrectly sold in Australia as *C. tanacetifolia* which differs in having yellow fruit.

***C. phaenopyrum* syn. *C. cordata* (Washington Thorn)** This North American species makes a striking round-headed tree to 7 metres and has shiny maple-shaped leaves that turn brilliant red in autumn. Its clusters of tiny white flowers, formed in late spring, are followed by large clusters of small bright red berries in autumn, birds allowing! Big woody thorns on this species, but they become fewer as the tree matures.

C. pinnatifida* var. *major A lovely, small, spreading deciduous tree to 5 metres or so from China with possibly the most beautiful foliage in the genus. It has cut almost maple-like leaves that colour well in autumn. Its small white flowers are followed by clusters of crimson berries.

***C. stipulacea* (Mexican Thorn)** Evergreen medium thornless tree with white flowers in spring and large yellow fruit that ripens in autumn and stays on the tree till the end of winter. It grows to about 7 metres and would make a good specimen tree or planted as a hedge or screen.

× *Crataemespilus grandiflora*

A rare hybrid between a Hawthorn and a Medlar found in France about 1800. It is a small spreading deciduous tree to 4 metres or so with large white flowers in spring followed by large glossy brownish-orange fruit. It also has lovely autumn foliage in shades of yellow, orange and red.

***Crinodendron hookerianum* (Chilean Lantern Tree)**

Evergreen shrub from South America for cool aspect with acid organic soil to 4 metres. Brilliant red lantern-shaped flowers in summer. A challenge worth taking!

C. patagua Large evergreen shrub with small round dark green leaves and white bell flowers with a frilled edge in summer and autumn. It grows to 5 metres and likes the same conditions as the above but is less difficult to please.

Cussonia paniculata

A strangely attractive small evergreen tree to 5 metres from South Africa that has stout branches topped with huge grey-green leaves divided into about 10 scalloped leaflets. Its tiny green flowers are born in large panicles adding much to its overall charm. Drought-tolerant but not for the really frosty areas.

***Cydonia sinensis* syn. *Pseudocydonia sinensis* (Chinese Quince)**

A lovely, small, deciduous tree to 7 metres from China related to the commercial quince. It has bright green foliage that turns red in autumn. In spring it produces solitary pale pink flowers, which are followed by its large yellow-green fruit that can be used in the same way as the quince. As it ages it produces bark rather like a crepe myrtle and as if this wasn't enough, it is as hardy as any apple tree and featured in my first book under its synonym.

Cyrilla racemiflora
Medium semi-evergreen shrub to 4 metres from North and South America with whorls of white flower spikes in summer that turn bronze when the flowers die. Many of the leaves turn bright red in winter. This hardy shrub has an open elegant habit so will not hide you well from the neighbours. It's in my first book.

Cytisus frivaldskyanus
A very prostrate to trailing evergreen shrub to 1 metre across, with tiny deep green leaves and stems, from the Balkans. It is drought-tolerant and sun-loving and ideal for a rock garden with masses of bright yellow pea flowers in summer.

C. × kewensis A charming semi-prostrate broom for a sunny well-drained site. Its green leafless stems produce masses of creamy-lemon, pea-like flowers in spring. This plant was raised in the Kew Botanic Gardens in 1891.

***Dais cotinifolia* (South African Daphne)**
An attractive drought-tolerant upright deciduous tree to about 7 metres with large clusters of pink daphne-like flowers in early summer. A good tree for small gardens or where room is limited; it loves a sunny, open aspect.

Daphne bholua
This rare upright semi-evergreen species comes from the Himalayas and has foliage and flowers that are similar to the common *D. odora* and, like pretty well all the genus, likes a sunny to semi-shaded aspect with well-mulched roots. This species produces its beautifully scented almost white flowers in late winter and grows to 3 metres tall.

D. b. alba A lovely white-flowered form of the above.

D. × burkwoodii Small deciduous shrub to 1 metre each way with masses of pink highly scented flowers in spring. Due to its heavy set of flowers and its almost naked frame at flowering it makes quite a show.

***D.* 'Carol Mackie' syn. *D. × burkwoodii* 'Somerset Variegata'** This form is like the above but has yellow-edged foliage that is later white-edged. Not a real improvement on the above at flowering but entertaining later in the season.

D. genkwa Very rare deciduous Daphne from China with masses of quite large mauve-blue scentless flowers up the bare stems in late winter. It grows to about 1.5 metres tall and has an open and some might say straggly habit, but I would contend that not everything in the garden needs to be bushy. The ideal plant to trick the less knowledgeable, as it looks more like a Lilac than a Daphne.

D. × houtteana A rare hybrid between *D. laureola* and *D. mezereum* that makes an evergreen shrub to 1 metre that has large purple leaves and clusters of night-scented, reddish-purple flowers in spring. No-one will guess it's a Daphne if they don't already know it.

***D. laureola* ssp. *philippi* (Spurge Laurel)** A European species that is very shade-tolerant. It is a small suckering shrub to 50 cm with leathery glossy evergreen foliage and small green night-scented flowers.

D. longilobata An erect small shrub to 1 metre with glossy deep green evergreen foliage and small white scentless flowers in clusters, followed by orange berries. From the Himalayas.

***D. mezereum* (Mezereon)** Hardy deciduous shrub to 1.5 metres with masses of purple-pink scented flowers on the bare stems in late winter, followed by bright orange poisonous berries in summer.

D. m.* forma *alba A rare white-flowered form which produces unusual soft apricot-yellow berries in summer.

***D. m.* 'Spring Wraith'** This is my own form of the above with the same white flowers and apricot-yellow berries. This differs in that its foliage is a soft buttery yellow in spring later turning green. Keep it in a light spot but out of direct sun as it will burn.

D. pontica Evergreen shrub for sun or shade from Europe to 1 metre tall. Rich, deep green foliage and clusters of night-fragrant green flowers in spring followed by deep red berries.

***D.* 'Rossetii'** A dwarf evergreen hybrid with strange green and pink slightly scented flowers in spring. This plant will rarely exceed 25 cm and its foliage is particularly rich and glossy.

D. tangutica Slow-growing evergreen shrub from China to 1 metre. It has clusters of pale pink to white fragrant flowers in spring.

Daphniphyllum himalaense ssp. *macropodum*

A handsome evergreen shade-tolerant shrub with deep green Rhododendron-like leaves from Japan that has a tiered habit and grows to about 7 metres. The flowers are very small and of no real interest. The plant, however, will keep them all guessing.

Davidia involucrata (Dove Tree)

Magnificent, large deciduous tree to 14 metres or more with large leaves colouring well in the autumn. The small flowers hang below the horizontal branches in spring. These flowers are surrounded by two large white bracts that look like wings, hence the common name. One of the best trees to come out of China. It likes deep cool soil and shelter from hot summer winds.

Decaisnea fargesii

A remarkable and attractive deciduous shrub to 3 metres from China. It is an upright, seldom branched plant with ash-like leaves that are blue tinged whilst young. It produces yellow-green racemes of blossom in spring followed by metallic-blue, broad-bean-like pods. It will grow in sun or semi-shade and likes a moist but well-drained aspect.

Dendriopoterium menendezii

This is a rare evergreen shrub in the rose family from the Canary Islands that loves open sunny well-drained sites and is drought-tolerant. It grows to about 2 metres each way and its leaves are grey and look as if they belong to a dwarf *Melianthus* and they cluster toward the ends of the copper-coloured stems. The tiny pink flowers with bright green calyxes are produced in slightly arching spikes in spring. What a relief to have something in this family that doesn't look like a rose!

Dendromecon rigida

This sun-loving and drought-tolerant evergreen shrub comes from California and grows to about 2 metres. Its leaves are blue-green and lovely and it produces its bright yellow poppy-like flowers throughout the year but mainly in the warmer months.

Desfontainia spinosa

South American evergreen shrub to 2 metres with foliage remarkably like a holly. It flowers in late summer and the blooms are waxy trumpets of bright orange with a yellow tip. A spot with morning sun and soil that doesn't dry right out suits best. This striking shrub features in my first book.

Deutzia crenata 'Nakaiana' (syn. *D.* 'Nikko')

Charming, deciduous dwarf shrub to 25 cm. Masses of tiny white flowers in spring. Like all the genus, it is a hardy shrub in both sun and semi-shade.

***D. × hybrida* 'Magicien'** A deciduous shrub to 1.5 metres tall with sprays of mauve-pink flowers edged with white in early summer.

D. × kalmiiflora Graceful, hardy deciduous shrub to 2 metres with masses of pale pink flowers in early summer.

D. ningpoensis A deciduous species from eastern China to 2.5 metres with long panicles of small white flowers in early summer.

Dichotomanthes tristaniicarpa

A spreading evergreen shrub from China that looks like a *Cotoneaster* and it is in fact closely related and just as hardy. It would make a good espalier that you can keep telling your friends isn't a *Cotoneaster.* The small rounded leaves start out copper, turn deep green and as they die, go red. It has, as you would expect, small white flowers in spring and red berries. If unpruned will grow to 1 metre tall by 3 metres or more across.

Dichroa febrifuga

A Chinese upright evergreen shrub to 2 metres related to the Hydrangeas that has heads of small pink-white flowers in summer followed by blue berries. Best in a cool moist aspect and not surprisingly likes to be pruned like its relatives, as do the following.

It is amazing that this useful genus has only recently found its way to Australia.

***D. f.* 'Golden Wings'** This form, discovered at Yamina Rare Plants at Monbulk, has yellow edges to the leaves.

D. versicolor This species has slightly larger leaves than the above with blue-stained leaf stems and larger heads of rich blue flowers followed by blue berries.

Dipelta yunnanensis

A hardy deciduous shrub to 4 metres from China with masses of pale pink to almost white flowers with orange spots inside. This spring-flowering shrub resembles a Weigela except that it has lovely copper-coloured papery seeds. The coppery exfoliating bark is also pleasing in winter. Sun to semi-shade will suit.

Dipteronia sinensis

A rare small spreading tree in the Maple family to 4 metres tall with compound almost Ash-like leaves that turn yellow in autumn and attractive red-winged seeds. It likes a site sheltered from hot winds. This is one of those off-beat plants that all collectors should want, which may keep me growing it!

Disanthus cercidifolius

Large shrub or small multi-stemmed tree to 3 metres from Japan with large heart-shaped leaves rather like those of a Judas Tree. One of the world's best autumn colouring plants but unfortunately only really growable in cool hill-station-type climates, but you can prove me wrong if you like! The foliage turns all shades of yellow, orange, red and burgundy. It's on the cover of my first book.

Distylium racemosum

A large, spreading evergreen shrub from Japan and Korea, to 4 metres tall. Glossy foliage and masses of dark red spidery flowers in winter. This elegant plant will cope with semi-shade or shade and is fairly drought-tolerant once established.

Dombeya natalensis

A sun-loving small to medium semi-deciduous tree of upright habit to 10 metres or so with soft green rounded foliage and masses of pure white blossom in high summer. It likes a sunny well-drained site and isn't cold hardy enough for very frost prone areas.

Drimys winteri (Winters Bark)

A tall, narrow evergreen shrub or small tree to 7 metres from South America with handsome bright green foliage. Clusters of ivory white, slightly scented flowers in early summer. It is in my first book with far more detail than I can give here. It requires cool root conditions and likes a well-drained but moist soil.

Edgeworthia chrysantha (Japanese Paper Daphne)

Deciduous shrub to 2 metres with masses of lemon yellow flowers in clusters like a Daphne but larger in late winter before the lance-shaped light green leaves appear. Slightly scented. This, as all the types, likes a well-drained soil in a morning sun aspect. The Japanese once made paper from the bark.

***E. c.* 'Grandiflora'** A smaller-growing form to 1.5 metres tall, with larger flower clusters and thicker branches. This one is in my first book.

***E. c.* 'Red Dragon'** This form has rich deep orange flowers set off by the white on the outside of each tiny flower making it an interesting addition to our late winter palate.

E. gardneri This rarely seen species is a semi-evergreen shrub to 3 metres with fully rounded heads of soft yellow scented flowers hanging like Christmas decorations, again in late winter.

Elaeagnus × ebbingei

A truly indestructible evergreen shrub to 3 metres each way. A very useful hedge or screening plant, it has grey foliage with a silvery reverse and tiny scented flowers in autumn.

E. macrophylla Hardy deciduous shrub to 2 metres, with a spreading habit wider than its height, from Japan and Korea. It has large silver-grey leaves and tiny scented flowers in autumn. Very hardy in sun or shade.

***E. pungens* 'Hosuba-Fukurin'** This form makes a speading shrub to 1.5 metres tall and usually wider with rich deep green comparatively narrow leaves neatly edged in white. A recent import into Australia.

***E. p.* 'Maculata'** A very hardy evergreen shrub to 2 metres or so, with brilliant yellow foliage edged with green. Its tiny flowers are produced in autumn and are scented.

***E.* 'Quicksilver'** This is a large deciduous shrub to 4 metres or so grown for its intensely silver foliage and small perfumed flowers. Like the rest of the genus it seems almost unkillable and there seems no reason for its obscurity in Australia.

Elaeocarpus reticulatus (Blueberry Ash)

An upright evergreen tree to 7 metres from N.S.W., with white bell flowers with fringed edges in spring, followed by dark blue berries in autumn. Will grow in sun or semi-shade and is slightly frost-tender when young, but tough as nails once established.

***E. r.* 'Prima Donna'** A lovely plant identical to the above except it has clear pink bell flowers.

Embothrium coccineum (Chilean Fire Tree)

Erect, evergreen small tree to 8 metres from Chile, with attractive rich green leaves and masses of orange-scarlet spidery flowers in spring. It likes a cool, moist root run in acid soils. If you don't get it right it will die promptly.

Emmenopterys henryi

A rare, small, open-canopied deciduous tree to 7 metres or so from China. It has large handsome leaves that start out bronze in spring. The flowers produced in summer are in flattish heads and white trumpets surrounded by large white bracts. It first flowered in Britain in 1987 and, as far as I know, hasn't flowered here yet. Be the first! It likes a sheltered site and good deep soil.

Enkianthus campanulatus

Deciduous shrub from Asia requiring an acid soil and cool moist conditions similar to Rhododendrons. Masses of bell-like flowers in pale pink, with deeper pink veining in spring and brilliant autumn foliage. This species has a charming tiered habit and grows to about 3 metres. Another plant that gets a guernsey in my first book.

E. cernuus* forma *rubens Flowers burgundy and autumn leaves red and burgundy. This species makes a twiggy dome-shaped shrub to 2 metres or so.

E. deflexus Very similar to *E. campanulatus* but the flowers slightly larger and petals curl back at the ends.

E. perulatus White flowers and burgundy autumn leaves. This species makes a dome-shaped shrub to 2 metres or so and is probably the hardest to propagate, so is always scarce.

E. serrulatus Large upright shrub to 4 metres with foliage much bigger than most species, colouring orange-red in autumn. The white flowers in spring are also much larger than other species and thus this one could be considered the one that is on steroids.

Escallonia bifida syn. *E. montevidensis*

Hardy evergreen shrub from Brazil. Good background plant to 5 metres, with masses of small white flowers in summer and autumn when they are most useful. This one is possibly the prettiest of the genus and is in my first book.

***E.* 'Iveyi'** A very hardy evergreen shrub to 4 metres or so, ideal for hedges or screens. It produces clusters of pure white flowers in summer and its leaves are a really shiny dark green.

E. laevis This 3-metre evergreen from Brazil has extra large glossy green, bronze-tinged leaves and large clusters of clear pink flowers in summer.

E. pulverulenta A hardy evergreen to 4 metres with large, glossy, rich green leaves and slender spikes of greenish-white flowers. Native to Chile.

Eucryphia cordifolia (South American Leatherwood)

Useful and attractive evergreen small upright tree to 7 metres or so from South America with masses of quite large white apple blossom-like flowers in summer, well set off by its rich green leaves. A cool root run out of the hot winds and an acid organic rich soil suits this and the following forms best.

E. cordifolia × lucida A hybrid between a South American and Tasmanian species with an upright habit and rich dark evergreen foliage and, as is usual, masses of pure white flowers in summer. Grows to about 7 metres. What will Australian plant purists make of this intercontinental hybrid?

E. glutinosa The only deciduous species. This one comes from South American and has masses of white flowers in summer and then in autumn the leaves turn a fabulous bright red. Spreading bushy habit to 5 metres.

E. × intermedia Evergreen hybrid between *E. glutinosa* and *E. lucida*. Some leaves are simple and others trifoliate and the flowers are the usual white summer things.

E. lucida (Tasmanian Leatherwood) Small-leafed species with upright habit to 7 metres or so. This famous Australian species has masses of small white flowers in summer and is well known for the strongly-flavoured honey the bees produce from it, so start your own cottage industry!

E. l. 'Ballerina' This form selected from the wild has quite deep pink flowers usually produced on small plants with very dark burgundy stamens. Much darker than *E. l.* 'Pink Cloud' and released somewhat later.

E. l. 'Leatherwood Cream' A lovely variegated form with grey-green leaves edged with creamy-white.

E. l. 'Pink Cloud' A form discovered in the wild by that well-known plantsman Ken Gillanders as was *E. l.* 'Ballerina'. This one has softer pink flowers and usually takes longer to flower.

E. milliganii Small-growing form to 3 metres or so resembling *E. lucida* with tiny leaves and white flowers. Possibly a high altitude form of *E. lucida*.

E. moorei Species from N.S.W. and eastern Victoria with pinnate leaves and masses of white flowers in summer, usually produced on quite young plants. It makes a small spreading tree to 5 metres and is probably the hardiest species.

E. 'Penwith' This hybrid between *E. cordifolia* and *E. lucida* was raised in Cornwall and resembles the second parent but has larger flowers and leaves.

E. wilkiei This is a brand-new species discovered on Mount Bellenden Ker in Queensland in 1997 and looking most like *E. moorei* with its pinnate leaves with tiny bronze bristles and masses of good-sized white flowers in summer. Even though it comes from Queensland, I haven't found it any harder to grow than the other species and forms.

***Euonymus alatus* (Cork Winged Spindle Tree)** Deciduous bushy shrub to 2 metres, from China and Japan, with brilliant pinky-red autumn leaves and strange wings of corky bark on the stems. Hardy and sun-loving, this plant's bare stems will excite any floral artist and, as if this wasn't enough, it features in my first book. This species has small deep pink berries with orange seeds inside. This and all the following species are hardy and will grow in sun or light shade although deciduous species colour better with lots of sun.

E. a. 'Compactus' This is a smaller growing form to 1 metre ideal for the acreage-challenged. It is, however, less impressive in the bark stakes.

E. cornutus This hardy semi-deciduous shrub from China has an open arching habit and narrow glossy leaves and grows to 3 metres. In spring it produces tiny brown flowers. But it is for its remarkable large pink berries with broad-ridged extensions that hang below the branches that it is chiefly grown. As these ripen they split to expose orange seeds. In cold areas it can be deciduous and often colours well, usually in shades of cream and palest pink.

E. europaeus (Spindle Tree) Large shrub or small tree with green stems to 5 metres. Pinky red autumn leaves and masses of pink fruit that split to reveal orange seeds in autumn and early winter.

E. e. 'Red Cascade' A selected form that is often pendulous under the weight of its rosy-red berries. Its leaves also turn a rich scarlet in autumn.

E. myrianthus An evergreen shrub to 2.5 metres each way, from western China. Glossy, lanceolate leaves and tiny green flowers. Its major claim to fame is the fruit that follows in autumn. When ripe, these yellowish-green berries split to expose bright orange seeds. Sun to semi-shade in well-drained to dryish soil is all this amenable shrub needs.

E. oxyphyllus This deciduous Asian species will in time make a small tree to 4 metres with foliage that can turn brilliant reds and purples in autumn. It produces tiny green flowers in spring and large round deep pink berries in autumn that split, exposing the orange seeds that often hang below on fine threads.

Euphorbia lambii

This is a very rare evergreen shrub from the Canary Islands with thick stems and a dome-shaped habit to 3 metres. It has large heads of green flowers in spring and is easy to grow in any open sunny site in even dry soils. This species is slightly frost-tender.

E. mellifera A rare, bushy, evergreen shrub to 4 metres from the Canaries, with attractive soft green foliage and heads of bronze-green, honey-scented flowers in spring. A sunny, well-drained aspect suits this bold feature plant. Yes, and it is in my first book!

Eurya emarginata

Medium evergreen shrub in the Camellia family to 3 metres from Japan that grows well in shade. The foliage is rich dark green and some older leaves will go red before shedding. It produces tiny yellow-green flowers in autumn.

Euscaphis japonica

A very rare large deciduous shrub or small tree to about 5 metres, from China and Japan, with Ash-like leaves and tiny greenish flowers. It is, however, in late summer to autumn that this plant comes into its own, when it is covered with bright pink-red berries that split open to expose dark blue-black seeds. A sheltered site with some moisture suits best.

Exochorda giraldii (Pearl Bush)

Hardy, deciduous sun-loving shrub to 4 metres from China. Masses of white flowers in spring from white pearl-like buds and yellow autumn leaves. Good as a cut flower.

***E. × macrantha* 'The Bride'** A large-flowered hybrid form to 2 metres tall that has attractive arching to weeping branches and is usually wider than it is tall.

Fagus grandifolia (American Beech)

Slow-growing, rare and eventually large deciduous specimen tree to 10 metres, although not in one lifetime! It has handsome bright-green foliage and smooth grey bark. This is one for the collector that likes to be one up on everyone else!

***F. sylvatica* (English Beech)** An eventually large deciduous tree that is truly a noble thing with age, reaching 20 metres and more over the generations. It has fresh bright green foliage turning bronze in autumn and lovely smooth grey trunks. The leaves drop slowly and in a sheltered site may hang on until spring. This is another classic deciduous hedging plant much used in Europe but not often used this way here.

***F. s.* 'Aurea Pendula'** This golden-leafed form has a weeping habit as I'm sure those with some Latin have worked out! It needs to be staked to encourage height and kept out of the really hot sun so it won't scorch. A good tub specimen or centrepiece for a rock garden.

***F. s.* 'Cristata' (Cock's comb Beech)** This slow-growing form has strange curled and tightly clustered leaves of green on an upright small tree. Not to everyone's taste but a real conversation piece.

***F. s.* 'Dawyck'** A pencil form of English Beech with normal green foliage and a habit like a broad Poplar. Will eventually grow to quite a tall tree but don't worry, we won't live to see it!

***F. s.* 'Dawyck Gold'** This is a gold-leafed pencil form for those who have everything else!

***F. s.* 'Dawyck Purple'** A form of pencil beech with deep purple foliage that could make up a trifecta!

***F. s.* 'Heterophylla' (Fernleafed Beech)** A form with finely cut ferny green foliage on a tree that is taller than wide and like most forms will take its time to get up there.

F. s. 'Pendula' A green-leafed form with beautifully weeping side branches and trunks that often lean over slightly creating a wonderful picturesque specimen that will in time make a large weeping tree. This form features in my first book.

F. s. 'Purpurea Pendula' A lovely weeping form of copper beech that requires staking to obtain height or spend a bit more and buy it on a standard.

F. s. 'Riversii' (Copper Beech) This well-known form will in time make a large spreading shade tree with dark burgundy foliage from spring till autumn.

F. s. 'Rohanii' A copper beech with lobed leaves remarkably like a burgundy form of English Oak. Although it will in time grow quite tall this form is narrower than the usual Copper Beech.

F. s. 'Rohan Obilisque' This form has the foliage of *F. s.* 'Rohanii' but the narrow form of the Pencil Beech and is fairly new in this country.

F. s. 'Roseomarginata' (Tricolour Beech) The coppery green foliage of this form is edged with pink and white variegation. Stunning to look up through into the sun when it's tall enough to stand under.

F. s. 'Tortuosa' This form has the classic green foliage of the species but it keeps falling over itself, slowly creating a weeping mound that in time (lots of it!) it will make a small weeping tree.

F. s. 'Zlatia' (Golden Beech) This form has lovely golden yellow foliage in spring and summer and will in time make a spreading tree of great beauty if it isn't burnt to death by hot winds.

Fatsia japonica 'Variegata'

This is a rare and lovely form of a common but indispensable shade-loving shrub. It has huge tropical-looking, hand-shaped leaves irregularly edged in white. The tips look as if they have been dipped in paint. It will grow into an open bush to 3 metres and is quite drought-tolerant as well. In late autumn it produces huge panicles of tiny white flowers that are clustered into balls.

Fieldia australis

This is a small evergreen Australian native shrub to 50 cm in the African Violet family that in the wild grows on the trunks of tree ferns and it could well be used in this way in the garden or as a pot or hanging basket subject. It is evergreen with slightly hairy mid-green leaves and has drooping pale lemon trumpet-shaped flowers in summer followed by large white berries. A cool moist aspect befitting its usual host suits best.

Firmiana simplex

A beautiful and hardy deciduous specimen tree from China that grows to about 15 metres and isn't used anywhere near enough. It has large impressive maple-shaped leaves that turn yellow in autumn. The flowers are in sizeable panicles and are yellow-green followed by seed capsules that split and expose the seeds well before they drop.

Fothergilla gardenii

This is a truly lovely North American deciduous shrub to 1 metre for a cool climate in a rich acid soil. It has fluffy white slightly scented flowers in spring and richly coloured foliage in autumn.

F. g. 'Mount Airy' This newly selected form has slightly smaller leaves of a slightly grey-green, really good autumn foliage and is reputedly a bit more drought-tolerant. I don't, however, think it will grow in the Mallee!

F. major Slow-growing deciduous shrub to 1 metre from North America with masses of fluffy white flowers before the leaves. The large leaves turn brilliant shades of yellow, orange and red in autumn. Like the rest of its relatives it likes a cool aspect in rich acidic soils.

Franklinia alatamaha

Rare, upright, small deciduous tree to 7 metres from Georgia in North America. Extinct in the wild since about 1790. It produces large white camellia-like flowers in summer and autumn. (It is related to the

Camellia.) The foliage turns brilliant orange and scarlet in autumn. Plant this stunner in a spot sheltered from hot winds.

***Fraxinus americana* (White Ash)**
A very fast-growing and hardy deciduous shade tree to 20 metres, with good, rich, yellow autumn foliage. This will make a good shade tree in no time and like most species in this genus it isn't fussy about soil or site.

***F. excelsior* 'Pendula' (Weeping Ash)** Handsome weeping deciduous tree with pinnate green leaves. Should be staked to give it a start but unlike many weepers it will increase in height over the years. One of my favourite weepers as it doesn't have that artificial umbrella-look that most of this style of plant has. It's also tough-as-they-come.

***F. griffithii* (Evergreen Ash)** This evergreen species comes from northern India and makes a medium-sized tree to 8 metres with glossy rich green compound foliage and masses of white fluffy flowers in late summer when few trees flower.

***F. ornus* (Manna Ash)** A charming medium tree to 10 metres with masses of fluffy white scented flowers in spring, and most unusual pale lemon and bronze-burgundy autumn foliage. This is the tree that the sweet liquid called manna comes from.

Fremontodendron californicum
A large upright evergreen shrub to 5 metres from California, with beautiful golden yellow flowers in summer and autumn. It likes a sunny well-drained site and once established is quite drought-tolerant. Shelter from strong winds is important as a horizontal specimen loses much of its appeal!

***Fuchsia excorticata* (Tree Fuchsia)**
A small tree to 7 metres from New Zealand with small, pink, bell flowers flushed purple, followed by deep purple to black edible berries. The flowers are not very showy but are often produced on the older stems and even the trunks. The main feature of this unique fuchsia is the lovely peeling light brown bark on the twisted trunks and branches. The leaves have a silver reverse.

F. minutiflora A dainty, arching evergreen shrub to 1 metre with tiny leaves and equally small pink flowers throughout the warmer months. Like its glitzier relatives a cool moist aspect suits best.

***Garrya elliptica* 'Evie'**
A new variety of Silk Tassle tree with smaller leaves, more compact habit than the following, and it sometimes has purple tinges to its long winter-produced catkins. Should get to 3 metres and will grow in sun or semi-shade in almost any well-drained site. All the plants in this genus are drought-tolerant.

***G. e.* 'James Roof' (Silk Tassle Tree)** Large evergreen shrub to 4 metres with long grey-green catkins during the winter. The 'James Roof' form has much longer catkins than the type generally available. They make very good plants for growing as an espalier.

G. flavescens A very rare evergreen species to 3 metres from California with 12 cm catkins in winter and very handsome silvery-grey foliage.

G. laurifolia* ssp. *macrophylla This rarely seen evergreen species from Mexico to 4 metres or so has large leaves and drooping catkins in late spring that are less spectacular than *G. elliptica* but the foliage is a vast improvement.

Gaultheria mucronata* syn. *Pernettya mucronata
This is an evergreen slightly suckering shrub to 1 metre from Chile, with dark green, slightly spiny leaves, tiny white flowers (like Lily-of-the-Valley) in spring, followed by large attractive berries in autumn. This plant needs a cool moist aspect to do its best and I have forms with berries that may be pink, red, white or mauve so take your pick or plant them all in a big drift.

***G. × wisleyensis* 'Wisley Pearl'** This is the original clone that originated at Wisley in 1929 and is a small suckering shrub to 30 cm. The flowers are white and the large berries are a rich burgundy.

***Genista hispanica* (Spanish Broom)**
Dwarf bushy shrub to 75 cm tall by as much as 3 metres across making a mound of deep green

prickly stems with masses of bright yellow flowers in late spring. Ideal for hot sunny areas where the hose rarely goes. For more information just turn to my first book.

***Gevuina avellana* (Chilean Hazel)**
A rare, small evergreen tree from Chile and Argentina in the Protea family and nothing to do with Hazelnuts (although it has an edible nut). The leaves are ferny and highly decorative and it produces spidery white flower clusters like a giant Grevillea in summer. A sheltered moist aspect in an acid humus-rich soil suits best.

***Greyia sutherlandii* (South African Bottlebrush)**
Large deciduous sun-loving shrub to 3 metres that is a little frost tender when young. It has very large soft green geranium-shaped leaves and spikes of rich red flowers in summer. Copes well with dry soil when established.

Griselinia jodinifolia
A rare South American evergreen shrub to 3 metres. It has an upright habit and tightly packed leathery dark green leaves. An ideal tub specimen or feature plant. The flowers like the rest in the genus are small brown and not very showy.

***G. littoralis* (Broadleaf)** A very hardy large evergreen shrub to 4 metres from New Zealand that will grow well in both sun and shade and will tolerate salt winds. It has very glossy mid-green leaves and is ideal for screens and hedges.

***G. l.* 'Bantry Bay'** This striking Irish selection has irregular yellow leaf centres with a narrow green edge, making it the most variegated clone. It is however not completely stable so a sharp lookout and sharp secateurs are important to keep it pure.

***G. l.* 'Green Jewel'** This form has yellow-green variegation mainly around the leaf's edge.

***G. l.* 'Variegata'** This variety has very bold foliage well edged with bright yellow.

G. scandens A very attractive low-arching shrub to 1.5 metres tall from South America. It has large leathery apple-green leaves and in winter it produces strange brown flowers that are about as showy as this genus gets. If it is any recommendation I like its subtle blossoms.

***Halesia carolina* (Snowdrop Tree)**
A large deciduous shrub or small tree to 5 metres each way draped with clusters of showy white bell flowers in spring followed by handsome ridged green fruit. This native to North America likes a cool root run and shelter from hot winds to do its best and would make a good companion for Rhododendrons and the like.

Halimium ocymoides
Spreading dwarf evergreen shrub about 50 cm tall and 1 metre across with silver grey foliage. Flowers in the summer are bright yellow with dark brown basal markings. A native to Spain and Portugal that is sun-loving and drought-tolerant as one would hope, considering its home.

***Hamamelis × intermedia* 'Arnold Promise' (Witch Hazel)**
Like all the following species and forms these are spreading deciduous shrubs to 4 metres or so for an aspect out of hot afternoon sun and hot summer winds. The tiny egg-yolk yellow, strap-petalled flowers are born in winter and are sweetly scented. Its large leaves turn yellow in autumn.

***H. × i.* 'Jelena'** Foliage yellow and orange in autumn, flowers orange-coloured.

***H. × i.* 'Ruby Glow'** Orange red autumn foliage and coppery red flowers.

***H. japonica* 'Zaccariniana'** This form has sulphur-yellow flowers that open quite late and rich yellow autumn foliage.

***H. mollis* (Chinese Witch Hazel)** Golden autumn leaves and bright yellow flowers that are sweetly scented.

***H. m.* 'Brevipetala'** Golden autumn leaves, short-petalled deep yellow scented flowers.

***H. m.* 'Pallida'** Yellow autumn foliage and large pale lemon scented flowers.

***H. vernalis* 'Sandra' (Ozark Witch Hazel)** Heavily scented yellow flowers in late winter and striking orange and red autumn foliage.

Hebe armstrongii

A charming little evergreen New Zealander to 30 cm that gives a good imitation of a tiny yellow-green conifer. Its leaves are tiny scale-like things pressed close to the stems and it will give the whole game away by producing tiny white flowers in summer. It's sun-loving, as are most in this genus.

H. canterburiensis A charming little mound, to 10 cm tall by a little wider, of minute deep green leaves and masses of tiny white flowers in summer.

H. chathamica As the name would suggest this species hails from the tiny Chatham Islands off the east coast of the South Island of New Zealand. It is a sprawling mat to 1 metre across with bright green foliage and short racemes of soft lavender-to-white flowers in summer.

***H. cupressoides* 'Boughton Dome'** Another tiny conifer look-alike that, in this case, rarely seems to flower thus not giving the game away! Its scaly foliage is sage green and it grows into a neat bun about 20 cm each way.

H. recurva This charming shrub grows to about 1 metre each way and has lovely grey, slightly recurved leaves and slender spikes of white flowers in summer.

***H.* 'Red Edge'** This neat rounded shrub grows to about 20 cm each way and has rounded grey leaves with a fine red edge as the name would suggest and in summer produces masses of spikes of white flowers.

Hedera helix 'Congesta'

A strange but attractive shrubby ivy with stiff upright stems to 1 metre and small deep green leaves arranged on opposite sides of the stem. A good pot or rock-garden plant that will have most of your guests guessing. It doesn't seem to flower so can't get weedy.

Heliohebe 'Hagley Park'

A small evergreen sub-shrub to 60 cm with small glossy green leaves edged with red and clusters of rose-pink flowers in summer. This is a hybrid of the following species and is more upright, with smaller flower clusters.

***H. hulkeana* (New Zealand Lilac)** This sub-shrub to 1 metre was once classed as *Hebe* and one has to draw a long bow to compare it with a Lilac. It is however a lovely thing in its own right, with dark stems supporting deep evergreen foliage topped in late spring with good-sized sprays of soft lavender flowers. A sunny aspect, and well-drained but not desperately dry soil, suits best. Prune very hard after flowering to keep it shapely.

Helwingia chinensis

This rare evergreen Chinese shrub grows to about 3 metres and has large rich green leaves that are ruby-coloured when young. The clusters of tiny green flowers due to the fusion of stems are held in the centre of the leaves. This is not just a novelty but a good foliage plant for semi to deep shade. I imported this from Heronswood Nursery in Washington State in 2003.

Heptacodium miconioides (Seven Son Flower of Zhejiang)

A comparatively newly-introduced deciduous shrub to 3 metres from China, first grown in the West in 1981. It has scented white trumpet-shaped flowers in summer that are followed by a good show of bright red calyxes. The peeling coppery bark is also a feature. A sunny aspect and almost any well-drained soil should do.

Hoheria glabrata (Mountain Ribbonwood)

A beautiful, small deciduous tree to 5 metres from New Zealand, as are all the species. It has soft, green, serrated leaves and masses of pure white slightly scented flowers in late summer. Hardy but not drought-tolerant.

***H. populnea* 'Alba Variegata' (New Zealand Lacebark)** A lovely evergreen tree to 10 metres or so with white flowers in late summer and in this form striking white-edged leaves.

***H. p.* 'Osbornei'** A medium evergreen tree to 10 metres with masses of white flowers in late summer. The foliage is stained a plum colour on the underside that is a lovely foil to the flowers.

H. sexstylosa A medium upright evergreen tree with drooping side branches. Masses of pure white flowers in the autumn. A lovely and elegant tree to about 10 metres.

***H. s.* 'Purpurea'** This stunning form has rich purple undersides to the leaves. I presume that the cultivar name is invalid as it shouldn't be in Latin and I can't find it listed anywhere. To die for, but try not to!

Holodiscus discolor (Ocean Spray)

This handsome North American shrub is related to the Spirea. It is hardy, sun-loving and deciduous. It grows to about 2 metres and in early summer it produces fluffy creamy-white panicles of tiny flowers. These then turn into less attractive, brown deadheads, so the secateurs come in handy.

Hydrangea angustipetala

A rare species from Japan and Taiwan that I bought from Dan Hinkley in the U.S.A. It gets to 2 metres or so and has fairly small foliage for a Hydrangea. The flowers which are formed in late spring (unusual for this genus) are quite good-sized white lacecaps.

***H. arborescens* 'Annabelle'** A new form of the following variety with larger heads of green to white flowers on stiffer, more upright stems. This form will make a slightly suckering clump to 1.5 metres.

***H. a.* 'Grandiflora'** A small deciduous shrub of loose suckering habit with round heads of lime green to white flowers. Ideal for dried flowers. The greener flower heads I still think are as good as the above 'steroidal' form.

H. aspera* ssp. *robusta A lovely Himalayan sub-species of *H. aspera* that makes a bushy shrub to 3 metres. It has attractive bright green leaves with red stems and white and blue lacecap flowers.

***H. a.* 'Rocklon'** A strong-growing form with attractive foliage, and lacecaps containing mauve fertile florets surrounded by white sterile florets.

H. a. sargentiana A form with huge furry leaves on heavily bristled stems to 4 metres or more. It produces large blue and white lacecap flowers in summer.

H. a. strigosa A late flowered lacecap with violet-blue fertile flowers surrounded by white-bracted sterile blooms. This form has narrow, deep green leaves and an upright habit to about 3 metres.

H.a.villosa A lovely furry-leafed form making a spreading shrub to 3 metres tall with lacecaps of a soft, rich mauve throughout.

***H. a. v.* 'Saw Point'** A seedling that popped up in my nursery in 1996 that differs from *H. a. villosa*, having very long narrow leaves with jagged, serrated edges and serrated bracts that are often stained green.

***H. heteromalla* 'Snowcap'** This selection is like the species on steroids with its quite large leaves and big white lacecaps on a deciduous shrub to 4 metres.

H. h. xanthoneura A large, almost tree-like species to 5 metres or more, with quite small, light green leaves attached to bronze stems. Its pure white lacecaps are produced in summer.

H. indochinensis This rare narrow evergreen shrub grows to about 2 metres tall and has rich green foliage with a purple reverse and small white lacecap flowers in summer.

H. involucrata A shrub up to 1 metre with rough bright green leaves and blue and white lacecaps during summer that open from a large bracted bud, which is most unusual for the genus.

***H. japonica* 'Intermedia'** Robust small shrub to 1 metre with blue fertile flowers surrounded blue ray florets that are purplish red in alkaline soils. The foliage turns burgundy before dropping.

***H. macrophylla* 'Oregon Pride'** I imported this form from my friend Sean Hogan in Oregon. It has deep pink mophead flowers that are rich blue in acid soils, and the new growth has attractive black stems.

***H. m.* 'Quadricolor'** A blue and white lacecap form with leaves irregularly edged with white and yellow-green.

***H. m.* 'Regula'** A good white-flowered, mop-headed hybrid hydrangea that has strong flower-supporting stems; the blooms turn shades of green and red in autumn.

***H. m.* 'Variegata'** A shrub to 2 metres with attractive, silver variegated leaves and blue and white lacecaps.

***H. paniculata* 'Burgundy Lace'** This form has large conical heads of white flowers in summer that turn pink and mauve in autumn. This is a good plant with a fairly inappropriate name and it grows to about 2 metres, as do the following unless specified.

***H. p.* 'Floribunda'** This hard-to-find cultivar has huge narrow conical heads of white flowers with a goodly proportion of fertile flowers amongst its large sterile ones. An award of merit was given in England in 1953 for this stunner.

***H. p.* 'Grandiflora'** Medium to large deciduous shrub with big white panicle-type flowers (like a huge Lilac) in summer, turning pink and green in the autumn.

***H. p.* 'Kyushu'** A new selection from Japan with more vigour than the above variety but with smaller daintier flower heads with more tiny fertile blooms amongst the sterile bracted ones.

***H. p.* 'Pink Diamond'** Another fairly new cultivar with white flower heads turning pink with age.

***H. p.* 'Praecox'** This form is out before Christmas with more fluffy fertile flowers and very large bracted sterile blooms. A very choice form with a strong constitution that will grow to at least 3 metres.

***H. p.* 'Tardiva'** This clone is quite late-flowering, with large conical heads of white flowers that turn pink and green in autumn. This got an award of merit in England in 1966.

***H. p.* 'Unique'** This form has huge heads of white flowers similar to the old cultivar *H. p.* 'Grandiflora' but even larger. I'm not sure that this qualifies it for its cultivar name but its yet another good selection given an award of merit in 1990.

***H. quercifolia* (Oakleaved Hydrangea)** Shrub to 2 metres, with white panicle-type heads of flower and large oak-shaped leaves that turn deep claret in autumn and winter.

***H. q.* 'Snow Flake'** A new form with very full double florets that last a lot longer than the single form, although their weight makes the heads more pendulous.

H. scandens* ssp. *liukiuensis A strange little twiggy deciduous shrub to 1 metre from Japan with tiny leaves that can colour well before shedding and tiny little white lacecap flowers in summer.

***H. sikokiana* (Japanese Oakleafed Hydrangea)** I imported this stunner from Crug Farm in Wales some time back. It grows to an upright shrub to 3 metres with large, light green lobed leaves with incredible presence topped in summer with light airy white lacecaps.

Hypericum 'Hidcote'

Hardy evergreen shrub to 2 metres both ways that has lovely golden-yellow flowers with a boss of yellow stamens from midspring till autumn. This one got an award of merit in 1954 and probably came as a seedling from Hidcote Manor so it must be good!

H. kouytchense This rarely seen species from China is an evergreen shrub to 2 metres with pretty leaves that are bronze-stained when young, green later. It has large, bright yellow flowers throughout summer and into autumn with conspicuous stamens, followed by bright red seed capsules.

***H. × moserianum* 'Tricolor'** A lovely dwarf arching shrub to 50 cm with evergreen white and pink-edged leaves and small pale yellow flowers throughout the summer.

***H.* 'Rowallane'** This magnificent evergreen shrub has larger flowers than *H.* 'Hidcote' and these are produced on an upright but arching plant to 3 metres tall. This was given its well-deserved award of merit in 1943 and probably originated in Rowallane Gardens in Ireland. This features in my first book as well.

H. uralum This rare species from China is an evergreen shrub to 2 metres with neat tiny little leaves that are scented when crushed. It produces bright yellow flowers during summer and autumn that are about 2 cm across and, like the rest of the genus, has lovely long stamens.

Ilex × altaclerensis **'Lawsoniana'**
This bold Holly has large usually spineless leaves splashed with yellow in the centre. It is a female form and, if pollinated, will produce huge crops of berries. It received a first class certificate in England in 2002 even though it's been in cultivation since 1894. Watch this one as its leaves can revert to the green form.

I. aquifolium **'Angustifolia'** An unusual form of English Holly with a neat upright habit and slow growth. It has small, narrow, dark green foliage and red berries in winter if, like most other Hollies, it has a boy friend. Funnily enough I haven't ever seen this form flower or fruit.

I. a. **'Bacciflava'** Indistinguishable from an ordinary English Holly except that it has attractive yellow berries.

I. a. **'Ferox Argentea' (Hedgehog Holly)** A sterile male variety that can't obviously fruit or pollinate the female forms and that has silver-edged leaves and spines on top of the leaves as well as the edges. A good, compact form.

I. a. **'Laurifolia'** A strikingly different Holly with completely spineless deep green foliage. It is a male clone so ideal to cross-pollinate fruiting forms or to grow in areas where self-seeding has created a weed problem.

I. cornuta **(Chinese Holly)** Large evergreen shrub to 3 metres with dark green leaves usually with three spines giving the leaves a somewhat triangular look. Produces crops of red berries.

I. c. **'Rotunda'** A charming dwarf female form with larger leaves than the type with more and larger spines on the leaves. It will slowly grow to about 50 cm each way and makes a charming tub specimen.

I. crenata **'Fastigiata'** A remarkable, narrow-growing shrub, to 2 metres tall by only a few cm wide, with small, deep green leaves. Just the thing if you are looking for something like an exclamation mark that isn't a conifer and nothing like most people's idea of a Holly.

I. c. **'Gold Gem'** Dwarf evergreen shrub to 50 cm with bright golden leaves and no thorns that – if it's possible – looks even less like a Holly than the above. Ideal for rock gardens or perhaps a dwarf hedge.

I. dimorphophylla **(Okinawan Holly)** I imported this lovely thing some years ago and don't know if I have a male or female form. Not that it matters too much as its foliage is the reason to grow it. As a juvenile it has small, bright green, closely-packed leaves with lots of spines. As it matures its leaves become rounded and spineless, not at all Holly-like. Makes a large shrub to 4 metres or so.

I. kingiana A truly bizarre Holly from Bhutan and Indian Sikkim that will grow to a tree of 10 metres or more. Its large evergreen leaves to 23 cm long look more like those of a Rhododendron. It gives itself away when it produces masses of red berries along last season's stems.

I. opaca **(American Holly)** This plant has lighter green and less spiny leaves than the English Holly. It is, however, faster growing and would make a good screen or hedge. Will grow to 4 metres.

I. purpurea **(Kashi Holly)** Another one of mine that I got from Dan Hinkley's fabulous nursery in the U.S.A., and again I don't know its sex. The foliage is large, thin and spineless with just fine serrations on the edges. Its young stems are a lovely black that sets off the leaves well. The flowers are supposed to be purple to pinkish and the berries red. A quick-growing, large background shrub or small tree up to 5 metres.

I. verticillata A large deciduous shrub to 3 metres known in its home of North America as Winterberry or Black Alder. I've no idea where this latter common name originates from. The foliage turns bright yellow in autumn. The large orange red berries persist on the bare branches all winter if a boy and girl are present. I often plant them in the same hole with the drabber male at the back so he doesn't take up space.

Illicium anisatum
A medium aromatic evergreen shrub to 2.5 metres from Japan, with attractive lemon flowers in spring. This shrub, like the other species that follow, likes a moist

well-drained soil and shelter from the hot afternoon sun.

I. floridanum A plant from the U.S.A. similar to *Illicium anisatum*, but with larger sparser leaves and longer petalled-maroon flowers.

I. henryi Smaller shrub than the other two species above, that will take some time to exceed 2 metres. It has light green leaves and rose pink flowers in spring. From western China.

I. mexicanum Its name gives away its origin and it is similar to *I. floridanum* but with larger flowers and more petals. In other words, the steroidal species.

I. parviflorum A rare, slightly suckering species from North America with heavily scented foliage and small deep yellow flowers in autumn.

Indigofera pendula

A fast-growing deciduous shrub to 3 metres from China with fine grey ferny foliage and drooping spikes of deep mauve pea flowers in summer and autumn. A well-drained site in a sunny aspect will suit.

Iochroma coccineum

A quick-growing semi-deciduous shrub to 2 metres from South America with large soft leaves and substantial clusters of drooping narrow orange trumpets throughout the warmer months. It likes a sheltered warm spot and will tolerate some shade. It is however frost-tender so not for really cold areas.

I. cyaneum This species differs from the above in being slightly cold hardier and producing similar narrow trumpets but in this case they are a rich dark blue-purple.

I. grandiflorum This is the hardiest species I have grown, but it can still frost, so be warned. It will grow to 4 metres and has rich blue trumpets about twice the length of the above. It will also (if it wasn't frosted down the previous winter) flower till the cold sets in.

Itea ilicifolia

Attractive evergreen shrub to 3 metres with Holly-like leaves (but not prickly) and drooping spikes of greenish white, slightly scented flowers in summer. This elegant Chinese plant likes a moist but not wet, acid soil in a spot sheltered from hot winds. If it doesn't like you it will die promptly! Want to know more? Check it out in my first book.

I. japonica A small deciduous species to 1 metre from Japan with upright spikes of white scented flowers in summer, and stunning autumn foliage. A morning sun aspect with moisture suits best as it does with the following.

I. virginiana An attractive, somewhat suckering deciduous shrub to 1 metre from North America that looks like a smaller leafed version of the above. It produces upright spikes of tiny, white, scented flowers in summer and richly coloured autumn foliage.

***I. v.* 'Henry's Garnet'** This is basically a selected form that (under the right conditions) has particularly good autumn foliage and doesn't grow quite as tall.

Jasminum fruticans

A shrubby Mediterranean Jasmine to 4 metres by the same across with arching branches and sprinklings of golden yellow flowers all during the warmer months and even regularly in winter. Hardy, with attractive foliage.

J. parkeri A tiny little evergreen ground-hugging shrub to 30 cm across from the western Himalayas. It has tiny pinnate leaves and yellow scentless flowers in summer. A sunny rock garden, or as a small bonsai, are two possible uses for this tiny Jasmine.

Jovellina violacea

Small evergreen shrub to 1 metre from Chile with masses of lavender flowers spotted purple and yellow during summer. It likes a moist soil in a semi-shaded spot and would blend well with (or replace) some Fuchsias.

Juglans nigra 'Laciniata' (Cut Leafed Walnut)

An extremely handsome deciduous tree that tends to come true from seed. It has deeply serrated leaves giving it a ferny look. The walnuts are usually produced in quantity and just as tasty as the non cut-leafed forms.

***Kalmia angustifolia* (Sheep Laurel)**
Evergreen, slightly suckering shrub to 2 metres from North America with masses of deep pink flowers along its stems in spring. This shrub is hardier than the better-known *K. latifolia* but still likes a cool aspect and a moist soil.

K. a.* var. *pumila A quaint dwarf form of the above, to 25 cm, with the same charming deep pink flowers.

***K. latifolia* (Calico Bush or American Mountain Laurel)** Handsome evergreen shrub that will grow slowly to 2 metres with large clusters of pale pink saucer-shaped flowers in spring. This is arguably one of North America's most alluring shrubs and is, like all aristocrats, a little difficult. It likes an acid soil and cool aspect to do well, and just because you can grow Rhododendrons don't assume you can grow this.

Kerria japonica
A dainty deciduous shrub to 1.5 metres with masses of single yellow flowers in late winter and early spring. It has pale green foliage and a slightly suckering habit. Hardy in sun or shade and not fussy about soil.

***K. j.* 'Pleniflora'** A more vigorous and upright form to 3 metres with double egg-yoke yellow flowers. This form will sucker into quite large clumps if allowed.

***Knightia excelsa* (New Zealand Honeysuckle)**
A very handsome upright evergreen tree to 13 metres with rich green serrated leaves and spikes of deep red flowers in late spring and early summer, rather like Grevillea robusta in form. It prefers a cool aspect and will cope with dry soil once established.

***Koelreuteria paniculata* (Golden Rain Tree)**
A picturesque deciduous tree to 15 metres or so from China with leaves divided into lots of leaflets that can turn rich yellow in autumn. The flowers are produced in large panicles in summer and are, of course, yellow and these are followed by large coppery, papery seed pods that are most entertaining. The rough, fissured bark on old gnarled trees is also a feature. A sunny well-drained site suits.

***Kolkwitzia amabilis* 'Pink Cloud' (Beauty Bush)**
A large arching deciduous shrub to 4 metres from China with masses of soft pink flowers with a yellow throat in spring. This cultivar, raised at Wisley in 1946, is deeper and larger flowered than the wild form.

+ *Laburnocytisus adamii*
A truly remarkable, small upright deciduous tree to 5 metres that arose as a graft hybrid between *Laburnum* and *Cytisus* in France in 1825. It produces flowers of three types, all on the one plant; some will be drooping spikes of yellow, typical of the Laburnum, some will be clusters of purple broom-like flowers and the rest, and by far the majority, are drooping spikes of apricot flowers that are between both parents.

***Laburnum anagyoides* 'Aureum'**
A small, upright deciduous European tree to 4 metres with drooping spikes of yellow Wisteria-like flowers in late spring and – in this form – attractive yellow-green leaves throughout the summer.

***L. × watereri* 'Vossii' (Golden Chain Tree)** This hybrid Laburnum has the longest drooping flower spikes of any form, up to 20 cm long and lots of them to boot. Often used over arches, like at Bodnant Gardens in Wales, but rarely on that scale. Igloo greenhouse frames just don't do it for me.

Latua pubiflora
An elegant small deciduous shrub to 2 metres from Chile. The slightly prickly arching stems support rich, purple, velvety trumpet flowers in late winter and spring. This plant likes a moist soil in a sunny or semi-shaded site. It was used by South American Indians to poison water to kill the fish. (Not the way I would recommend fishing but could be useful if unwanted guests drop in!) It will be found in my first book.

Laurelia sempervirens

A hardy, conical small tree with drooping branches to 7 metres or so from Chile. Its deep evergreen foliage smells like aniseed jellybeans so don't tell the children or it could become deciduous! The flowers are tiny and of no importance but this plant is elegant and will make a good screening tree. Seems to cope well with sun or shade and is fairly drought-tolerant once established.

***Laurus azorica* (Canary Island Bay Tree)**

A very rare form of Bay Tree, differing from the usual species only in that it has larger leaves. This tree can reach 10 metres or so but can be pruned or shaped (even into a ball on a stick) and tastes much better than those dried things bought from supermarkets.

***L. nobilis* 'Aureus' (Golden Bay)** A form of the classical Bay Tree that has soft gold-green foliage; otherwise it looks much the same as the normal Bay Tree and tastes just the same in your cooking! Although it could grow to 8 metres or more, it could be a gold ball on a stick!

Lepechinia hastata

This plant could be a shrub or a slightly woody perennial and comes from Mexico and surrounds. It is related to Salvia and grows to 2 metres or more tall. Its large leaves are a lovely grey-green and very aromatic and the long upright panicles of purple flowers are produced almost non-stop. A sunny well-drained site is all that is needed and if you want more information turn to my second book.

Lespedeza thunbergii

Oh, I hate plants that don't easily fit into any category, and this woody perennial is probably a shrub that dies down and needs cutting, just as a classic perennial, so a shrub it is! It has arching stems, to 2 metres or more long, with pretty leaves divided into three leaflets. In late summer and autumn it has cascading masses of tiny, rosy-purple pea flowers. It likes a well-drained site in sun or semi-shade and hails from China and Japan.

Leucothoe davisiae

Shade-loving evergreen shrub to 50 cm with a slightly suckering habit. Rich, dark green leaves topped with upright spikes of Lily-of-the-Valley-like flowers in summer. Native of North America.

L. fontanesiana Evergreen shrub to 1 metre with drooping branches, white Lily-of-the-Valley flowers in spring and burgundy-tinged leaves in winter. Like all the species, treat it like a Rhododendron.

***L. f.* 'Rainbow'** Form with cream, yellow and pink variegated leaves.

L. keiskei A tiny little Japanese species, to 20 cm, with an arching habit and very dark foliage. It in fact looks like a reduced version of the above and could be ideal for the truly space-challenged.

Leycesteria crocothyrsos

Hardy evergreen shrub to 3 metres with attractive foliage on horizontally arranged branches. The flowers are yellow in drooping spikes and produced in summer followed by small green fruit not unlike gooseberries to look at but I doubt they taste like them. Native of Assam, and in my first book.

***Ligustrum japonicum* 'Rotundifolium'**

A slow-growing upright and compact shrub with glossy deep green leaves. Grows to 2 metres and is an ideal tub specimen in sun or shade. It occasionally produces heads of small white flowers. In a genus that does 'boring' so well this is a remarkably good textural foliage plant that is tough-as-guts to boot!

Lindera obtusiloba

A magnificent large shrub with large entire (or sometimes three-lobed at the tip) leaves. The foliage is bright green in summer and gold with pink tints in autumn. The tiny flowers are yellow and cluster along the stems before the leaves appear. This native of China, Japan and Korea is also in my first book, but if you haven't got your copy yet plant this in a spot sheltered from hot winds.

Liquidambar orientalis

This Liquidambar to 10 metres from Asia is a smaller and daintier species of Liquidambar than its North American relative, making it much more appropriate for small gardens. Its foliage turns to brilliant colours in autumn and the foliage has more rounded lobes.

***L. styraciflua* 'Festeri'** A form of Liquidambar having larger leaves than the type and which colour deep claret-red in autumn and hold well into winter. An Australian selection.

***L. s.* 'Gum Ball'** A fascinating dwarf Liquidambar which makes a dense bushy shrub to about 2 metres. Its foliage colours brilliantly in autumn and holds well into winter. Can also be purchased as a standard that will make its own ball on a stick.

***L. s.* 'Silver King' syn. *L. s.* 'Variegata'** A medium deciduous tree to 7 metres, with foliage margined creamy-white and flushed with pink later in the summer, turning burgundy and pink in autumn.

***L. s.* 'Worplesdon'** A lovely, tall tree with weeping side branches in time, heavily cut foliage that colours well in autumn and early winter. It also has attractive corky bark.

Liriodendron tulipifera (Tulip Tree)

Large deciduous North American tree to 30 metres or so with green and orange tulip-shaped flowers in spring and large leaves that turn bright yellow in autumn. Seedling trees will take many years to flower, so some people may prefer the following grafted forms as they flower young.

***L. t.* 'Aureomarginatum'** A form with golden edges to the leaves in spring, which fade to straight green by midsummer.

***L. t.* 'Fastigiatum'** Very tall but narrow form to 20 metres with the classic leaves and flowers but a slender form ideal where space is of a premium and won't grow over the fence and annoy those next door!

***L. t.* 'Glen Gold'** A lovely form of Tulip tree with light yellow foliage in spring that fades a bit as the season advances then turns bright yellow again in autumn.

Lomatia dentata

An evergreen shrub to 3 metres from South America with glossy deep green foliage and greenish-white spidery flowers. It will grow well in sunny to semi-shaded aspects.

L. ferruginea A truly spectacular species from Chile and Patagonia to 4 metres or so with stiff fern-like leaves on bronze stems and flowers somewhat like a Grevillea in shades of buff and scarlet. It prefers a cool aspect and acid soils and will be a challenge to those away from the cool hill-station areas.

L. fraseri A lovely shrub to 5 metres or so from N.S.W. and Victoria with ferny, rich green foliage and white scented spidery flowers in summer. It grows well in semi-shade and is fairly drought-tolerant once established.

L. hirsuta This rare Chilean and Argentinian shrub grows to about 5 metres and produces clusters of spidery white and green flowers in spring set off well by its comparatively large leathery evergreen leaves. A spot in moist soil and out of the afternoon sun will suit it best. I saw huge plants of this in Argentina at the base of the Andes.

Lonicera fragrantissima

A large semi-deciduous arching shrub from China to 3 metres that produces highly scented small cream-coloured flowers in winter. It is very hardy but inclined to be a bit straggly and uninteresting to look at. Plant it in an out of the way corner and enjoy the perfume.

L. pileata An evergreen horizontally-branched shrub to 50 cm tall by up to 2 metres wide that makes an ideal ground cover in heavy shade. Leaves rich green. Its inconspicuous lemon flowers hide between the leaves but are sweetly scented, these are followed by translucent violet berries.

***L. p.* 'Gold as Green'** This is my own selection and it has lighter green foliage than the species and a slightly taller arching habit.

L. tartarica A hardy deciduous shrub to 1 metre from Central Asia and Russia with masses of rose pink scentless Honeysuckle flowers in summer followed by red berries.

Lophomytus × ralphii 'Pucker's Red'

An attractive upright narrow evergreen shrub to 2.5 metres from New Zealand with small rounded bronze leaves that darken with frosts in winter. It also has crops of small white flowers in summer followed by black berries. It likes a sunny site and is reasonably drought-tolerant.

***L. × r.* 'Red Dragon'** This form has slightly smaller smoother leaves and richer burgundy colour.

Loropetalum chinense

Evergreen arching shrub to 2 metres from China in the Witch Hazel family, ideal for a tub or of course the open ground. The white strap-petalled flowers appear mainly in late winter-spring. A hardy plant that will do well in sun or part-shade and a photo can be seen in my first book.

***L. c.* 'Burgundy'** This form has deep pink flowers and rich burgundy leaves and as there are few evergreens with such dark foliage this makes it a very valuable plant. Treat it just as you would the green form.

Lotus hirsutus syn. *Dorycnium hirsutum*

A small deciduous shrub from the Mediterranean to 1 metre tall with grey furry leaves and clusters of softest pink pea flowers in summer. These are followed by reddish seed pods. Prune back really hard in winter and plant it in a well-drained sunny aspect. It does feature in my tree and shrub book under its synonym.

Luma apiculata syn. *Myrtus luma* (Cinnamon Barked Myrtle)

Moderate-growing evergreen tree to 7 metres from Chile and Argentina with dark green leaves and masses of white blossom in the summer and autumn. Black, edible but boring berries in winter. The bark is a lovely cinnamon colour with white patches. It also makes a very good hedge although this will hide the trunks. This tree will grow well in most aspects and is fairly shade-tolerant. It is prone to red spider mite in sheltered sites. It is in my first book, and to stand in a forest of these in Argentina was truly amazing. I expected to see Hobbits peering out at me!

Mackaya bella

A charming evergreen shrub with glossy deep green foliage and pale pink trumpet flowers veined with burgundy in late spring. This South African shrub can reach 3 metres and grows well in dry shaded areas, which makes it ideal under trees, although it is fine in the sun to. It is slightly frost-tender but its preferred aspect will give it enough protection as a rule.

Maclura pomifera (Osage Orange)

An almost indestructible large deciduous tree to 15 metres with thorny branches and rich yellow autumn foliage. It produces on female trees large, warted yellow inedible fruit the size of a well-grown Grapefruit that show up in nurseries every year for identification. Once used as a windbreak and shelter-tree in farming areas but rarely used today. It comes from the U.S.A. and will tolerate very alkaline and dry soils.

Macropiper excelsum (New Zealand Pepper)

An attractive evergreen shrub to 3 metres with large heart-shaped rich green leaves to 10 cm each way. The flowers are small and of no real consequence, looking (if this makes any sense) like green chocolate bullets. It will grow both in sunny or shaded aspects, is drought-tolerant, and its foliage colour will be yellow-green in the sun. A good tub specimen. The foliage is aromatic and has been used to alleviate toothache. It will be nipped by heavy frost.

M. melchior This form comes from the Three Kings Islands of New Zealand and has larger, more heavily veined and brighter, glossy green leaves than those of the more common *M. excelsum*. It is a dramatic foliage plant, ideal in dryish shade but is slightly frost-tender so those of you in cold areas, take note!

Magnolia acuminata var. *subcordata* (*M.* cordata)

A large bushy deciduous shrub or small tree to 6 metres from North America with light green foliage and scented pale yellow goblet-shaped flowers in late spring. This and most of the following species will grow well in sun or semi-shade in a well-drained friable soil.

***M.* × *brooklynensis* 'Woodsman'** A strange but attractive hybrid produced in the Brooklyn Botanic gardens when they crossed *M. acuminata* with *M. liliiflora*. The result is a small upright deciduous tree to about 4 metres with tulip-shaped flowers that are dusty-pink and green outside, and green and creamy-white inside.

***M.* 'Caerhays Belle'** A lovely hybrid with huge semi-double bright pink flowers on a small deciduous tree to 7 metres.

M. campbellii This Magnolia must be one of the world's most spectacular flowering trees. The large goblet-shaped pale pink blooms are produced in early spring on a tree that can reach 17 metres or more. It may take up to 20 years to flower, but usually doesn't, so be patient.

***M. c.* 'Alba Group'** A white-flowered form of the species that flowers at a comparatively early stage usually due to being grafted.

M. c. mollicomata This form is almost identical to the species with slightly deeper pink flowers produced as a younger plant; perhaps as young as five years old.

M. delavayi A rare evergreen Chinese tree to 7 metres or so with large leathery olive green leaves and scented parchment-coloured, saucer-shaped flowers in summer, to 25 cm across.

***M. denudata* (Yulan)** A truly lovely plant in a stunning genus. This is an upright, small deciduous tree from China to 5 metres or so that has tulip-shaped pure white flowers before the leaves break in spring.

***M.* 'Elizabeth'** A newish American hybrid with soft yellow sweetly scented tulip-shaped blooms in spring. It is a cross between *M. acuminata* and *M. denudata* and the flowers are shaped like the second parent. Once established, this selection can also produce flowers till after Christmas.

***M. grandiflora* 'Exmouth'** Large evergreen tree from North America with huge cream-coloured scented flowers in summer and autumn. The 'Exmouth' form flowers at a younger age than seedling plants, often in just three years.

M. hypoleuca A rare deciduous Magnolia from Japan to 7 metres tall, with very large paddle-shape leaves and large open cup-shaped cream-white, highly scented flowers in late spring and early summer. A stunning medium tree with an almost tropical look.

M. macrophylla An amazing deciduous species from the south-east parts of the U.S.A. that in a sheltered spot could get to 20 metres or more. Its huge paddle-like soft green leaves can exceed 60 cm in length and in years to come it will produce fragrant white flowers with stains of purple toward the petal base in early summer.

***M.* 'Royal Crown'** This hybrid makes a small tree to 4 metres or so with large deep pink flowers with a white interior before the leaves open.

M. salicifolia A lovely upright conical deciduous tree to 4 metres or so from Japan with narrow leaves and narrow-petalled starry flowers in early spring rather likes those of *M. stellata* without the shrubby habit.

M. sieboldii Wide-spreading deciduous shrub or small tree to 4 metres with nodding fragrant white flowers with burgundy stamens in summer. Native of Japan and Korea.

M.* × *thompsoniana A large bushy deciduous shrub or small tree to 5 metres with attractive bright green foliage and narrow tulip-shaped scented flowers of a strange buff-cream colour during summer.

M. wilsonii A spreading large shrub or small tree with upside-down white flowers with burgundy stamens in late spring. It differs from *M. sieboldii* in its narrower leaves and daintier flowers.

× *Mahoberberis aquisargentii*

A strangely beautiful evergreen hybrid between *Mahonia aquifolium* and *Berberis sargentiana* that I brought back from Oregon in 2003. The foliage is somewhat Holly-like and a truly glossy rich green with vicious spines! The flowers are bright yellow and followed by black berries. If the books I have are to be believed this slightly suckering shrub of 1 to 1.5 metres will grow in sun or shade, moist or dry.

***Mahonia aquifolium* (Oregon Grape)**
Small evergreen shrub to 1 metre from North America with dark green foliage, bronze-tinged in winter. The bright yellow flowers are produced in early spring and followed by decorative blue-black berries. Suckering habit, good as a taller ground cover and, like the rest of the species, it likes shade in cultivation.

M. confusa This rare species from China is a narrow upright shrub, eventually up to 2 metres, with deep green leaflets on purple leaf stems. Its clusters of yellow flowers are on upright spikes in autumn and these are followed by blue-black berries.

M. fortunei A lovely slender upright evergreen shrub from China to 2 metres with narrow, thornless, rich green leaflets and upright small clusters of yellow flowers in winter.

M. japonica Handsome shrub to 3 metres with deep green prickly leaflets and long outward-pointing racemes of sweetly scented soft yellow flowers in midwinter.

***M. j.* Bealei Group** This form differs from the species in having few, larger and greyer leaflets on a narrower bush. The flowers are in shorter more pendulous paler yellow spikes. It all sounds second best but be assured it isn't as this plant can hold its own with the best.

M. lomariifolia Large, stiff upright shrub to 4 metres with very long leaves and upright spikes of rich golden yellow flowers in winter. Like most of the larger growing species it will eventually expose its trunks, which have lovely furrowed parchment coloured bark. Probably the most impressive species and comes from China.

M. napaulensis This species grows to about 3 metres and has large olive-green spiny leaflets and rich yellow flowers in slightly drooping spikes in mid- to late winter.

***M. × wagneri* 'Moseri'** This slightly suckering shrub grows to about 1.5 metres and has mid-green, non-prickly foliage that can colour richly in frosty areas. The new growth is usually an amazing orange shade. The flowers are born in short upward-facing spikes along this year's stems in winter.

***Malus* 'John Downie' (Crab apple)**
This is probably the best of the Crab apples if jelly is your aim! It makes an upright small deciduous tree to 7 metres with white blossom in spring and large red fruit. The autumn colour can be quite showy as well. Like all the following species and forms it is a hardy sun-loving tree that will grow in most soils.

***M.* 'Pioneer Rose'** A hybrid between an ornamental Crab apple and an eating apple discovered by my good friend Helen Serpells in Victoria's North East. It makes a lovely small spreading shade tree to 4 metres with cerise flowers in spring followed by burgundy-tinged foliage and large deep burgundy red fruit almost the size of a commercial apple. When cooked, you will get pink stewed fruit.

M. × platycarpa An American selection that makes a small spreading shade tree to 6 metres with large single soft pink flowers followed by impressive almost eating apple-sized, slightly flattened green fruit that smells delicious as it ripens on the tree.

M. toringoides A small deciduous tree from western China that produces slightly scented white flowers in spring. It has unusual lobed leaves and little round coral-coloured fruit with red blushing. It makes a graceful spreading small tree to 7 metres.

M. transitoria This is a lovely and hardy small deciduous tree from north-western China with an open arching form to 7 metres tall. The foliage is lobed and turns brilliantly in autumn and it has white blossom followed by small round yellow fruit in autumn.

M. tschonoskii This lovely rare Crab Apple hails from Japan and makes an upright conical tree to 10 metres or so with grey-green leaves and white blossom followed by yellowish-green fruit and brilliant autumn foliage. It has a string of British awards to its credit and I find it hard to understand its rarity in this country.

M. trilobata A rare and remarkable Crab Apple from Greece with almost maple-shaped leaves that turn brilliant red in autumn. Its large white scented flowers are followed by green fruit and it makes a tidy upright tree ideal where space is limited. This species is so unique that it is sometimes listed as another genus (*Eriolobus*). This is so good that it features in my first book and I think I may have over-popularised it!

***M. yunnanensis* var. *veitchii* (Pencil Crab Apple)** A lovely very narrow-growing tree to 7 metres with large leaves turning bright colours in autumn. It produces clusters of small white flowers in spring and deep pink-red fruit in autumn and early winter.

M. × zumi* var. *calocarpa A lovely hybrid Crab Apple with flowers pink in bud opening white and scented. These are followed in autumn by tiny bright red persistent fruit (birds allowing). It has a spreading habit to 4 metres or so making it a good small shade tree.

Manglietia fordiana

A rare evergreen conical tree to 7 metres from Hong Kong. It is closely related to the *Magnolia* and like *Michelia* will probably be sunk into *Magnolia* if the taxonomists have their way. It has white scented flowers in spring that are, funnily enough, very like those of a *Magnolia*!

Maytenus boaria

An elegant small to medium evergreen tree from Chile, to 10 metres. It is quite drought-resistant and has a lovely weeping habit with age. So if you can picture an evergreen weeping willow you have a mental picture. If this tree was more available I would recommend it as an elegant farm tree that in times of drought could be fed to cattle as it is in South America. It will sucker a bit which could be a way of getting more plants.

M. magellanica A bushy evergreen shrub to 3 metres from Chile with leathery dark green leaves. It also has small red flowers followed by bright yellow fleshy berries. This could make a good hedge in areas that don't get too dry in summer.

Melanoselinum decipiens (Tree Angelica)

A very strange evergreen monocarpic plant (flowers only once, then dies) that looks like a palm with Angelica leaves that can be 1 metre long. As each leaf dies it leaves a ring around the trunk. The plant can live to ten or more years before blooming and when it does it looks like a giant parsnip in flower. This wonderful plant gives the garden a tropical look but is actually native to Madeira and is in my first book.

Melia azedarach 'Jade Snowflake' (Variegated Bead Tree, Variegated White Cedar)

This is a remarkable form of a commonly planted medium shade tree that is native to Asia and Australia. Like the common form this is a quick-growing deciduous tree with fine ferny foliage, clusters of mauve fragrant flowers in summer and hard yellow bead-like fruit that often hangs on well into winter. This form differs due to its pure white mottled variegation that lifts it well and truly beyond the mundane.

Melianthus major

A very hardy South African shrub to 3 metres that should be cut down to ground level every summer to stop it getting leggy. Its leaves are large, compound, serrated and to die for. Its tall spikes of burgundy-bracted flowers are produced in summer and much-loved by wattle birds. Sun to semi-shade and drought-tolerant.

M. villosus This rarely seen species has green foliage. Its flower spikes are a more brown-red and in its own way it's as attractive as its better-known relative.

Meliosma dilleniifolia ssp. *cuneifolia*

A large deciduous Chinese shrub to 3 metres with panicles of creamy-white scented spirea-like flowers in summer followed by small black fruit.

Mespilus germanica 'Dutch' (Medlar)

A lovely small spreading picturesque deciduous tree to 4 metres or so related to the Hawthorns and once an important fruit tree. It has large single white flowers in midspring followed by strange brownish fruit with persistant calyx lobes that can be eaten when soft and/or turned into jellies and pastes. The foliage also turns beautifully in autumn.

***M. g.* 'Nottingham'** This form has a more upright habit and slightly smaller fruit which makes this one the one to choose if space is limited. Those in the know suggest that the flavour of this form is stronger than the above. It still has the lovely flowers and good autumn foliage.

Metapanax delavayi

A rare evergreen shrub to 4 metres or so from China with compound leaves that have a passing resemblance to marijuana so plant it and wait for the strange looks! The foliage does lend a tropical look to the garden and it will grow in sun or semi-shade. Its tiny green flowers in clusters are subtle to say the least and are followed by black berries.

Mitraria coccinea

A low, spreading, evergreen shrub from Chile with masses of bright orange, tubular flowers from late spring through summer. This plant can also be grown as a light climber, open ground cover, trailing over a wall or in a hanging basket. It prefers a semi-shaded moist aspect and is in my first book if you need more.

Montanoa leucantha ssp. *arborescens* (Mexican Tree Daisy)

A fast-growing shrub to 4 metres or so that is usually cut to near ground level each spring as one would to a tree Dahlia. It has attractive leaves and heads of white scented daisies in winter. Wants a sunny, well-drained site.

Muehlenbeckia astonii

A rare but tough-as-guts evergreen shrub to 2 metres from New Zealand with tiny bronze-green leaves on zig-zagging branches. It looks like a mound of exploding wire and is far more attractive than this description suggests!

Musschia aurea

An extremely rare woody perennial to 1 metre from the sea-cliffs of Madeira, where it is almost extinct. This strange Campanula relative has large, glossy green leaves and clusters of upward-facing yellow bell flowers in summer. It likes a sunny, well-drained site and its foliage is so attractive that its lovely flowers are almost an over-indulgence! I include it with shrubs with a little reluctance as it could easily be with perennials.

Myrtus communis (Common Myrtle)

Aromatic dark green evergreen shrub to 2 metres with masses of white flowers in summer, followed by black fruit. It comes from southern Europe is heat and drought-tolerant and is the Myrtle of the ancients.

***M. c.* 'Nana'** Attractive form to 1 metre, smaller in all parts than the above.

Nandina domestica 'Richmond'

This form of Japanese sacred bamboo is in every way the hardy sun or shade-tolerant, drought-proof, upright evergreen bamboo-ish shrub with masses of white flowers that the usual form is. It was selected in New Zealand many years ago due to it being a reliable fruiting form producing large heads of bright red fruit that are held for months.

Neillia sinensis

An elegant arching deciduous shrub to 2 metres with spikes of tiny white flowers in summer and rich-coloured autumn leaves. It is hardy, shade-tolerant and quick-growing although don't let this or the following species get too dry. Its bristly seed pods are also entertaining.

N. thibetica A very elegant, hardy deciduous shrub to 3 metres from western China. It produces arching coppery canes supporting bright green leaves, that turn gold in autumn, and narrow spikes of soft pink flowers in late spring and early summer.

Neolitsea sericea

Hardy evergreen tree from China, Japan and Korea that grows to about 10 metres. The handsome grey-green mature foliage is topped in spring by furry yellow-brown new growth. Its small flowers are yellowy-green, and form in small clusters in late autumn.

Nothofagus alpina syn. *N. procera*

A fast-growing deciduous tree to 14 metres or so from South America which colours brilliant orange in autumn. Like the rest of the genus they like a deep well-drained soil that never gets too dry.

N. antarctica A charming deciduous species from Chile, to 8 metres. It has a gnarled habit and small crinkled leaves that turn brilliant colours in autumn.

N. betuloides This South American species makes a lovely upright evergreen tree with small rich dark green leaves not unlike those of *N. dombeyi* so it is one to add to the collection in a very large garden!

***N. cunninghamii* (Myrtle Beech)** Native large-growing evergreen tree to 17 metres or more. It has small dark green leaves and the new growth bronze-red. This species is found widely in Tasmania and in cool gullies in parts of Victoria.

N. dombeyi A large evergreen species from South America to 17 metres with small deep green leaves. I saw monsters of this species in the wild in Argentina and only metion this so that you will know how well travelled I am!

***N. fusca* (New Zealand Red Beech)** The delicate bronze-red evergreen juvenile foliage becomes olive green as the tree matures. It is upright to spreading with age (as we all seem to be!); to 17 metres or more.

***N. gunnii* (Tanglefoot)** Small tree, rarely seen more than a couple of metres tall, with attractive autumn foliage and a rustic habit. One of the very few deciduous Australian natives and definitely the most challenging species to grow away from its Tasmanian mountain haunts. A couple of really hot days can see it off to that Beech forest in the sky!

***N. moorei* (Antarctic Beech)** A lovely large evergreen Australian species to 20 metres from N.S.W., with (for the genus) big, deep green leaves and brilliant lobster-coloured new growth.

N. nitida A lovely, rare, evergreen South American species with foliage similar to *N. cunninghamii* but larger. The tree is, however, smaller and more irregular in outline but will still reach 10 metres if you live long enough.

***N. obliqua* (Roble Beech)** Upright, birch-like deciduous species from Chile that will grow extremely quickly, if conditions suit, with rich green foliage of medium size with good autumn colour.

Nyssa sinensis

Chinese upright tree to 10 metres with large coppery red leaves in spring followed by rich-coloured autumn foliage. This is one of this world's great autumnal trees as are the following. All the species and forms grow best in a sunny but moist to wet site.

***N. sylvatica* (Tupelo)** A beautiful small to medium tree to 10 metres with a much more irregular outline than the above. This species is from North America and has brilliant orange and red autumn foliage.

***N. s.* 'Autumn Cascade'** Upright tree with weeping branches discovered as a seedling in this country. The green leaves, larger than the species, turn brilliant red in autumn.

Oemleria cerasiformis syn. *Osmaronia* (Oso Berry)

A hardy upright deciduous shrub to 3 metres from California. It is one of the first deciduous shrubs to form leaves before the end of winter and at the same time it produces dainty pendant spikes of sweetly scented white flowers rather 'coconuttish' at least to my nose. This made it into my first book if you want to see a picture.

Olearia insignis syn. *Pachystegia insignis* (Marlborough Rock Daisy)

This extremely rare evergreen shrub comes from New Zealand and makes a neat rounded shrub to 1 metre with large leathery leaves with white furry reverses and large pure white daisies in summer from white furry buds. It likes a sunny aspect with a root system that is kept cool under rocks or a good mulch.

O. rufa* syn. *P. rufa Slightly smaller in all respects than the above, but with bronze fur below the leaves and on the flower buds.

Oplopanax horridus (Devil's Club)

This strange deciduous shrub comes from the U.S.A. around the Pacific North West and grows in damp forests so a cool moist aspect will suit. Its thick stems are usually unbranched and are always armed with strong spines. Its large, soft green, maple-shaped leaves are clustered towards the top and have thorns down the midrib underneath (a great practical joke!). It produces panicles of small greenish flowers followed by clusters of stunning red berries.

Osmanthus armatus

Large evergreen shrub to 4 metres or so from China with Holly-like leaves and tiny white scented flowers in the autumn. This genus are all hardy, evergreen, sun and shade-tolerant, drought-tolerant and extremely good screening plants.

O. × burkwoodii A hybrid to 3 metres with small rich deep green foliage and a compact habit, making it ideal for hedging. The small but showy white flowers are well-scented. It is a hybrid of the following. (It looks like *O. delavayi* on steroids.)

O. delavayi Beautiful Chinese species to 2 metres with small dark green leaves and masses of white 'coconut suntan lotion' scented flowers in spring. This one trims well so would make a good low hedge.

***O. decorus* 'Baki Kasapligil'** A newly imported form that I got from Dan Hinkley's fabulous Heronswood Nursery in Washington State (that now is no longer, unfortunately). It will make a shrub to 2 metres and has large unarmed deep green leaves so that no-one will pick what it is. Its scented tiny white flowers are formed in early spring.

O. × fortunei Similar to *O. armatus* (which is one of its parents) in foliage and size. Tiny extremely fragrant white flowers in autumn and Holly-like leaves in youth, less spiny with age.

O. fragrans A large evergreen shrub with dark green non-spiny foliage and tiny heavily scented cream flowers in summer. This Japanese and Chinese native has one of the plant kingdom's strongest perfumes.

O. f.* forma *aurantiacus This form only varies from the above in that its tiny flowers are orange.

O. heterophyllus A hardy evergreen shrub to 3 metres with Holly-like leaves that with age tend to lose their teeth a bit (much like us really!). Its tiny white scented flowers are formed in late autumn and will really spice up your life.

***O. h.* 'All Gold'** This form has bright golden Holly-like leaves and tiny white scented flowers in autumn. I imported it from England a few years ago and you'll be glad I did.

***O.h.* 'Fastigiata'** I recently imported this form from America and it has foliage identical to the species but will grow to 3 metres tall by only about 40 cm wide. A great addition to a great genus.

***O. h.* 'Goshiki'** This form came home with me from the U.S.A. in 2003 although I have since found out that someone beat me to the punch (which is one of the downsides to importing plants). It has the classic Holly leaves and the scented flowers but this one has conspicuous yellow and white marbling in the foliage.

***O. h.* 'Purpurea'** Medium evergreen shrub to 3 metres with the usual Holly-like leaves, dark green when mature but deep purple whilst young. It has the same sweetly scented tiny white flowers in autumn. Any form of this species will make a good screen or hedge.

***O. h.* 'Rotundifolius'** This strange but attractive form makes a neat, dense bush with very dark green, round leathery leaves that make it a good feature plant. The same flowers as the species.

***O. h.* 'Sasaba'** Another of my recent imports that will have them all guessing! It will grow to a 3-metre shrub and has the same scented flowers, but the leaves that in this genus are usually simple have become three spiny leaflets. A fabulous textural plant.

***O. h.* 'Variegatus'** A charming form with silver edges to the leaves and of slow, compact growth habit to 2 metres or so with the same scented flowers.

***Ostrya carpinifolia* (Hop Hornbeam)**
Medium deciduous tree to 6 metres or so from southern Europe and Asia Minor with yellow autumn leaves and hop-like seed pods. Lovely male catkins hang in the tree in spring.
O. japonica This species from Japan and China is quite similar to *O. carpinifolia* but is smaller in all its parts.

***Oxydendrum arboreum* (Sorrel Tree)**

Small upright tree to 5 metres from North America with white Lily-of-the-Valley-type flowers in summer and exquisite crimson autumn foliage. It requires a cool aspect and compost-enriched acid soil but is worth any trouble and even made it into my first book.

***Paeonia* 'Alice Harding'**
This is a quite small-growing tree peony rarely exceeding 75 cm tall but in time making a large suckered clump. Its flowers are very full double and yellow with a very pleasing scent. Like all the following forms it likes a sunny well-drained aspect with vegetable-garden-like soil without competition from tree roots. Unlike the herbaceous species and hybrids these forms don't need a winter chill to get them to bloom.
***P.* 'Angelet'** A lovely hybrid to 1 metre with semi-double cream flowers with red flares at the base of the petals.
***P.* 'Arcadia'** This cultivar grows strongly to 1.5 metres with large more or less single yellow flowers with central red flares.
***P.* 'Artemis'** This variety grows to about 1 metre and has single soft lemon flowers.
***P.* 'Black Panther'** A hybrid from America, with large semi-double dark blood-red flowers with yellow stamens. It grows to about 2 metres and its fine foliage often colours well in autumn.
***P.* 'Black Pirate'** This form has deep black-red single flowers very like the above in colour but smaller.
P. delavayi* syn. *P. lutea* var. *delavayi A charming wildling with finely cut foliage that is burgundy as it emerges, and single, deepest crimson flowers to 10 cm across with golden stamens. It grows to about 2 metres and although it has small flowers compared to many of its relatives they are big compared to many other plants and it is so lovely it should not be ignored. Remember I know about such things!
***P.* 'Destiny'** Probably a seedling form of *P. rockii* that found its way into Australia so long ago that it may have been the Chinese gold miners that did it. A strong shrub to 2 metres with huge single flowers that are so pale pink as to be almost white with large cherry-coloured blotches in the centre.
***P.* 'Etienne de France'** This extremely old form probably came to Australia with the Chinese gold miners and, despite its French name, was named here. It is a large shrub to 2 metres or so with large scented, double mid-pink blooms that would have got Barbara Cartland very excited!
***P.* 'Flambeau'** This old form has huge heavy double soft tomato-red sweetly scented flowers that, like so many of the Chinese doubles, is lovely to float in a bowl but too heavy to hold itself up so bamboo staking of the individual stems is needed to show it off on the bush. Grows to about 1.5 metres.
***P.* 'Gauguin'** This rare hybrid to 1.5 metres tall has large semi-double flowers that are ivory, heavily overlayed with wine-red. Hard to describe and hard to resist.
***P.* 'Gessekai'** This stunning Japanese hybrid is almost single pure white and has huge upward-facing flowers, almost the size of the proverbial dinner plate on a shrub to 1 metre or so.
***P.* 'Golden Bowl'** This variety to 2 metres has large, single, rich yellow flowers with red flares towards the centre.
***P.* 'Hana Daigin'** This is a lovely loose semi-double deep purple from Japan with incurved petals and yellow stamens. The stems are strong and hold the flower up well on a 1-metre bush.
***P.* 'Happy Days'** A strong grower to 1.5 metres with medium-sized single flowers that are a lovely soft apricot with central burgundy flares.

***P.* 'Harvest'** This form grows to 1 metre and has large semi-double flowers that are a soft apricot-pink with darker central flares.

***P.* 'Hesperus'** This form has large, single, rose pink flowers on a shrub to 2 metres. A lovely plant if you like pink!

***P.* 'Kinshi' syn. *P.* 'Chromatella'** This old Chinese form grows to about 2 metres and has huge double lemon flowers with reddish petal edges. It is heavily scented but is so large it can't hold its heads up. It is, however, stunning picked and floated in a bowl.

***P.* 'Kumagai'** This Japanese hybrid has huge single lavender-pink blooms on a bush to 2 metres.

***P.* 'Kronos'** A stunning, large, double black-red with handsome cut foliage that grows to about 1.5 metres.

***P.* 'L'Esperance'** This form grows to about 1.5 metres and has large sweetly scented semi-double soft yellow flowers with burgundy stains at its centre.

P. lutea* var. *ludlowii Hardy deciduous plant to about 4 metres with attractive pale green foliage and single yellow flowers to 12.5 cm across. From south-east Tibet.

***P.* 'Marchioness'** A lovely single apricot flower on a strong-growing shrub to 1.5 metres tall.

***P.* 'Marie Laurencin'** A variety with huge double flowers that are lavender-pink with an ivory base colour. Another hard-to-describe form that is worth looking out for.

***P.* 'Renown'** This form has large semi-double flowers that are a stunning peach-pink on a strong bush to 1.5 metres.

***P.* 'Thunderbolt'** A very striking robust form to 1 metre with very big single scarlet-red flowers with a boss of yellow stamens.

***P.* 'Zephyrus'** This American hybrid grows to about 1.5 metres and has large semi-double, soft apricot-pink flowers with a dark centre.

Parrotia persica

Small wide spreading deciduous tree from Iran to 8 metres or so with small red flowers in late winter and beautiful autumn foliage, mainly yellow with some red tints. The bark is flaky and exposes browns, creams and greys somewhat like that of a crepe myrtle. A sunny aspect suits best and it is fairly drought-tolerant once established.

Parrotiopsis jacquemontiana

A rare large shrub to small tree, to 7 metres, from the western Himalayas. Lovely white-bracted flowers very like those of the Dogwood are produced in spring, followed by yellow leaves in autumn. This lovely thing needs a sunny spot sheltered from hot winds and all the soil preparation you can give it.

Perovskia atriplicifolia 'Blue Spire'

Hardy deciduous semi-woody shrub to 1 metre tall from Afghanistan to Tibet. The lovely, mealy, silvery white, feathery foliage is topped in summer by spikes of deep lavender-blue flowers. This is a charming quick-growing sun lover that is an insect magnet. Prune it almost to the ground each winter to keep it compact.

Peumus boldus

A hardy, upright evergreen shrub to 4 metres or so from Chile with attractive deep green foliage and small fluffy white flowers in spring. The leaves are used in its homeland to make a kidney-cleansing tea. It makes an attractive screening shrub or hedge. If both sexes are available the berries formed are edible.

Peucedanum multiradiatum

A charming evergreen shrub in the carrot family from the Cape area of South Africa that grows to about 2 metres or so. It has umbels of tiny yellow flowers in summer but it is for the foliage that one would grow this plant. Like all good carrots this has fine ferny foliage and in this case it is smoky-grey and supported by mauve leaf stems. A sunny well-drained site is all it should need.

Phellodendron amurense (Amur Cork Tree)

A quick-growing, large, deciduous tree, eventually to 20 metres or so in both directions, from Asia – although we won't be around to see it this size. It is grown for its large pinnate leaves and the corky bark it produces on its trunk. This handsome shade tree turns bright yellow before shedding.

***Philadelphus* 'Belle Etoile'**

Bushy deciduous shrub to 2 metres with lovely scented single white flowers flushed burgundy at the centre in early summer. Like the rest of the genus it is a hardy undemanding shrub.

P. caucasicus Hardy deciduous shrub to 3 metres from Russia with highly scented creamy-white flowers in short spikes of five to nine blooms in late spring and early summer.

***P. coronarius* 'Aurea' (Gold Leafed Mock Orange)** Deciduous shrub to 2 metres with bright gold foliage and sweetly scented white flowers in summer. Like many other gold foliage plants this one needs a spot with lots of light to keep the leaves well-coloured but not so much that it will burn in the sun. Worth any effort and featured in my first book!

P. 'Manteau d'Hermine' A dwarf deciduous shrub to 1 metre with very fragrant creamy-white double flowers in early summer.

P. 'Natchez' A good upright deciduous variety 4 metres tall with large single to semi-double white scented flowers in early summer. This one is so showy that I sell out every year so you should definitely have one!

P. 'Silberregen' A dainty dwarf variety to 1 metre with extra small leaves and single white, wild strawberry-scented flowers. This plant is usually sold as *P.* 'Silver Showers' which is taken to be the translation of its German name but, as we all know, 'Silver Rain' is a more precise translation of the German.

P. 'Virginal' Strong-growing, virtuous, upright deciduous shrub to 3 metres with double, pure white, scented flowers. Like most virgins it's a bit rigid!

Philesia magellanica

A very rare dwarf suckering evergreen shrub from southern Chile related to Lapageria. It has small dark green leaves and quite large waxy red trumpet flowers in summer and autumn. Ideal in a pot or tree-fern log in shade. In the wild it will grow up through the moss on the side of trees making large suckering colonies.

***P. m.* 'Rosea'** An extremely rare form with rose pink flowers originally imported in the 1970s from Hilliers nursery in England by Otto Fauser (one of Australia's best-known plantsmen) and kindly passed on to me.

Phillyrea angustifolia

A dense bushy evergreen shrub to 3 metres from the Mediterranean closely related to Osmanthus. It has narrow deep green leaves and tiny white, slightly fragrant flowers in late spring, followed by black berries. Could make a good hedge and will grow in sun or shade as well as dry soil. Not, perhaps, the most significant plant but very useful and attractive enough to use in difficult spots. I have it under large Blackwoods (*Acacia melanoxylon*) and never water it.

P. latifolia Does all the things of the above species but has shiny, more rounded leaves. As a hedging plant it may even be superior due to the healthy gloss of the leaves. It comes from southern Europe through to Turkey so should be tough. This species can get even taller, growing up to 4 to 5 metres.

Photinia arbutifolia* syn. *Heteromeles arbutifolia

A hardy evergreen large shrub to small tree to 4 metres from California with attractive deep green serrated leaves and panicles of small white flowers followed by red berries.

P. beauverdiana A small to medium spreading deciduous tree from China to 6 metres. Large clusters of small white hawthorn-like flowers in spring followed by clusters of red berries and rich orange autumn foliage. This hardy tree is one of my favourites and features in my first book that by now you must realise you can't live without (both the book and the *Photinia*).

P. villosa A large deciduous fan-shaped shrub to 5 metres from China and Japan. The clusters of white flowers are followed by red berries and rich autumn foliage. A very elegant plant and ideal where the previous one is too large.

Phymosea rosea
A tall upright evergreen shrub to 5 metres or so in the Hibiscus family from Central America. It has deep lipstick-pink flowers in the warmer months. In very cold districts it is a tad frost-tender. It likes a sunny well-drained and sheltered site.

***Physocarpus opulifolius* (Nine Bark)**
A hardy quick-growing deciduous shrub to 3 metres from North America. Clusters of small white flowers in spring are followed by bronze-pink papery seed pods and rich yellow and orange autumn foliage. The bark peels each year and is a nice shiny bronze in the winter.

***P. o.* 'Diabolo'** A stunning newish variety with dark plum-coloured foliage from spring to autumn when the leaves turn richly.

***P. o.* 'Luteus'** A form with lovely yellow leaves in spring fading to yellow-green in summer, often with some copper tints. The combination of this and the above will knock your socks off!

Picrasma quassioides
Ornamental small tree to 7 metres or so from Asia with brilliant coloured autumn leaves in shades of orange and scarlet. Similar to and an ideal alternative for the *Toxicodendron* (Rhus) which many people are allergic to. A well-drained soil in sun or semi-shade will suit.

***Pistacia chinensis* (Chinese Pistachio)**
A hardy, small, deciduous tree to 7 metres from China with an elegant habit and brilliant scarlet autumn foliage that will be reliable even in areas that normally aren't renowned for autumnal glory. Also a good alternative to the dreaded *Rhus* tree that many people are allergic to (which is in fact now known as *Toxicodendron).*

***Pittosporum tenuifolium* 'Tom Thumb'**
Dwarf evergreen shrub from New Zealand to 1 metre, ideal for rock gardens or a very different dwarf hedge. Its leaves are rich burgundy, almost black, but green when young in spring.

P. tobira A very hardy bushy evergreen shrub or small tree to 4 metres with glossy bright green leaves. It produces highly fragrant flowers that start creamy white and become yellow with age. Native to Japan and China grows well in dry shade although it doesn't need it.

***P. t.* 'Wheeler's Dwarf'** A dwarf bun-shaped form rarely exceeding 1 metre each way. This makes a truly impressive plant that some smart-Alec nursery person released under the tacky trade name of 'Little Miss Muffet'. I can see where they were coming from but it put me off this great plant for quite a while.

Plagianthus regius
A quick-growing upright deciduous tree from New Zealand, to 10 metres. It has soft green serrated leaves and masses of tiny fluffy green flowers in spring. It looks a bit like a soft-leafed silver birch without the white trunk. A sunny site that isn't too dry will suit.

Plectranthus argentatus
A soft wooded slightly frost-tender shrub to 1 metre from Queensland and N.S.W. It has large, glistening, silvery leaves topped with narrow spikes of small bluish flowers. It is one of the very few silver foliage plants that grow well in shaded aspects and it copes well with dry soil as well. It features in my first book.

***Polyscias sambucifolia* 'Fernleafed' (Elderberry Panax)**
A truly stunning evergreen native shrub to 5 metres or so that is fairly drought-tolerant and will grow well in sun or semi-shade. The flowers are tiny green things in umbels followed by blackish berries but it is for its incredibly fine ferny brilliant green leaves that it is grown.

***Prunus incisa* 'Praecox'**
This is a spreading shrubby cherry to 3 metres or so each way with small white blossom on the bare branches in winter and pretty yellow and orange autumn leaves.

***P. laurocerasus* 'Otto Luyken'** This is a truly useful compact dwarf ground cover shrub to 50 cm tall by 1.5 metres or more across. It has the large glossy leaves of the tall-growing Cherry Laurel and masses of tiny white flowers in impressive spikes in spring. Its branches sit in upward-facing, fan-like sprays that would make it worth growing if it did nothing else. Good in sun or semi-shade.

***P. lusitanica* 'Variegata' (Variegated Portugese Laurel)** A very hardy conical evergreen to 7 metres or so with rich green leaves edged with white and red young stems to show it all off. It has spikes of white Hawthorn-scented flowers in spring followed by black berries. A good hedge or screening plant that will cope with sun or shade.

***P. padus* (Bird Cherry)** Medium deciduous tree to 10 metres that is remarkably quick growing for the impatient gardener that wants almost instant shade. Spikes of small white almond scented flowers in late spring. Bright autumn foliage.

***P. serrula* (Tibetan Cherry)** Medium spreading tree to 7 metres or so with narrow willow-like leaves and white flowers in spring if the wind doesn't get them first! This tree has shiny mahogany-coloured bark that will turn you into an instant tree hugger; it features in my first book.

***P. spinosa* (Sloe or Blackthorn)** A large suckering deciduous shrub to 3 metres with spiny branches and masses of tiny white flowers in spring followed by shiny black fruit used to make Sloe Gin (its most important feature). Good, tough thing that could be used in hedgerows or bits of rough ground that you will see as butterfly habitat and others may see as messy!

***P. subhirtella* 'Autumnalis' (Autumn Cherry)** A small spreading tree to 7 metres which has small white flowers throughout autumn and winter to early spring. A very desirable tree for winter colour and with pleasant autumnal foliage as well.

***P. s.* 'Autumnalis Rosea'** A lovely soft pink version of the above.

***Pseudopanax crassifolius* (Lancewood)**
A truly bizarre evergreen New Zealander that for some years grows as a single stem until it gets to about 3 metres and has long, bronze, green narrow leaves that are so stiff that they snap if bent. Eventually it branches out and makes a round-headed tree to 5 metres with shorter deep green leaves and it looks like a vegetable lollypop. Sun or semi-shade tolerant and drought-tolerant once established.

P. ferox This species has the same growth habit of the above with juvenile foliage that is even harder and dead-looking. Something more like a collection of hacksaw blades on a stick would be hard to imagine. Also from across the Tasman.

P. laetevirens This species comes from Argentina and Chile and grows to a small shrub about 1.5 metres tall with glossy mid-green leaves consisting of five leaflets. Good pot plant or garden shrub, lightly shaded sites.

P.* × *lessonii A New Zealand shrub to 3 metres or so with leaves divided into several deep green leaflets which will give a tropical look to almost any garden outside the tropics! Will cope with fairly dry shade and also makes a good pot plant (even indoors), as do the following forms.

***P.* × *l.* 'Cyril Watson'** An interesting evergreen foliage shrub to 3 metres with rich, olive green, three-lobed leaves that give a somewhat duck-footed effect. Lord knows who Cyril Watson was but he didn't do badly in the naming stakes; however, the plant may have drawn the short straw!

***P.* × *l.* 'Gold Splash'** This form has leaves divided into 5 or so leaflets that are liberally splashed with yellow and will easily exceed 3 metres. This variegate isn't completely stable and will throw some green shoots that will need to be dealt with.

***P.* × *l.* 'Purpurea'** This form grows like, and requires the same conditions as, the previous ones; however its leaves are divided into 3 to 5 leaflets that are a lovely glossy bronze whilst young and become a greener shade as they mature.

Pseudowintera colorata
An interesting shade-loving evergreen shrub to 3 metres from New Zealand with most unusual yellowish green foliage, variously blotched and margined with deep burgundy-red, particularly in winter with a whitish reverse. As most shade lovers tend to be deep green this is a great change of pace.

***P. c.* 'Red Glow'** This rare selection has red-stained leaves that intensify in colour in winter with the same whitish reverse. This one has to be seen to be believed.

***P. c.* 'Red Leopard'** This new form is madly spotted with burgundy over the whole leaf and it is also richest in winter. This amazing form isn't for the faint of heart and I love it!

***Pterostyrax hispida* (Epaulette Tree)**
Small deciduous tree to 6 metres from China and Japan with large, soft green leaves turning yellow in autumn. In summer the tree has long drooping panicles of tiny white scented flowers. A sheltered site with morning sun will suit best. If you want to see what it looks like look it up in my first book. It must be on your shelf by now!

***Pyracantha atalantioides* (Firethorn)**
Hardy evergreen shrub to 2 metres with glossy deep green leaves and brilliant red berries in winter. Ideal for an espalier. Native to China.

***Pyrus calleryana* 'Bradford'**
A clone of a Chinese pear selected in America. It is a hardy and highly ornamental tree to 10 metres or so with lovely white blossom in spring and rounded leaves that colour well in autumn.

***P. nivalis* (Snow Pear)** A very hardy deciduous tree to 10 metres with masses of white blossom in spring, and attractive silver foliage throughout the growing season, turning yellow and apricot in autumn. Native to southern Europe.

***P. pashia* (Indian Pear)** An elegant medium tree to 10 metres with arching branches clothed with smallish persistent leaves that often shed in spring in mild years so that autumn colour can be late or even not at all. The dainty white blossom is followed by small round brown fruit.

***P. ussuriensis* forma *ovoidea* (True Manchurian Pear)** Unlike what is usually sold as a Manchurian Pear, which is probably a form of *P. calleryana*, this is a true form and differs by having longer leaves on longer leaf stems, a more irregular habit and more various autumn foliage. It is a more elegant tree that is far more wind-tolerant. It also has quite large rounded brown fruit that can weigh the branches down in autumn.

***Quercus dentata* (Daimio Oak)**
A striking slow-growing deciduous tree from Japan, Korea and China, to 7 metres, with a rustic irregular form and huge English Oak-shaped leaves that can be up to 30 cm long. It usually colours well in autumn and regularly holds its dead leaves well into winter.

***Q. × firthii* (Macedon Oak)** This hybrid found at Macedon in the 1920s by the head propagator at the state nursery is thought to be a cross between the Pin Oak, *Q. palustris* and one of the evergreen species. It is a large semi-evergreen tree to 20 metres or so with glossy green leaves that often turn in mid- to late winter. Dame Elisabeth Murdoch planted two that are now on the National Tree Register – now, how is that for a challenge!

Q. × heterophylla Another strange hybrid, this time between *Q. rubra* and *Q. phellos*, that has shiny leaves of various shapes and sizes as its strange parentage would suggest, and quite good late autumn foliage. Eventually a largish tree that you may live to see up to 20 metres or more.

***Q. ilex* (Holm oak)** A very hardy evergreen tree that will slowly grow to 10 metres with deep grey-green foliage that would make a worthy drought-tolerant windbreak or hedge that for no apparent reason is overlooked in favour of disgusting Leyland Cypress by all and sundry. It is native to the Mediterranean region.

***Q. phellos* (Willow Oak)** This rarely seen very hardy deciduous shade tree to 20 metres comes from the United States and has tiny narrow willow-like glossy green leaves that can colour extremely well in autumn. Stump your friends by planting this remarkably un-oak-like oak.

***Q. robur* 'Concordia' (Golden English Oak)** The golden-leafed oak is a slow-growing tree with bright yellow spring and summer leaves. Shelter it from the hottest winds and sun so that it doesn't burn.

***Q. r.* 'Fastigiata'** Narrow pencil form of the English Oak that makes a great alternative to the troublesome Lombardy Poplar. Will in time grow to a quite tall tree.

***Q. r.* 'Pectinata' (Cut Leaf Oak)** A vigorous variety with very finely cut ferny foliage most unlike what one would expect of an oak. Highly recommended and will fool all your 'smart Alec' horticultural friends.

***Q. r.* forma *purpurascens* (Purple English Oak)** An extremely rare form that has rich burgundy leaves that are strongest in colour when young and is usually a medium tree to 7 metres or so.

***Q. rubra* 'Aurea' (Golden Red Oak)** A large deciduous tree from North America with large-lobed leaves that start gold in spring, turn greenish in summer, and can turn quite good red in autumn before it sheds.

***Q. suber* (Cork Oak)** The classic species that will be found in the neck of your wine bottle (at least its bark will). A very hardy picturesque evergreen tree to 10 metres or so from southern Europe and northern Africa with leathery deep green leaves and thick, rugged and (funnily enough) corky bark as it matures. Full sun and quite dry conditions suit it well and it should be used more as a specimen or screening plant.

Rehderodendron macrocarpum

A very rare deciduous tree from China to 7 metres. It produces masses of tiny white snowdrop-like flowers in spring followed by pendulous ribbed woody seeds that are red in colour and as big as a pecan nut. The foliage turns orange-red in autumn. It has only been known in Western horticulture since 1930. It prefers a cool aspect and moist acid soil.

Rhaphiolepis umbellata

This is a remarkably hardy dome-shaped evergreen shrub to 2 metres each way from Japan and Korea that would make a great screen or hedge. It has rounded leathery deep green leaves that are almost enough to make you plant it. It does however also produce spikes of slightly fragrant white flowers in early summer followed by black berries.

Rhaphithamnus spinosus

A large bushy evergreen thorny shrub to 4 metres from Chile and Argentina with small light blue flowers in spring followed by large pea-sized deep blue berries. Happy in any well-drained aspect with good light and good for stopping kids from cutting corners!

Rhododendron nuttallii

A stunning open-growing upright shrub to 3 metres from north-eastern India with light green heavily veined leaves and huge cream trumpets in spring with a strong scent.

R. prinophyllum* syn. *R. roseum A North American deciduous shrub to 2 metres with highly scented mid-pink flowers in spring and lovely yellow and apricot autumn foliage. An acid soil and a cool aspect is needed for this and most other species in this genus.

R. spinuliferum A rare evergreen species from Yunnan with an open willowy habit to 3 metres. It has bronze-tinged leaves especially in winter and narrow upward-pointing scarlet trumpets with petals that turn inward instead of outwards as all other Rhododendrons do.

***R. stenopetalum* 'Linearifolium'** A strange evergreen shrub to 60 cm from Japan with extremely narrow furry leaves and flowers that consist of almost thread-like bright pink petals in spring. One to trick your friends with.

***R. viscosum* (Swamp Honeysuckle)** This deciduous species has soft pink well-scented flowers that are produced quite late in spring. In North America this plant grows in wet to boggy soils. So if you have such a spot and hadn't before considered a *Rhododendron* now you can. It doesn't require wet conditions by the way.

R. williamsianum A lovely dwarf evergreen shrub to 1 metre from China with rounded heart-shaped leaves that are rich copper when young and beautiful bell-shaped pink flowers in spring.

R. yakushimanum A rare Japanese species that slowly makes an evergreen mound to 1.5 metres or so each way. It has lovely long narrow leaves usually rolled down at the edges that are covered with brown fur while young and retaining it under the leaves with maturity. The flowers are produced in small heads and are pink in bud and usually white when open.

R. yedoense A small deciduous shrub to 1 metre from Japan with double mauve flowers in midspring. This makes a lovely flat-topped bush in time. As this form is double it isn't a true species although it has been named as one and is more likely to be a form of *R. poukhanense*.

Rhodoleia championii

Small tree with large shiny evergreen leaves to 7 metres from China for a sheltered semi-shaded site with an upright habit and tiered branch arrangement. Small deep pink, thick petalled flowers are born in clusters in spring.

Rhodotypos scandens

A very hardy deciduous shrub to 2 metres from China and Japan. It produces lovely single white Dog-rose-like flowers during summer followed by conspicuous shiny black fruits. The leaves turn soft yellow in autumn. A sunny to semi-shaded site in any reasonable soil will do.

Rhus × pulvinata (Hybrid Sumach)

This deciduous small tree from North America has large Ash-like leaves that colour superbly in autumn. If left alone it will grow into a small round-headed tree to 4 metres otherwise it can be treated as a perennial and pruned to the ground which will encourage larger leaves as can both of the following. This is a hybrid of two eastern North American species *R. glabra* and *R. typhina.*

***R. × p.* 'Autumn Lace Group'** This form has foliage that is heavily cut giving it a ferny look and it has smooth stems and smooth leaflets. A good picture of this one is to be found in my first book.

***R. typhina* 'Dissecta'** Similar to the above but this form has furry stems and mat leaves and is as good as the above, so you choose.

Ribes × gordonianum

An interesting hybrid flowering currant, whose parents are *R. odoratum* and *R. sanguineum*, that was bred in 1837. It makes a light, open suckering shrub with scented burnt-apricot flowers with a yellow centre in spring. A pleasing and different shrub in an unusual colour.

***R. odoratum* (Buffalo Currant)** Hardy, slightly suckering deciduous shrub from North America, to 3 metres with attractive glossy green foliage that colours richly in autumn and masses of clove-scented golden yellow flowers with a red centre in spring. Like the following it likes a sunny well-drained site.

***R. sanguineum* (Flowering Currant)** A very hardy deciduous shrub to 3 metres from North America with drooping spikes of soft pink flowers in late winter and early spring. These flowers have a strange scent loved by some but loathed by others. It is universally enjoyed by nectar-feeding birds.

***R. s.* 'Albescens'** This rare form has lovely white flowers tinged with pink.

***R. s.* 'Splendens'** This form has extra dark flowers and tends to make a smaller bush to about 2 metres.

R. speciosum A rare and beautiful semi-deciduous arching shrub to 2 metres from California. It has prickly stems, gooseberry-like leaves as well as pendant waxy scarlet Fuchsia-like flowers in spring. Used a lot in England as a wall shrub and could be used here in the same way.

Robinia hispida (Rose Acacia)

This extremely hardy suckering deciduous shrub grows to about 2 metres tall and has clusters of rich pink pea flowers in spring. It is native to the U.S.A. and any well-drained sunny site will do.

Rubus 'Benenden'

A stunning deciduous shrub to 2 metres with soft green leaves and glorious pure white flowers to 7.5 cm across with a boss of yellow stamens that will be one of spring's great joys once the two of you are introduced. A sunny to semi-shaded aspect with fairly good soil will suit this must-have shrub.

R. lineatus A truly impressive evergreen foliage plant from Asia with large pleated leaves divided into five leaflets. It has a satiny sheen on top and a silvery reverse. It produces 3 metre arching canes and has a suckering habit so be warned or keep it in a tub. This one found its way into my first book.

R. leucodermis A North American suckering deciduous shrub to 2 metres with arching prickly canes that are ghostly white in winter. The compound leaves are a lovely grey colour and if the old canes aren't removed each year like those of most raspberries it will produce tiny boring white flowers that give away its relationship to the common blackberry. Will grow well (as all blackberries will!) in almost any aspect that isn't really dry.

***R. phoenicolasius* (Wineberry)** A lovely arching deciduous shrub to 1.5 metres or so from Japan, Korea and China with red bristly canes in winter and small pale pink flowers followed by small edible red berries.

***R. spectabilis* (Salmonberry)** A vigorous, slightly suckering shrub to 2 metres, with spiny stems and bright green foliage. It produces its scented, magenta, single rose-like flowers in early summer followed by edible yellow fruit.

Ruscus aculeatus hermaphrodite form (Butchers Broom)

Useful European evergreen shrub to 50 cm (really an evergreen perennial) ideal for dry shade under trees. The leaf-like cladodes are very dark green. The tiny greenish flowers have a purple centre and are produced in the centre of the cladodes. If both male and female forms are grown, the females will produce large red berries in the usual forms. This type, which I raised from seed collected at Great Dixter gardens in Sussex, is self-pollinating so it fruits alone.

R. hypoglossum Attractive dwarf suckering shrub to 1 metre inches from southern Europe. With small greenish flowers in the centre of the leaf-like cladodes. This is a very useful plant for dense shade even amongst tree roots.

Salix caprea 'Pendula' (Weeping Pussy Willow)

A charming weeping umbrella-shaped tree usually grafted onto 2 metre standards, with grey-green foliage in spring turning yellow in autumn, and masses of fluffy female grey-green catkins in late winter. This cultivar is fertile but for some reason I'm allowed by law to grow this one!

***S. myrsinifolia* (Black Stemmed Willow)** A fast-growing deciduous shrub to 6 metres with rich very dark green foliage and black first year canes in winter. Best if it is coppiced every couple of years.

Sambucus nigra 'Aurea' (Golden Elder)

A very hardy deciduous shrub up to 4 metres with attractive yellow pinnate leaves throughout the warmer months. It also produces (as do all in this genus) flat clusters of tiny, sweetly scented white flowers in spring, followed by black berries. The flowers, just as in the plain green-leafed form, can be used to make fritters, cordial and champagne, and the berries (if any flowers were left) can be made into the famous wine. I now hold a national collection of this genus in my garden at Macedon for the Ornamental Plants Conservation Association of Australia.

***S. n.* 'Black Beauty'** This fairly new form grows to about 3 metres tall with heads of soft pink flowers (perhaps the makings of pink champagne!), set off extremely well by its extremely dark burgundy foliage. This form is darker and not as tall growing as the older *S. n.* 'Guincho Purple'.

***S. n.* 'Black Lace'** A medium shrub to 2.5 metres with finely cut, deep purple foliage and heads of tiny, soft pink flowers in early summer. One of the most stunning forms only recently making it to Australia. It, like *S. n.* 'Black Beauty', was raised at Horticulture Research International at East Malling in the U.K.

S. n. forma *canadensis* 'Maxima' This form I imported from England and it's a real stunner. It has large green Ash-like leaves and huge flat heads of tiny white flowers in summer, to 35 cm or more across. (One fritter per family!) This vigorous form will quickly grow to 3 metres or so.

S. n. 'Castledean' I recently imported this form from Dan Hinkley's Heronswood nursery (now sadly closed). It has classic green leaves but the petioles (leaf stems) are black which contrasts well with its heads of white flowers. It will probably grow to 3 metres.

S. n. 'Guincho Purple' A large-growing form to 5 metres or more with light chocolate foliage and almost white flowers followed by black berries.

S. n. 'Laciniata' (Fern Leafed Elder) Another of my imports that in this form makes an upright shrub to 2.5 metres with rich green deeply cut ferny leaves. Clusters of white spring flowers and the usual black berries.

S. n. 'Linearis' This strange form is yet another of my imports and makes a bushy shrub to about 2 metres with green leaves that are almost reduced to the central veins giving the whole plant a remarkably fluffy look.

S. n. 'Madonna' This newish form has leaves that have golden edges that take up about half the leaf area making it the boldest of the variegated forms. It will grow to about 2 metres tall.

S. n. 'Marginata' This older form has silver-edged leaves and will grow into a large bushy shrub to 3 or 4 metres.

S. n. 'Pulverulenta' This strangely beautiful form grows to about 2 metres and its claim to fame is the lovely white marbling throughout its leaves. The flowers and fruit are still as for the species.

S. n. 'Pyramidalis' This unusual form I imported from America from Heronswood Nursery and its claim to fame is its narrow upright form to 3 metres and its largish rich green foliage.

S. n. 'Witches Broom' This novelty was obtained from Oregon by me in 2003 and makes a round bun to 25 cm each way with smaller than normal green leaves. This form is sterile, as many witches' brooms are, so it won't annoy you with any pesky flowers!

***S. racemosa* 'Plumosa Aurea'** This stunning form to 2 metres has finely cut golden-yellow leaves from spring till autumn although they do green a bit as the season advances. This species has small clusters of yellow flowers followed by red berries and needs some shelter from the hottest sun. Apparently we can use the seeded fruit of this one to make wines and jellies too.

S. r. 'Sutherland Gold' I imported this form from England and it is very like the above but the cut foliage is a little courser and it is supposed to stand a bit more sun.

Sapium japonicum

A lovely open, irregular, large shrub or small tree to 4 metres or so, with large leaves that turn exquisite reds and oranges in autumn. It also has entertaining spikes of tiny green flowers in summer. The sap is poisonous so don't be silly enough to eat it! A sunny, well-drained site should suit this plant from Japan, Korea and China.

Sarcococca confusa

A small evergreen shrub to 50 cm, with deep green leaves and tiny white highly scented flowers, and deep red to black berries in winter. All species are useful in dry shade, as tub specimens, as a dwarf hedge and cut foliage and are native to China.

S. hookeriana A more erectly branched variety to 50 cm with somewhat lanceolate deep green leaves with the classic white scented flowers and black berries.

S. h. var. *humilis* Dwarf suckering shrub with dark evergreen foliage, grows to about 50 cm. Tiny white flowers and black berries.

S. orientalis This species is similar to *S. cofusa* but with larger leaves.

S. ruscifolia Small arching evergreen shrub 2 metres with dark glossy green leaves and small white scented flowers in late winter to spring followed by red berries. This one made my first book. It's the only one I had a photo of or any of the others could have made it in!

Schima wallichii

A large handsome evergreen shrub or small tree to 7 metres from Asia, related to the Camellia. It produces white scented flowers in late summer and has attractive salmon new growth. Look it up in book number one!

Sinocalycanthus chinensis

A rare deciduous shrub to 3 metres from China, it was only introduced to Western horticulture in 1983. It is closely related to the American *Calycanthus* and will probably be sunk in with them in due course, as hybrids between the two have already been bred in America. Its leaves are large and glossy, bright green and the flowers produced in early summer are white with a slightly pink tinge and a yellow centre. Although not long grown here it seems hardy, liking a well-drained, leafy soil that isn't too dry and a morning sun aspect.

Sinojackia xylocarpa

A very rare, deciduous, large shrub to 2 metres from eastern China. Its arching branches support drooping white bell-like flowers in spring. The foliage goes pale yellow before shedding and it likes a moist lime-free soil.

Skimmia × confusa

A shade-loving evergreen shrub to 1 metre tall and wider than tall with leathery dark green leaves and upright spikes of scented cream flowers in late winter. This male form obviously can't produce fruit but it has its uses when girls are about and its flowers are possibly the best in the genus.

***S. japonica* (hermaphrodite form)** A dense dome-shaped evergreen shrub to 2 metres with spikes of scented white flowers and red berries in late winter. Like the rest of the genus a good shade-tolerant shrub. This form doesn't need a boy friend but is more productive with one!

***S. j.* 'Bronze Knight'** A male clone that, like any other male clones, will help pollinate the above form to help it set more berries or any female forms as it isn't all that fussy! It makes a compact shrub to 1 metre with white scented flowers in winter from bronze buds.

***S. j.* 'Kew White'** I imported this form from England and it has lighter green leaves and if pollinated will produce lovely white berries from its scented white flowers. Grows to about 1 metre and is a good addition to any harem.

***S. j.* 'Nymans'** A female form to 2 metres with large abundant red berries after sex.

***S. j.* 'Rubella'** Another male clone of compact habit that has panicles of tiny burgundy-red flower buds opening to white scented blooms. Possibly one of the showiest male forms.

***S. j.* 'Wisley Female'** This form was obviously raised at Wisley in England and named by someone with no sense of adventure. It has a bushy habit, to 2 metres tall by a little wider, and if it is planted with a boy friend will produce crops of red berries much like *S. j.* 'Nymans' so I really don't know why I am growing both.

Sophora davidii

A hardy arching deciduous sun-loving shrub to 3 metres from China with fine grey-green foliage on its slightly prickly stems and masses of small blue-white pea flowers in summer.

***S. microphylla* 'Dragon's Gold'** This is an evergreen shrub to 3 metres with fine feather foliage and drooping yellow flowers flushed with orange. A sunny well-drained site suits, as it does for all the species.

***S. tetraptera* (Kowhai)** New Zealand's floral emblem makes an elegant upright medium tree to 10 metres with small ferny leaves that are even smaller on young plants and drooping clusters of rich yellow flowers in spring. Like many plants from New Zealand, as youngsters their branches zigzag all over the place.

S. toromiro An evergreen hardy shrub to 3 metres with attractive small pinnate leaves and pendulous yellow flowers. A native of Easter Island where it has been extinct since the 1960s due to the introduction of sheep and overlogging by the natives. It was, in fact, thought completely extinct till quite recently. It is now being re-introduced via the Melbourne Botanic Gardens.

Sonchus congesta

A small, sparsely-branched shrub to 1 metre from the Canary Islands, with rosettes of large, soft green leaves with jagged edges and bright yellow flowers in summer. Think giant woody Dandelion! It likes sun to semi-shade and is fairly drought-tolerant. It is a bold foliage plant and well worth growing. (So just forget the dandelion reference as it will probably put you off!)

S. leptocephalus A quite different-looking, upright sparsely-branched shrub to 1.5 metres with fine, wispy green foliage like puffs of green smoke and tiny yellow dandelions in summer. A sunny, well-drained aspect is about all this Canary Island plant needs.

Sorbaria aitchisonii

Hardy deciduous shrub to 3 metres from Kashmir with large, elegant, soft green, ash-like leaves and large panicles of tiny white flowers in summer. This genus likes a sunny to semi-shaded site and isn't too fussy about soil. It is in the first book.

S. arborea Taller grower than the previous species to about 4 metres with larger leaves and panicles up to 50 cm long of tiny white flowers. Native of central and western China.

Sorbus aria 'Lutescens' (Silver Whitebeam)

A hardy upright deciduous tree to 9 metres from Europe with large grey-white felty leaves that turn gold and russet in autumn. It produces white flowers in spring and bunches of crimson fruit in autumn.

***S. aucuparia* 'Beissneri' (Golden Fern Rowan)** An upright deciduous tree to 9 metres with soft yellow-green foliage. The trunk and stems are a coppery-orange colour particularly effective in winter. The white flowers are followed by red berries. I assume this golden form will keep witches away as well as its green equivalent is meant to!

S. cashmiriana A lovely medium deciduous tree to 8 metres from Kashmir with rich autumn foliage and pearl white berries with a pink blush that often hang on well into winter.

***S. commixta* 'Embley'** A superb small upright tree to 8 metres with brilliant red autumn foliage and clusters of good quality orange-red berries.

S. hupehensis This Chinese species to 9 metres has grey-green foliage that turns deep burgundy in autumn and its white flowers are followed by clusters of berries that are white tinged with pale pink.

S. megalocarpa A most unusual Rowan to 4 metres with an arching habit and entire leaves that start ruby-red in spring turning green in summer and then reds and oranges in autumn. It has large brown berries.

***S. reducta* (Dwarf Rowan)** A dwarf suckering deciduous shrub to 50 cm from China with compound leaves that turn brilliant red in autumn. Clusters of small white flowers in spring followed by pink and white berries.

S. vilmorinii This small spreading tree from China rarely exceeds 7 metres. Its deep green foliage turns a brilliant glowing burgundy in autumn and its lovely deep pink berries fade to white flushed rose.

Stachyurus himalaicus

This rare evergreen arching shrub grows to about 3 metres and has glossy good-sized leaves that are smaller that the more commonly available *S. praecox* and soft pink flower buds that open to soft yellow flowers in winter.

***S. leucotrichus* 'Magpie'** This form was until recently thought to be a form of *S. chinensis* and it differs from the following *S. praecox* in that it has grey-green leaves boldly edged with creamy-white and splashed with pale green and pink. It flowers later than *S. praecox* and also regularly sends out branches with all-white foliage.

***S. praecox* (Early Spiketail)** Medium to large deciduous shrub to 4 metres with pendulous spikes of lime-yellow flowers along the branches in winter. This Japanese plant sometimes holds foliage when growing vigorously or in mild winters.

S. salicifolius I raised this one from seed, released it in 2005 and it's stunning. (Take my word for it!) Like the other species it has long arching branches and should grow to about 3 metres tall and as wide. The flowers are the usual drooping spikes of soft yellow bells in late winter but its best feature is its long narrow rich green evergreen leaves that will impress all but the most jaded!

S. yunnanensis I imported this obviously Asian species from North America in 2003, and it has rounded evergreen leaves and an arching habit and drooping pale yellow flowers in midwinter.

Staphylea colchica (Bladder Nut)

Strong-growing deciduous suckering shrub to 4 metres from the Caucasus with attractive clusters of coconut-scented white flowers in spring followed by curious, inflated, bladder-like seed pods. For more, check out my first book.

S. holocarpa A lovely species from China, with a more tree-like habit (it doesn't sucker like *S. colchica*). The flowers are white and born in drooping clusters in spring, followed by good crops of inflated seed pods.

Stephanandra incisa

A charming and elegant arching deciduous shrub to 1 metre from Japan and Korea. It has attractive clusters of tiny white flowers in summer, good autumn foliage and bronze twigs in winter.

***S. i.* 'Crispa'** I imported this from England a few years ago and it has foliage that is crinkled and grows into a ground-hugging mound rarely taller than 20 cm but may reach 1 metre or more across. Like the species, it colours well in autumn.

S. tanakae A medium-sized deciduous shrub to 2 metres from Japan. Attractive arching branches with copper bark in winter. The foliage turns yellow before shedding and the tiny white flowers are born in clusters in summer.

Stewartia malacodendron

A small spreading deciduous North American tree to 5 metres tall in the Camellia family with white flowers in summer with a purple eye and rich autumn foliage. Like all the following this tree likes a cool moist soil and shelter from hot summer winds. A good companion for Rhodos and the like.

S. monodelpha Similar to the above with slightly larger less glossy foliage and bigger white flowers with lovely purple stamens. This North American species also colours well in autumn and grows to 5 metres.

S. pseudocamellia This Japanese species is probably the most popular and has attractive flaky bark, yellow stamens in the white flowers and rich red and yellow autumn colour. This one has a more upright vase-shaped form and will grow to at least 7 metres.

S. pteropetiolata A very rare evergreen species from Yunnan with very dark green foliage and classical white flowers in summer. This one will make a narrow vase-shaped tree to 7 metres or so.

S. sinensis A very rare Chinese species rather like *S. pseudocamellia* with slightly fragrant white flowers and brilliant scarlet autumn foliage.

Styrax hemsleyana

A lovely small open-branched tree to 7 metres with large green deciduous leaves slightly smaller than those of the better-known *S. obassia*. Its white scented flowers are produced on drooping spikes in summer.

***S. japonica* (Snowbell Tree)** A beautiful, small, spreading deciduous tree to 7 metres from Korea and Japan. The light green foliage turns a lovely pale yellow in the autumn and the clusters of white bell flowers hang below the branches in late spring. This well-loved species features in my first book.

***S. j.* 'Emerald Pagoda'** This cutting-grown selection would seem to have been on steroids, as it grows faster and larger than the type, its leaves are about three times bigger as are its flowers. For the size queens amongst you!

S. obassia A handsome, upright deciduous tree from Japan. Very large, soft green leaves turning yellow in autumn. The fragrant white flowers hang in spikes in late spring and the chestnut-coloured bark peels in strips in the winter.

Sycopsis sinensis

A weeping evergreen small tree to 4 metres from China that looks a little like the weeping fig *Ficus benjamina*. The winter flowers have no petals but are clusters of lemon stamens with red tips, surrounded by brown scales. Does well in sun or shade.

Symphoricarpus × chenaultii 'Hancock'

A tough little deciduous ground cover shrub, to 20 cm tall by at least a metre wide, with little bright green leaves, tiny white flowers and some dark pink berries. Will grow in sun or shade and will layer where it hits the ground.

Syringa × chinensis (Rouen Lilac)

A hardy deciduous sun-loving shrub to 2 metres with medium-sized panicles of scented soft mauve flowers in spring. Much daintier and, in my humble opinion, superior to the usual hybrid Lilacs, as are all of the following.

S. × diversifolia A charming deciduous shrub to 2 metres with heavily scented clear mauve flowers in dainty small sprays. The very unusual foliage is rich green and divided giving the shrub a ferny appearance.

S. microphylla A charming Chinese species with small rounded leaves and goodly clusters of small soft pink slightly scented flowers in spring. This one will eventually grow to 2 metres tall and as wide if the secateurs can't be found.

***S. meyeri* 'Palibin'** A delightful dwarf shrub to 1 metre with pretty rounded leaves and masses of well-scented tiny mauve flowers in spring and pleasant autumn foliage. This one rightly made it into my first book.

***S. patula* 'Miss Kim'** This is yet another semi-dwarf form to 1 metre with heads of mauve, perfumed flowers in spring and, unlike most Lilacs, it produces fabulous purple autumn leaves. Should have made it into my book!

***S. × persica* (Persian Lilac)** A dainty, medium shrub to 1.5 metres with clusters of pale lilac flowers with a good perfume.

S. reflexa A large-leafed shrub to 4 metres with long narrow drooping spikes of rich mauve non-perfumed flowers in spring.

***S. wolfii* (Pink Lilac)** A tall, upright deciduous shrub to 4 metres with quite large leaves and large upright panicles of soft pink slightly scented flowers in spring.

Tagetes lemmonii (Mexican Bush Marigold)

This is fast-growing, short-lived (but easy to propagate) evergreen shrub to 1.5 metres has stunningly scented foliage that releases its aroma with the slightest touch. It also has masses of single egg yoke-yellow (free range of course!) daisies mainly in the winter. It likes a sunny well-drained site and a bit of shelter in really frost-prone gardens. Prune hard after flowering to keep it bushy. The leaves have been used as a flavouring and to make tea try it and let me know how you got on, if you can!

Tamarix ramosissima

A hardy (in fact almost indestructible) quick growing shrub to 4 metres from western and central Asia with scale-like grey foliage that will convince most that it is a conifer. In summer the whole thing will turn pink with its tiny flowers giving the game away. Sun-loving and will laugh at drought.

Telopea oreades (Victorian Waratah)

Upright evergreen tree to 7 metres with large rich green leaves and attractive cherry-red pinwheel flowers in spring and early summer. This and the following species like a cool aspect and moist but not wet soils.

***T. truncata* (Tasmanian Waratah)** This is an open-growing evergreen shrub to 3 metres or so with pinwheels of scarlet flowers in late spring. It likes similar conditions to the above and made it into my first book.

Tetradium daniellii syn. *Euodia daniellii*

A rare but hardy deciduous shade tree to 8 metres from China and Korea with Ash-like leaves that turn yellow in autumn and clusters of white pungently scented flowers in late summer when few trees flower followed by small red to black berries.

Tilia americana (Basswood)
A beautiful medium to large deciduous tree to 15 metres or so with very large coarsely-toothed leaves that can be 25 cm or more long. A lovely shade tree which turns soft yellow in autumn.

T. amurensis This Asian Linden will make a small spreading tree to 10 metres with largish heavily cut leaves turning yellow in autumn.

T. cordata (Small Leafed Linden) A large deciduous tree from Europe to 20 metres or more with attractive heart-shaped leaves that turn yellow in autumn. In spring it produces masses of tiny ivory-coloured flowers that aren't very showy but are highly scented and loved by bees that are often found drunk under the trees.

T. platyphyllos (Broad Leafed Linden) Much like the above except it has larger leaves and flowers earlier in the season.

Toona sinensis 'Flamingo' syn. _Cedrela sinensis_
A very hardy upright slightly suckering tree to 7 metres, that in this form arose in cultivation in Australia. Its leaves are Ash-like and start out a striking pink in spring, fade slowly to white and then turn green. After all that effort it doesn't bother to do much in autumn. It is very upright and so ideal where space is at a premium.

Trachelospermum jasminoides 'Tricolor'
A strange dwarf shrubby form of what is usually a climbing plant. It will slowly grow to about 30 cm tall and 1.5 metres across and likes sun or semi-shade. It produces lovely white and pink mottled variegation mainly on the new growth. It seems not to flower but its foliage effect is there all year.

Trachycarpus fortunei (Chinese Windmill Palm)
One of the world's most cold-hardy palms that will grow slowly to 7 metres or so with a shaggy trunk topped with large fan-shaped leaves. Gives a tropical look to even 'less than tropical' Mt Macedon!

Trochodendron aralioides
Large slow-growing evergreen shrub to 6 metres from Japan with an elegant layered habit and large bright green leaves. The small lime-green flowers are produced in clusters during spring and early summer. An effective garden shrub for dense shade and useful for floral art. It is in book number one.

Ugni molinae syn. _Myrtus ugni_ (Chilean Guava)
Medium evergreen shrub to 2 metres with dark green foliage and bronze new growth the pink, urn-shaped flowers are produced in spring followed by dull-red strawberry-flavoured berries in autumn. The fruit makes lovely jelly and is great to pick and eat straight from the bush. It tastes rather like wild strawberries and will grow in sun or semi-shade and is drought-tolerant once established.

Ulmus davidiana 'Nirekeyaki'
This tiny deciduous tree only grows to about 25 cm with minute foliage. Ideal for rock gardens and bonsai. A surprisingly tough plant for a sunny aspect.

U. parvifolia 'Frosty' A small-growing form of Chinese Elm with lovely white leaves in spring. The white colouring recedes as the season advances until only the teeth are white, giving the tree a frosty appearance. This hardy deciduous tree, to 8 metres or so, features in my first book.

Vaccinium glaucoalbum
An attractive small evergreen shrub to 60 cm in height from Tibet with rounded grey-green leaves and tiny pale pink Lily-of-the-Valley-type flowers in spring followed by black berries. Like all its relatives it likes a moist acid soil in a coolish aspect.

V. ovatum (Box Blueberry or Huckleberry) An evergreen shrub to 1.5 metres from western North America with dark green leaves that are coppery-red when young, small pink tinged white bells in summer followed by edible red berries ripening black. A moist cool aspect suits best. Huckleberry ice-cream is delicious!

V. koreana A dwarf deciduous shrub to 50 cm, from guess where? It has tiny white flowers in spring followed by very bright red berries and red autumn foliage.

Vestia lycioides

Small erect evergreen shrub from Chile, to 2 metres. It produces attractive pale greenish-yellow trumpet flowers in spring and summer. The foliage if crushed smells like burning rubber, a great surprise to the unknowing! Want to know more then look it up in my first book.

Viburnum awabuki

A handsome evergreen shrub to 7 metres with large, very shiny rich green leaves and clusters of scented, white flowers followed by red berries that turn black with age. This is usually sold in Australia as *V. odoratissimum* but this species has a smell to the crushed foliage, which *V. awabuki* doesn't have.

***V. a.* 'Emerald Lustre'** A lovely form with even bigger lighter leaves. It almost looks like a tropical plant!

V. bitchiuense Deciduous upright shrub for sun or semi-shade, to 3 metres, from Japan. Clusters of pale pink to white scented flowers in early spring and attractive autumnal colour. Most *Viburnum* are hardy and will cope happily with sun to semi-shade and are comparatively drought-tolerant once established, exceptions will be noted.

***V. × bodnantense* 'Dawn'** A hybrid of *V. farreri* and similar to it but with larger clusters of flowers which may or may not be an improvement.

V. buddleifolium Medium semi-evergreen shrub to 3 metres from China with handsome foliage. Clusters of tiny white flowers in summer, followed by red berries that turn black with age.

V. burejaeticum Large deciduous shrub, to 4 metres from China, that is fairly rare in cultivation. White flowers in spring followed by bluish-black berries.

***V. × burkwoodii* 'Anne Russell'** A fairly dense, bushy plant to 3 metres with compact heads of highly scented, white flowers from pink buds. Far less gawky than the original clone of this hybrid, which I have always had a love-hate relationship with.

V. carlesii Deciduous shrub to 2 metres with sweetly scented pink to white flowers in spring. This plant is rare in Australia, and its hybrid *V. × juddii*, which is easier to grow in any case, is often sold as it.

V. × carlcephalum A lovely hybrid between *V. carlesii* and *V. macrocephalum* that makes a large deciduous shrub to 3 metres, with rounded heads of white scented flowers, from pink buds in spring.

V. cylindricum A large evergreen shrub to 4 metres from China, with deep green leaves and panicle-shaped clusters of small white flowers in summer, followed by black berries.

V. davidii Dwarf evergreen shrub from China to 1 metre with very large, glossy, dark green leaves and small white flowers in clusters appearing off and on throughout the year. To produce the grey-blue berries on female plants, a male form is usually required. Ideal in large rock gardens, tubs and as a tall ground cover. This species doesn't like it too hot and dry.

V. farreri* syn. *V. fragrans A deciduous shrub to 3 metres or so from the Himalayas with masses of highly scented pale pink flowers on the bare stems throughout winter. Old plants develop peeling coppery bark.

V. henryi An open evergreen shrub to 4 metres or so with very long, narrow, dark green leaves. It comes from central China and produces white fragrant flowers in summer followed by red berries that turn black with age.

V. japonicum A hardy evergreen shrub from Japan to 3 metres with very glossy bright green leaves. It produces clusters of small white flowers in summer followed by masses of brilliant orange-red berries.

***V. j.* 'Variegatum'** This form has leaves irregularly blotched and streaked with creamy-white. Some leaves or entire shoots can be completely without green pigment. It also produces good crops of red berries.

V. × juddii A bushy deciduous shrub to 2 metres with clusters of heavily scented pale pink to white flowers in early spring. Similar to *V. carlesii*, which is one parent and considered by some to be better.

***V. lantana* 'Aurea' (Golden Wayfaring Tree)** A deciduous shrub to 4 metres with broad leaves that are gold in spring and slowly fade to pale green by autumn when it can turn to brilliant autumnal tones. Its flat heads of creamy-white flowers are followed by red berries that blacken with age.

***V. l.* 'Variifolium'** This form has lovely mottled leaves splashed with yellow.

***V. macrocephalum* 'Sterile'** A semi-evergreen shrub to 4 metres from China. It has massive ball-shaped heads of flowers starting green and ending up white. Flowering time is late winter to spring.

***V. opulus* 'Notcutt's Variety'** Large deciduous shrub to 4 metres with white lacecap-type flowers in spring and richly coloured autumn foliage. In the summer it produces drooping clusters of translucent orange-red berries, which are lovely for picking. One of the best Viburnums for its fruit display, it is naturally in my first book!

***V. o.* 'Xanthocarpum'** A lovely form identical to the above except for its wonderful amber-yellow berries and yellow autumn foliage. Plant this and the above next to each other for a stunning display.

***V. plicatum* 'Grandiflora' (Japanese Snowball)** Medium to large deciduous shrub to 3 metres with horizontal branches. The round white heads of flower form along the top of the branches in late spring, and last well.

***V. p.* 'Lanarth'** Resembles the following better-known cultivar but is stronger in growth and a little less horizontal in its habit of branching. This one can easily reach 3 metres tall by nearly as wide, so leave room.

***V. p.* 'Mariesii'** A superb variety with very flat branches on a bush to 2 metres tall and wider than that. It is topped with white lacecap blooms in spring.

***V. p.* 'Pink Beauty'** A smaller-leafed form to 3 metres, with white lacecap flowers ageing to soft pink.

***V. p.* 'Rosace'** A lovely sterile form, with rounded heads of softest pink.

***V. p.* 'Summer Snowflake'** A lovely form that differs from the others by being fairly dwarf, only to about 1.5 metres tall by a little wider, and producing its white lacecaps off and on from spring to autumn.

***V. prunifolium* (Black Haw)** A hardy deciduous shrub to 3 metres from North America with richly coloured autumn foliage. The small white flowers are produced in clusters during spring and are followed by blue-black edible berries. You could make Black Haw jelly to delight all your friends!

V. rhytidophyllum A large evergreen shrub from China to 6 metres with very big leathery leaves. It produces creamy white flowers in late spring. If two clones are planted, both will produce huge clusters of bright red berries that turn black with age, so this is one of the few times when buying seedlings would make good sense!

***V. sargentii* 'Onondaga'** A spectacular form to 3 metres, originating at the US National Arboretum Washington in 1959. Its leaves start deep maroon and turn green in summer then reddish purple in autumn. Its lacecap-type flowers have deep cerise fertile flowers surrounded by pure white bracts.

V. setigerum An erect deciduous shrub to 3 metres from China. The lovely foliage is metallic blue-green in spring with bronze tinges, turning green in summer and orange-yellow in autumn. The clusters of white flowers are produced in summer and are followed by slightly flattened bright red berries.

V. suspensum An attractive, hardy evergreen shrub to 2 metres from Japan with clusters of soft pink to white scented flowers in spring followed by small red berries.

V. wrightii A deciduous shrub to 2 metres with clusters of small white flowers in spring followed by bright red berries in late summer and autumn. The foliage colours well before shedding.

Weigela middendorffiana

A rare species of deciduous shrub, to 1.5 metres or so, from Japan and China and of great appeal. It has lovely soft yellow trumpet-shaped flowers with orange spotting inside that are produced in spring. The foliage turns yellow before shedding.

Weinmannia racemosa
A hardy evergreen large shrub or small tree to 7 metres from New Zealand. Its major asset is its attractive bronze-tinged foliage particularly strong coloured in winter. It produces spikes of tiny white flowers in spring.

Wigandia caracasana
A fabulous, small, evergreen to semi-deciduous suckering tree, to 4 metres or so, from Mexico. It has huge paddle-shaped leaves and heads of rich mauve flowers in spring and summer. Give it an open sunny aspect and shelter from frost in cold districts. This plant features in my first book and in my garden.

Xanthoceras sorbifolium
A very hardy sun-loving deciduous shrub, to 3 metres or so, from northern China, with Ash-like leaves that turn soft yellow in autumn, but more importantly it has spikes of pure white flowers with a yellow centre that turn burgundy as it ages. These are produced in spring and followed by small walnut-like capsules containing black seeds. The flowers and leaves can be eaten and the seeds are said to be as yummy as Macadamia nuts.

***Xanthorhiza simplicissima* (Yellow Root)**
A strange little deciduous suckering shrub in the Ranunculus family from the eastern woods of the U.S.A., to 30 cm tall, with Ash-like leaves turning yellow in autumn and open panicles of tiny purple-brown flowers in spring. Its roots and inner bark are bright yellow and have a bitter taste. None of this of course adds to its ornamental value. Likes a moist semi-shaded aspect.

***Zanthoxylum piperitum* (Japanese Pepper)**
A deciduous shrub to 4 metres with tiny Ash-like leaves, that turn rich yellow in autumn, attached to thorny brown stems. It has small yellowish flowers in spring. It is an important condiment in Asia and seems to be getting a profile in Australia as Sechuan Pepper.

Zelkova serrata
A medium to large deciduous tree to 17 metres with an elegant spreading habit, from China, Korea and Japan. The dainty Elm-shaped green leaves turn brilliant yellows, oranges and sometimes reds in autumn. This tree is pretty tough and it is a bit surprising that it isn't used more often – perhaps it now will be!
***Z. s.* 'Kiwi Sunset'** A new form obviously found in New Zealand (it's another Kiwi Fruit thing!) which has nice yellow foliage but is otherwise like the species.

Zenobia pulverulenta
A beautiful deciduous to semi-evergreen arching shrub to 1 metre from North America. It produces masses of pure white bell-shaped flowers in late spring, which are good for picking and a good enough plant to be found in my first book. It likes a cool moist aspect just like Azaleas and Rhododendrons.

Conifers

Larix decidua 'Pendula'

***Abies amabilis* 'Spreading Star'**
A flat-growing deep green Fir with lovely pale green new growth in spring. It will be little more than 20 cm tall by 1 metre across in ten years.

***A. balsamea* Hudsonia Group** A ball-shaped dwarf to 30 cm each way in about ten years. It has dark green needles that start pale green and will make a good bonsai, tub specimen or feature plant in a rock garden. A sunny but not too dry an aspect suits best.

***A. × bornmuelleriana* 'Compacta'** This rare dwarf Fir will make an irregular shrub to 2.5 metres in ten years with tightly packed deep green needles.

***A. cephalonica* 'Meyer's Dwarf'** A lovely low-spreading conifer to 30 cm tall by a metre or more across in ten years with rich deep green needles.

***A. concolor* 'Compacta'** A lovely blue needled conical dwarf Fir that could get to 1 metre in ten years.

***A. c.* 'Winter Gold'** A slow-growing conical bush to 2 metres tall in about ten years. Its quite long needles are pale green in summer and then turn golden in winter.

***A. koreana* (Korean Fir)** A slow-growing dark green conifer with a classical Christmas-tree-like habit. The cones are purple when small and are produced on quite young trees. Will eventually reach 10 metres or more if you live long enough! Like many in this genus a sunny but not too dry an aspect suits. A good tub specimen whilst young.

***A. k.* 'Krystall Kugel'** A tiny little globe-shaped muppet to 20 cm each way in about ten years. Can be found room for, even in the tiniest garden!

***A. k.* 'Silberlocke'** This slow-growing form has twisted needles that expose their white undersides which makes it an ideal Christmas tree as it looks like it has its own Santa snow! A unique and arresting plant raised in Germany sometime before 1983.

***A. k.* 'Tundra'** This selection makes a dense, dark green mound to 30 cm by 30 cm wide in about ten years.

***A. lasiocarpa* 'Compacta'** A bright silver-blue needled conifer of compact conical habit, which slowly grows to about 3 metres in ten or so years. A better tree than the 'Blue Spruce' especially if you have a smallish garden.

***A. nordmanniana* 'Golden Spreader'** This dwarf form of Caucasian Fir (as its unimaginative name suggests) has yellow needles and a spreading habit. A ten-year-old plant should be 30 cm tall and about 1 metre across. Keep this one out of the really hot sun, as it may burn, and not too shady, as it might green!

***A. pinsapo* 'Glauca' (Blue Spanish Fir)** A lovely slow-growing tree of conical habit to 5 metres or so in ten years but which, one day, may be 20 metres or more. It has rich blue-grey needles and, eventually, handsome erect cones. It will tolerate more heat and drier conditions than most Firs.

***Agathis australis* (New Zealand Kauri)**
A conifer that in a thousand years may be 50 metres tall with a trunk diameter of 8 metres. This shouldn't worry you! As a young tree it has an open upright habit with large brown leaf-like needles that make it look very little like a conifer and not very well!

***A. robusta* (Queensland Kauri)** This Australian native grows very like its cross-Tasman relative but has even larger dead-looking leaves!

***Araucaria angustifolia* (Parana Pine, Candelabra Tree)**
A very rare South American conifer that will grow to 30 metres or so if you live long enough! It sheds its lower branches so that in time it looks like its second common name. Its large needles are dark green and slightly sharp on the ends but nowhere near as 'ouch-making' as the following species. It grows 7 metres or thereabouts in the first ten years.

***A. araucana* (Monkey Puzzle Tree)** A large tree of very rounded outline from South America that can possibly grow to 25 metres or more. The foliage is very dark green, triangular in shape and prickly. This tree, much loved in Victorian times, is making a comeback. If we wait long enough everything comes back into fashion, even your old flares!

A. bidwillii **(Bunya Pine)** A very large impressive tree from Queensland to 7 metres or so in the first ten years but eventually reaching 50 metres with dark green prickly foliage and huge cones that contain edible seeds although it takes years to produce them. Hope you don't starve in the meantime!

A. cunninghamii **(Hoop Pine)** This tall tree from northern Australia and New Guinea has an open habit and branchlets in clusters giving it a more irregular outline that most species in this genus. With adequate water whilst young it can grow quite quickly to 10 metres and can in time get to 50 metres, so give it room.

Athrotaxus cupressoides (Tasmanian Pencil Pine)

An upright native conifer of slow growth to 2 metres in ten years, and in time perhaps up to 10 metres, with rich green scale-type foliage. As it comes from such a cool climate it would make an ideal tub specimen in a fernery or semi-shaded courtyard, as would the two following plants.

A. laxifolia This is a bushier-growing species, which appears to be intermediate between *A. cupressoides* and the following species. It is in fact thought by many to be a naturally occurring hybrid and its bright green scales stick out a little from the branches. It can also be expected to reach about 2 metres in ten years and perhaps to 20 metres long after you are gone!

A. selaginoides **(King Billy Pine)** A slow-growing Tasmanian forest tree with firm triangular needles. Can eventually grow to a very large tree of up to 40 metres but has a growth rate about the same as the preceding forms, so would also tub up well.

Calocedrus decurrens (Incense Cedar)

An elegant slow-growing tree from North America with a narrow upright habit that will reach 3 metres or so in ten years but in time will grow very tall even up to 50 metres and make an ideal accent plant. The foliage is rich green and arranged in fans and as the common name suggests it has a strong scent. A moist, deep soil suits best.

Cedrus deodara 'Lime Glow'

A charming rugged dwarf Cedar to 1 metre tall by a little wider in ten years. Its needles are a soft goldy-grey.

C. d. **'Mountain Beauty'** A dwarf rugged-looking shrub with gold-green needles growing to about 2 metres in ten years (and, in my garden, still going) that is ideal for the very large rock garden.

C. d. **'Pendula'** A lovely weeping form that will only grow as tall as it is staked and then will cascade back to the ground. Obviously if not staked it will creep along the ground. The needles are the same long grey-green of the species.

C. libani **ssp. *atlantica* 'Glauca Pendula' (Weeping Blue Cedar)** A silvery-needled, weeping conifer that requires staking to gain initial height and will then cascade back to the ground. The weeping side branches spread out as well as down so a twenty-year-old at my nursery is 3 metres tall and 5 metres across.

C. l. **ssp. *brevifolia*** **(Cyprian Cedar)** A slow-growing, small to medium tree from Cyprus with the smallest needles of the genus that in old age could reach 15 metres. A good tub specimen for years before becoming a lawn specimen. Also ideal for Bonsai.

C. l. **'Sargentii'** Another weeping or trailing form that will follow the contours of the ground unless staked up.

Cephalotaxus harringtonii 'Fastigiata'

A narrow pencil-shaped conifer to about 3 to 4 metres over many years with long dark green needles. An ideal centre-piece for a rock garden or tub specimen or even as a pair on either side of the front door.

Chamaecyparis nootkatensis 'Pendula' (Weeping Nootka Cypress)

A beautiful, upright conifer with very dark green foliage. The side branches cascade down like long streamers. This strangely beautiful tree could grow to 10 metres or more and not only would it look stunning near water but it quite likes damp soil.

C. obtusa **'Bassett'** An extremely dwarf conifer, to 15 cm each way, with deep green, scale-like foliage in tiny swirling fans.

***C. o.* 'Flabelliformis'** A slow-growing, bun-shaped variety that will get to about 30 cm in ten years.

***C. o.* 'Sparkles'** This selection, with its open sprays of deep green foliage liberally splashed with yellow, will make a rustic shrub to 60 cm each way in about ten years.

Cryptomeria japonica 'Araucarioides'

A strange, dark green, slow-growing conifer with long whip-like branches, often with clusters of smaller branches at their tips. It will eventually form a leader and become a conical tree to 7 metres. As a young plant it looks like some sort of device for punishing naughty boys!

***C. j.* 'Globosa Nana'** An attractive semi-dwarf conifer with light green needles that grows into an irregular ball-shape approximately 1.5 metres each way in about ten years. I have a thirty-year-old one that is 3 metres each way and stunning.

***C. j.* 'Sekkan'** This fairly quick-growing form grows to an upright small tree of 3 metres within ten years and in spring all its new growth is a lovely creamy-white.

Cunninghamia lanceolata 'Glauca' (Chinese Fir)

A handsome medium to tall tree with long curled needles of a grey-green colour. I grow my plants from lateral cuttings and this makes them into a spreading ground cover of great elegance that will rarely produce a leader. (If it does this can be removed to keep the low habit.)

Cupressus cashmiriana (Kashmir Cypress)

A quick-growing conical tree to 5 metres within ten years with drooping grey foliage which makes it the essence of elegance. Quite hardy which belies its looks.

***C. lusitanica* 'Glauca Pendula'** A hardy quick-growing weeping grey-blue cypress to about 7 metres that makes a lovely lawn specimen with an elegant spreading habit.

Dacrycarpus dacrydioides syn. *Podocarpus dacrydioides* (New Zealand White Pine)

This bizarre tree spends its youth producing sparse dark brown ferny foliage that to the uninitiated would suggest it had long since died. As it matures its foliage does get a hint of grey-green to give its secret away if its increase in size isn't enough. Grows well in moist to damp soil and can become a forest giant in a couple of generations. Its common name refers to its wood, not its appearance.

Dacrydium cupressinum (Rimu)

A slow-growing New Zealand tree for a cool moist aspect. The foliage is dark green and pendulous making this a most graceful plant for a tub in a fernery. If you don't believe me look at the photo in my first book. It can get to about 2 metres in ten years and after that it just keeps going. You won't see it at 60 metres.

Diselma archeri

A small arching shrub from Tasmania that will slowly grow to 2 metres and would make a charming tub specimen or rock garden plant in a cool aspect. Why not bonsai your own Tasmanian!

Fitzroya cupressoides (Patagonian Cypress)

A rare and interesting conifer from Chile and Argentina. It produces graceful, drooping grey-green foliage and will become a large shrub or small tree in one lifetime, to about 3 or 4 metres, 50 metres in the wild.

Fokienia hodginsii

A lovely, small to medium tree from China with rich green foliage arranged in fan-like sprays. This tree requires a sheltered semi-shaded aspect for best results and will probably get to 3 metres in about ten years.

Ginkgo biloba (Maidenhair Tree)

A very primitive deciduous tree related to the conifers with large green leaves, which turn rich gold in autumn. It will eventually become a large spreading shade tree to 30 metres. However, 4 to 5 metres will often see us out. Fairly drought-tolerant, once established and capable of ignoring air pollution in car-clogged cities. Old trees (Oh, how I wish for an old one!) can produce bizarre, rooty things from the trunk that add to the aged look.

***G. b.* 'Autumn Gold'** A male selection with good autumn foliage, otherwise much the same as the species which as seedlings you don't know what you are going to get. (Sex-wise that is!)

***G. b.* 'Fastigiata'** A beautiful narrow-growing form of Ginkgo that makes an ideal vertical accent tree. It features in my first book and like the following selection is a male form so that you don't have any smelly fruit to deal with in years to come.

***G. b.* 'Saratoga'** This interesting form has long two-lobed leaves and a rustic irregular shape that lends itself to bonsai or tub culture. It will, however, with the fullness of time, make a sizeable tree if you don't own secateurs! Its autumnal yellow is as good as any.

***Glyptostrobus pensilis* syn. *G.lineatus* (Pond Cypress)**

A rare and upright deciduous conifer from Canton. It will slowly grow to 7 metres with soft grey-green ferny foliage that turns bright coppery-pink before shedding, which happens throughout the winter. It grows best in moist to wet soils. Probably the smallest growing species of deciduous conifer and it features in my first book.

***Juniperus communis* (Common Juniper)**

The well-known addition to Gin! This tough-as-guts small tree, to 4 metres in ten years, has sharply pointed needles and on female forms it produces the classic small black berries.

J. rigida A strange name for an elegantly weeping tree from Japan, Korea and Manchuria that in ten years could be 3 metres tall and eventually much taller. The new needles are buff-coloured in spring and turn a slightly bronze-green later and are as sharp as needles.

***Lagarostrobos franklinii* (Huon Pine)**

The well-known, slow-growing forest tree from Tasmania. It has weeping, rich green foliage and because of its slow growth makes an ideal tub specimen for a shady area. In a few hundred years you can cut it down and make some small decorative item like a letter opener!

***Larix decidua* (European Larch)**

A large deciduous conifer with soft green needles that turn pale yellow before shedding in autumn. It can grow to 30 metres or more in cool hill gardens where it and its relatives are happiest.

***L. d.* 'Hilliers Weeper'** The branches of this variety sweep out and down gracefully unlike the following variety that has branches hanging straight down. This form requires staking to acquire the desired height.

***L. d.* 'Julians Weeper'** Another weeping form of European Larch that also requires staking to gain height. This variety makes a very good tub specimen staked to 2 metres or so.

***L. d.* 'Little Bogle'** A bizarre semi-dwarf to 1.5 metres in ten years with tightly congested foliage and curled and twisted branches. Great off-beat tub specimen.

***L. kaempferi* (Japanese Larch)** A conical elegant deciduous tree differing from the European species mainly in its greyish foliage.

***Metasequoia glyptostroboides* (Dawn Redwood)**

A handsome, quick-growing deciduous conifer from China to 30 metres or so. It has soft green ferny foliage that turns rich pinky-bronze before shedding. It is an upright conical tree ideal as a lawn specimen. This very ancient tree was first described from fossil remains and discovered as a living plant in China about 1941.

***Microcachrys tetragona* (Strawberry Pine)**

A rare small-growing dark green conifer native to Tasmania. It can be trained as a small semi-pendulous plant by staking and makes a good tub specimen in the shade. In time you may get the tiny red fruit that gives this plant its common name, but they don't, however, taste of strawberries!

Microstrobus fitzgeraldii

A charming small arching shrub, to 1 metre over quite some years, with grey-green foliage. This native comes from one area in the Blue Mountains that is within a haze of mist from nearby waterfalls. This probably isn't needed in the home garden but a cool moist spot is.

Phyllocladus alpinus 'Cockayne's Blue' (New Zealand Alpine Celery Pine)

A form of Alpine Celery Pine selected for its blue-grey cladodes (pretend leaves). It slowly grows to about 1 metre in ten years and like all the species in this genus doesn't like it too hot and dry. Great novel tub specimen.

***P. asplenifolius* (Celery Topped Pine)** A strange Tasmanian native conifer with rich green cladodes with an outline not unlike celery. It is a slow-growing tree for a moist semi-shaded aspect and makes a good tub specimen and a great plant to check the knowledge of smart-arsed supposed experts!

***P. trichomanoides* (New Zealand Celery Pine)** This species is similar to the above with regards to its growth and requirements, but has larger and more intricate cladodes. Trust the New Zealanders to have a prettier one!

Picea abies 'Acrocona'

A dwarf-spreading form of Norway Spruce with dark green needles that can also be trained upright with staking. It produces quite large cones even as a young plant that start burgundy and go brown with age. Expect a plant about 1 metre tall and wider in ten years.

***P. a.* 'Inversa' (Weeping Norway Spruce)** A dark green form that must be staked to reach the required height and then will cascade back to the ground; otherwise it is a ground-hugging trailer that could cover about 1.5 metres in ten years.

***P. breweriana* (Brewer's Spruce)** A much sought-after species comes from North America where it has a very restricted range in the Siskiyou Mountains. It can grow very tall although it isn't likely to exceed 3 metres in the first ten years. Its needles are deep green and its side branches so droopy that no Christmas decoration will be able to hold on!

***P. mariana* 'Nana'** A tiny slow-growing conifer with a bun shape and grey needles, never exceeding 30 cm each way. This tiny plant is ideal for tubs, rock gardens and bonsai.

***P. omorika* (Serbian Spruce)** A rare narrow tree that could reach 35 metres tall and yet stay only 3 metres wide. In ten years it will probably be pushing it to be more than 4 metres tall.

***P. o.* 'Nana'** A dwarf bun-shaped form with tiny needles that could grow to 30 cm before you're gone!

***P. orientalis* 'Aurea'** A lovely deep green Christmas-tree-shaped conifer with very small needles. The new growth in spring is a rich golden yellow that contrasts well with the older needles. Expect a tree to 4 metres in ten years if it is doing well. Eventually a very tall tree.

***P. pungens* 'Early Cones'** An amazing little blue Spruce selected here in Australia that has short grey needles and will grow to 20 cm tall by 30 cm across in ten years. Its major claim to fame, however, is the fact that it produces tiny cones even from a baby plant.

***P. p.* 'Fat Albert'** A newish selection of Blue Spruce from North America (with this name from where else but, in this case, Iseli's Nurseries in Boring, Oregon) that makes a very compact broadly conical small tree, to 3 metres by 2 metres wide in ten years, far better than most previously available.

***P. p.* 'Fat Mac'** This selection makes a tight grey bun to 40 cm each way in ten years.

***P. p.* 'Iseli Fastigiate'** An amazing Spruce with rich blue needles and a narrow upright habit to 2 metres tall in ten years and yet less than 30 cm wide.

***P. p.* 'Montgomery'** A lovely, irregular, dwarf, bun-shaped form of Blue Spruce growing slowly to 2 metres. The needles are an intense silver-blue.

***P. p.* 'St Mary'** A charming small Blue Spruce that will make an irregular dome-shaped shrub to 30 cm tall by 60 cm wide in about ten years.

***P. sitchensis* 'Papoose'** A very compact and almost formally ball-shaped conifer with rich green needles. It will get to 1 metre each way in about ten years.

P. smithiana (Himalayan Spruce) A slow-growing large tree with rich dark green needles and elegant weeping branches. The new growth in spring is a soft pale green.

P. s. 'Ballarat' A locally selected dwarf that makes a small conical shrub to about 1 metre in ten years with attractive weeping side branches. Could be just the thing, as a tub specimen, to spend a bit of time with tinsel on it!

Pinus coulteri (Big Coned Pine)

This large drought-tolerant tree from North America has long needles, attractive bark and stunning huge cones that weigh up to 2 kg that could stun a Grizzly Bear! Not for the small garden but well worth it if you have the space for the large free fire-lighters, if for nothing else!

P. densiflora 'Alice Verkade' A tight little hedgehog with long bright green needles to 30 cm each way.

P. d. 'Pendula' A very strange pine that, if untrained, will trail along the ground or cascade over banks. It can also be staked up to make a weeping shrub to the height of the stake. It has long, dull green needles.

P. halepensis (Aleppo Pine) A very hardy large tree from the Mediterranean with bright green needles that will make a specimen tree or a windbreak. It will grow to 4 metres in ten years and then keep going.

P. leucodermis 'Schmidtii' A tiny little dwarf ball to 20 cm each way with tightly packed deep green needles.

P. mugo 'Amber Gold' A lovely bun to 50 cm tall by 75 cm across in ten years. The needles are green in summer and a lovely yellow colour in winter.

P. m. 'Mops' A rugged little bun-shaped pine, to 40 cm tall by 60 cm wide in ten years.

P. m. 'Pincushion' Another 'cute as a bug' bun of rich green foliage, to 80 cm wide by 25 cm tall in ten years.

P. patula (Mexican Pine) A quick-growing elegant pine to 15 metres or more with long drooping needles of rich green on coppery branches. I have no idea why this drop dead gorgeous tree isn't used a lot more.

P. pinea (Stone Pine) This Mediterranean species is the one that pine nuts are collected from. Not that I would grow it for this reason, as I am not tall enough to pick the cones, and don't expect to live long enough for my first crop – and the cockatoos will beat me to them anyway! The tree, however, will in time become a tall umbrella-shaped thing with lovely coppery bark, and be a feature wherever it is planted. So, go on!

P. strobus 'Torulosa' A form of Weymouth Pine that grows into a small bushy tree with curious twisted grey-green needles. Will reach about 3 to 4 metres in ten years.

P. sylvestris 'Fastigiata' A very narrow pencil form of Scots Pine with blue-grey needles that can grow to 7 metres or more but rarely wider than 30 cm. It also produces cones from an early stage which is quite endearing.

P. s. 'Hillside Creeper' As the name this form suggests, it creeps across the ground and rarely exceeds 30 cm tall but will reach at least a metre wide in ten years.

P. s. 'Repens' Another creeping form with the tips of the branches pointing up. A rugged and attractive rock garden or bonsai specimen. Perhaps, if trained up a bit, an elegant weeping tub specimen could be created. It will get to 1 metre or so wide in ten years.

P. s. 'Saxatilis' This form makes a rugged bun to 25 cm tall by 35 cm across in ten years.

P. thunbergii 'Emery's Dwarf' A lovely little, deep green bun to 25 cm each way in ten years.

P. t. 'Kotobuki' An interesting upright pine to 2 metres tall by 1 metre across in about the mandatory ten years, with comparatively short dark green needles and attractive candles of whitish new growth in the spring.

P. wallichiana (Bhutan Pine) A truly lovely pine that will grow to 40 metres or more with blue-green drooping needles and long narrow pendulous cones. It is, however, unlikely to be more than 5 metres in ten years.

Podocarpus alpinus
An attractive dwarf-spreading native conifer, to 1 metre tall and wider than that, that grows wild in the mountains of Tasmania and Victoria. It has rich grey-green needles and red berry-like arils.

P. lawencei A lovely rugged-looking spreading native conifer, to 60 cm tall by at least half as much again, with small grey-green needles.

***P. totara* 'Aurea' (Golden Totara)** A New Zealander that in time will make a large tree but in ten years is likely to be little more than 2 metres tall. It has a rugged outline and fairly sharp bronzy-yellow foliage. Would be a good tub specimen for many years.

P. salignus An elegant large shrub or small tree from Chile. It has long flat grey-green needles and an arching almost willow-like habit. A good screening plant and an attractive tub specimen whilst young. It will be unlikely to be more that 2 metres in ten years.

***Pseudolarix amabilis* (Golden Larch)**
A rare slow-growing, conical deciduous tree with soft green needles that turn a rich yellow before shedding. When mature this tree produces lovely cones that resemble green roses. It is a native to damp hilly areas of China and is unlikely to exceed 4 metres in ten years.

***Sciadopitys verticillata* (Japanese Umbrella Pine)**
A slow-growing conifer with an upright conical habit to 1 metre in ten years, but eventually a large tree. It has long needles (radiating like the spokes of an umbrella) that are actually two needles fused together along their lengths. While young, this tree makes a lovely tub specimen. Shade tolerant.

***Sequoia sempervirens* (Giant Redwood)**
The world's tallest tree and specimens have been recorded at more than 120 metres (not that we will be around for the eight hundred years required to reach such heights). It should, however, get to at least 6 metres in ten years. The form is upright and the foliage deep green and ferny.

***Sequoiadendron giganteum* (Big Tree)**
This will in time (lots of it!) become the biggest living thing. Not as tall as the Redwood but with a much wider trunk. The foliage is grey-green and scaly and the trunk develops thick spongy bark. Plant your own local landmark!

***S. g.* 'Pendulum' (the Weeping Californian Big Tree)** This is a unique form, growing to a tall tree with all the side branches weeping straight down the trunk. Possibly the world's tallest tree with narrowest width ratio. A very striking feature tree that can be seen in my first book.

***Taxodium acendens* (Pond Cypress)**
A rare deciduous conifer from the U.S.A. that grows well in damp to wet sites. It is upright in form with billowy clouds of bright green foliage that tends to point upward, which gives it a quite unique look. In autumn it turns fox-red before shedding.

***T. distichum* (Swamp Cypress)** A beautiful North American deciduous conifer to 20 metres or more ideal for damp to wet soils where it often produces woody lumps rising from the roots called cypress knees through which it takes in oxygen that is lacking in wet soils. Its soft green feathery foliage turns a rich rusty brown before shedding. Could get to 5 metres in ten years.

***T. d.* 'Cascade Falls'** This selection is pendulous and usually grafted onto standards and will grow no taller. It would make a stunning tub specimen or feature plant behind a pond.

***T. d.* 'Secrest'** A newish selection that has a flat branching arrangement and is grafted onto 1-metre standards so it looks like an open umbrella and will grow to about 1 metre across.

***Tsuga canadensis* 'Bennett'**
A dwarf-spreading form of Hemlock, to 60 cm tall by 1 metre across, with rich green

foliage and pale lime-green new growth. All the forms of *Tsuga* like a moist aspect and will tolerate some shade.

***T. c.* 'Cole'** A very flat-growing form with dark green needles that will hug the contours unless staked up and spread to about 1 metre in ten years.

***T. c.* 'Gentsche White'** An upright shrub to about 2 metres with rich green foliage and white tips to the branches. It is ideal as a Christmas tree in a tub and it already has its own Santa Snow.

Wollemia nobilis (Wollemi Pine)

Almost too famous now to describe, since its discovery in the Blue Mountains in 1994, but I will anyhow! Its needles are long, dark grey-green and stiff, and plastic-looking. It will grow to about 3 to 4 metres in ten years and will, in time, develop bubbly-looking bark. Only a hundred or so exist in the wild but by now some millions are probably in cultivation. A great conversation piece and perhaps the ideal native Christmas tree as it almost looks like the fake ones!

Climbers

Lapageria rosea

Actinidia kolomikta
A rare deciduous vine related to the 'Kiwi Fruit' but grown for the fact that the leaves will sometimes have pink tips and sometimes have white ones which makes for a truly fascinating light deciduous vine. This strange variegation doesn't usually develop in young plants so look it up in my second book. It likes a spot in morning sun sheltered from hot winds. The flowers produced in spring are small, white and slightly scented. If we had both male and female forms we would get sweet yellowish fruit. Will slowly cover an area of 3 metres each way.

Adlumia fungosa
A charming biennial climber to 5 metres native to North America. For the first year it looks a bit like a soft grey-green Maidenhair Fern until you look more closely. In its second season it will gently run up any support it can find and in summer produce tiny soft dusty pink flowers very similar to its relative the Bleeding Heart. It will then shed its seed and the whole thing should start again.

Ampelopsis aconitifolius
A rare grapevine relative from northern China and Mongolia with deep glossy green leaves that are deeply divided and turn a soft yellow in autumn. Likes a sunny spot and is drought-tolerant once established. Ideal up poles, on arches or through other climbers. Unpruned (all these grape relatives prune well), expect 4 metres each way.

***A. glandulosa* var. *brevipedunculata* (Blueberry Climber)** Hardy deciduous climber with pale green leaves and masses of berries in autumn, ranging in colour from green to aquamarine, turquoise, blue and purple. The leaves are slightly lobed and soft yellow in autumn. This native of north-eastern Asia is vigorous and sun-loving but quite controllable and could grow to 6 metres or more each way. This lovely thing is in my second book.

***A. g. b.* 'Elegans'** A smaller growing form with grape-shaped leaves with white mottled variegation that becomes more striking as the season advances. It has pink stems and tendrils and as if this isn't enough it has the same coloured berries as the species. Will rarely grow more than 3 metres and is also open and light thus it is an ideal candidate to mix with other vines or to grow through a shrub that won't be harmed by its attentions.

A. vitifolia* syn. *Vitis persica Hardy deciduous vine with attractive serrated foliage colouring richly in autumn. Native of Iran to the north-western Himalayas. This plant is not overly vigorous but can reach 5 metres each way.

Asteranthera ovata
A charming small evergreen climber from Chile probably more at home in a hanging basket or trailing along the ground, although it can reach 1 to 1.5 metres in a very cool moist aspect. This strange relative of the African violet produces deep cherry-pink flared trumpets amongst its tiny dark green leaves, from late spring through summer. It likes fernery-type conditions and is in my second book.

Berberidopsis beckleri* syn. *Streptothamnus beckleri
A lovely light evergreen climber from northern Australia, to 4 metres each way, for a cool moist aspect and out of the frost. It produces small deep pink waxy flowers with a white tip hanging below the branches during the summer. These are followed by large pink berries that turn black with age. The new growth is bronze-tinged. Both species feature in my second book.

B. corallina Elegant evergreen climber from Chile that may slowly grow to 3 metres or so for moist shady aspects. It has rich dark green foliage and brilliant red waxy flowers in small clusters during summer and is much more cold tolerant than its Aussie relative.

***Bomarea multiflora* (Climbing Alstroemeria)**
South American climbing lily to 4 metres with clusters of orange flowers spotted brown at the end of the stems for all of the warmer months. Those stems that have flowered die to the ground to be replaced by new ones. It prefers a sunny well-drained site and grows

well on a tall tripod or over a large shrub. Looks great in my second book!

B. salsilla An unusual species from South America with a completely herbaceous habit, dying down soon after flowering in mid-summer. Its stems will grow to 1.5 metres tall and are topped with clusters of waxy, cherry-red bells in summer. This one will look fabulous over a shrub or up through a hedge.

Clematis armandii 'Apple Blossom'

Strong-growing, large-leafed evergreen climber from China that could grow to 7 or more metres long with masses of scented pale pink to white blooms in early spring. Like almost this entire genus it likes a cool root run with its top into the sun. This much-loved variety is hard to strike and always scarce.

***C. a.* 'Hendersonii Rubra'** This form is very similar to the above but has slightly more pink in the flowers.

***C. a.* 'Snowdrift'** This variety, as its name would suggest, has pure white, scented flowers.

C. campaniflora A lovely deciduous species from Spain and Portugal that will grow to 3 or 4 metres and best cut really hard in winter as it flowers on its new wood. In summer it has nodding icy-white bells that are quite small but charming none the less.

***C. cirrhosa* var. *balearica* (Fern Leafed Clematis)** Dainty evergreen climber with dark green leaves from the Balearic Islands to 3 or 4 metres. The dainty creamy-white bells with purple spots inside are produced from April to October.

***C. c.* 'Freckles'** A recently released form with larger more open flowers heavily spotted inside with burgundy.

C. fasciculiflora This recent introduction to our shores will make quite a splash when it is better known, despite its hard-to-say name! It is an evergreen, quick-growing but light species from China, Myanmar and northern Vietnam with dainty, nodding, white bells in late winter. Pretty as the flowers are, it is for the foliage that you grow this one. (Which one doesn't say for this genus often!) It has large green leaves marbled with silver with a burgundy underside. Buy one immediately!

C. ladakhiana A dainty small deciduous climber from northern India that, unlike most species, is sun-loving and dry-tolerant. Prune hard in winter and it will probably grow no more than 2 metres or so each year. Its leaves are finely cut and grey-green and throughout the summer it will produce nodding yellow bells so heavily spotted red-brown as to look more that colour. It also has lovely fluffy seed heads.

***C. macropetala* 'Markham's Pink'** A dainty deciduous climber to 3 metres that was selected from a species native to Mongolia, China and Siberia that has large double cherry-coloured pendulous flowers in late spring.

C. montana Quick-growing deciduous climber from China, to 10 metres or so, that will cover all and sundry before your very eyes with pure white flowers in early spring.

***C. m.* 'Elizabeth'** Larger pale pink flowering form with a pleasant perfume that at least to me is somewhat like the smell of Teddy Bear biscuits! Yum.

***C. m.* 'Marjorie'** This fairly new form has lovely double flowers, which are cream touched with soft salmon-pink. It seems also to be a little less vigorous than other forms of this species.

***C. m.* 'Tetrarose'** Extra large flowered tetraploid form raised in Holland with very deep pink scented flowers with bronze tinted leaves that are also bigger than the species. It doesn't, however, seem to grow any larger.

C. napaulensis A curious summer deciduous species from North India and China to 4 or 5 metres each way. The flowers are produced in winter and are lime green bells with purple stamens. These are followed by large white feathery seed heads. This species is tolerant of sun or fairly heavy shade but will often take some time to start blooming. This is worth the wait for both you and your Honeyeaters. This one made it into my second book.

***C. texensis* 'Duchess of Albany'** This lovely plant, like all the hybrids in the *C. texensis* Group, should be cut to the ground each winter. They will then flower almost all summer and autumn with upward facing tulip-shaped flowers on 4 metre long stems. In this case the flowers are a lovely rich pink.

***C. t.* 'Gravetye Beauty'** This selection has rich cherry-red, tulip-shaped flowers and is one of my personal favourites.

***C. t.* 'Sir Trevor Lawence'** This selection has pink on the outside of the flowers with a crimson interior.

***C. viticella* 'Abundance'** This Clematis and the rest of the *C. viticella* Group are deciduous vines that should be cut almost to the ground each winter and will usually then flower from late spring to autumn. The flowers are usually small compared with the large-flowered hybrids but bigger than the *C. montana* types and are great to grow over other plants and may even hide the odd rose bush! This form has deep cerise-pink flowers with textured petals.

***C. v.* 'Alba Luxurians'** A lovely white-flowered selection with irregular green floral bracts behind the flower and often green stained petals.

***C. v.* 'Betty Corning'** A lovely form with nodding bells of soft smoky-blue fading to white in the centre.

***C. v.* 'Carmencita'** This form has medium-sized flowers of a rich carmine with dark stamens.

***C. v.* 'Huldine'** A lovely pure white selection that is almost up to large-flowered hybrid size and is often sold as one. It has slightly cupped flowers with a faint mauve bar down the backs of the petals.

***C. v.* 'Kermisina'** A smallish flower produced over a long period that is a rich cerise-red.

***C. v.* 'Madame Julia Correvon'** A lovely largish flowered form with widely spaced petals of rich cerise-red. This one usually needs a prune after its first flush to encourage an autumn crop of flowers.

***C. v.* 'Margot Koster'** This form has large flowers that are rich deep pink and tend to be produced from early summer until the end of autumn.

***C. v.* 'Pagoda'** This dainty little form flowers all season with nodding bells of soft mauve with a white centre and the outside is mauve with a white edge. An appealing plant at close quarters.

***C. v.* 'Polish Spirit'** This strong doer has quite large flowers from midsummer that are a rich purple with a paler central bar.

***C. v.* 'Purpurea Plena Elegans'** A truly lovely, full double, dusty red-purple that flowers from midsummer.

***C. v.* 'Royal Velours'** A smallish almost black-purple with a velvety sheen that needs a spot with some light or the colour disappears. Try it over a silver foliage plant like a Silver Weeping Pear and wait for the praise.

***C. v.* 'Triternata Rubromarginata'** This lovely plant flowers for months with small mauve flowers with a white centre and a sweet almond scent.

***C. v.* 'Venosa Violacea'** This charmer has smallish rich purple flowers with an irregular white central stripe and a long flowering period.

Decumaria barbara

A semi-evergreen, self-clinging climber from North America related to the Hydrangeas. It has bright green leaves and clusters of small white flowers in summer. Ideal up walls or tree trunks and can in time reach 9 metres.

Dicentra macrocapnos

A lovely fine herbaceous perennial climber to 3 metres with soft green foliage stained with splashes of white and golden yellow locket-shaped flowers in summer. Ideal for clambering over shrubs or other climbers. It features in my second book, as such a fine thing should.

Euonymus fortunei 'Coloratus'

A very handsome more or less evergreen climber or ground cover that will cope with poor soils in either sun or heavy shade. The deep green foliage often turns burgundy in winter – cold and stress allowing. It produces small lemon-green berries in autumn that split to reveal orange seeds. It is an ideal plant to grow amongst invasive tree roots and features in my second book and in a very difficult spot in my garden.

Ficus pumila 'Minima' (Dwarf Climbing Fig)
A dainty little evergreen, self-clinging climber with small deep green leaves, native to China. Ideal over rocks or low walls in sun or shade where it could in time grow to 3 metres or so each way and is so tightly pressed to its support that it looks like it was ironed on!

Forsythia suspensa
This is a hardy deciduous shrub but its lax spreading branches make it far better to be trained as a climber or allowed to spill over banks. It produces masses of bright yellow flowers through late winter. It is a native to China and made its way into my second book which will hopefully promote sales of both! Sun to semi-shade.

Heteropteris angustifolia
A light airy semi-deciduous climber from sub-tropical Brazil. It has bronze coloured new growth in spring, little yellow flowers that start in early summer and continue till winter. By midsummer it is producing its red winged maple-like seeds and these remain on the plant till winter. A sunny well-drained aspect suits best and possibly the only place you will find a picture is in my second book.

Humulus lupulus 'Aureus' (Golden Hop)
A rarely seen and beautiful golden-leafed form of the commercial Hop. It is a vigorous, suckering, herbaceous perennial climber for a sunny well-drained aspect. It will grow to about 4 metres in a season and will produce papery seed heads in late summer and autumn. (Make your own beer!) Another plant that made it into my second book.

Holboellia latifolia
A rare Himalayan evergreen twiner with deep green foliage usually consisting of three leaflets. It produces both male and female flowers on the one plant, the boys are greenish-white and the girls are purplish. These are followed by edible sausage-shaped purple fruit. A moist soil in morning sun or semi-shade is best.

Hydrangea anomala ssp. _petiolaris_
A self-clinging, deciduous climbing species from Asia with white lacecap flower heads in summer. This plant, like the following species, will cling to walls or tree trunks and likes a cool but light aspect and could in time cover a cathedral if you happen to live in one. It is, however, just as happy over a 2 metre tree stump.

_H. p._ var. _cordifolia_ 'Brookside Littleleaf' As its name would suggest this form has much smaller foliage than the type that almost approaches the diminutive size of a climbing Fig. I imported this one quite recently and am finding it a good doer and think it may well grow as big as the other forms given the room.

_H. p._ 'Miranda' Another of my recent imports that in this case has attractive white to soft yellow variegated edges to the leaves. The colour does seem to fade a bit as the season goes on.

H. seemanii A very rare evergreen species from Mexico with leathery dark green foliage and lacecap style creamy-white flowers from prominent buds in summer. Like other climbing Hydrangeas, it will adapt to cover whatever you want.

H. seemanii × _serratifolia_ This rare evergreen self-clinging climber came to these shores very recently when I imported it from America. It has long deep green serrated leaves that just alone make it worth having. It produces white lacecap flowers in late summer.

_H._ species I imported this as _Schizophragma corylifolium_, however when Dan Hinkley (the famous person who started Heronswood Nursery) was visiting me in 2007, he told me that he had flowered it and it is an unnamed Hydrangea. It does have pretty, bright green leaves with red petioles and Dan assures me these are accompanied by small, white lacecap flowers. One day we will work it out, but in the meantime enjoy growing it!

***Jasminum nudiflorum* (Winter Jasmine)**
A charming hardy, winter flowering lax shrub from China with masses of golden-yellow trumpet-shaped flowers right through the colder months. Although it can be grown as a free-standing shrub it is far more useful trained up a fence or wall where it can get to 4 metres or so and is hardy enough to grow up through the lower branches of a tree to give it an interesting skirt.

***Lapageria rosea* (Chilean Bell Flower)**
Slow-growing evergreen climber for moist shady aspects with large waxy deep cherry-red bell flowers in summer and autumn. Give it good leafy soil and good light without any direct sun and you will have one of the world's great climbers. It is stunning up the posts in a fernery or quite suitable as a tub specimen. It is the floral emblem of Chile and naturally made it into my second book.

***L. r.* 'Angol'** One of the newish Chilean selections that in this case has the largest flower of any in a rich rose-pink. This one is named after the town in Chile where the nursery that did the selections was found and I am reliably informed that most of these selections were done by local people from the wild and not as one might think as an organised breeding program.

***L. r.* 'Arco Iris'** This rare form has medium-sized white trumpets with irregular cerise edges to the petals.

***L. r.* 'Chequecura'** This form has its three inner petals of a lovely soft pink and its outer three are white although some early flowers may be pure white.

***L. r.* 'Colinge'** This selection has comparatively short white trumpets completely netted with cerise veins.

***L. r.* 'El Vergel'** This form has large very soft pink flowers.

***L. r.* 'Nube Blanca'** A large flowered pure white of good vigour.

***L. r.* 'Nuhuelbuta'** This clone has large white flowers spotted and marked with soft plum-purple, which is subtle but arresting at close quarters.

***L. r.* 'Pan de Pedra'** This form has white flowers lightly stained with palest shell pink. Some of the earlier flowers can be straight white.

***L. r.* 'Quilipichum'** This form has flowers of the classical cherry-red colour but has double blooms. The extra petals hang out from the centre of the trumpet, like a giant Zygocactus.

***L. r.* 'Rosada Fuerte'** This form has long deep rose-pink trumpets from cream buds.

***L. r.* 'Toqui'** This is an extra long trumpeted white with cream to green shading on the outer petals.

Lardizabala funaria
A light-growing, rare evergreen twiner from Chile to 4 metres or so with attractive dark green foliage composed of up to nine leaflets. The flowers are purple and white; the male ones in drooping spikes the females solitary. These appear in winter and may be followed by edible dark purple sausage-shaped fruit. A semi-shaded to sunny aspect.

***Lonicera hildebrandiana* (Giant Honeysuckle)**
A large evergreen climber from the Himalayas that may grow without constraint to 20 metres or more. It has very large pale green leaves and the tubular flowers grow to 15 cm and start white, turn yellow and finish apricot. This plant is strongly scented and blooms all summer and these are followed by large green berries that taste like a gin and tonic! This worthy plant is in my second book and is, in my humble opinion, the triumph of its genus.

***Parthenocissus henryana* (Silver Vein Creeper)**
Attractive, deciduous, lightly self-clinging climber from China. The leaves usually have five leaflets, are dark green with white veins and a plum reverse and turn rich red in autumn. Unlike most autumnal colourers this plant will still perform in fairly heavy shade, in fact its white veins disappear in full sun. See it growing up my shed in my second book.

P. quinquefolia **(Virginia Creeper)** A self-clinging climber from the U.S.A. with large bright green leaves consisting of usually five leaflets that turn bright scarlet in early autumn. Looks stunning dripping out of trees or from a pergola.

P. sikkimensis This evergreen species that is quite new in this country has small leaves divided into five deep green serrated leaflets. This charming plant makes a great ground cover in semi-shade or small climber over low walls. It may yet prove not to belong to this genus but time will tell.

P. tricuspidata **'Beverley Brook'** A small-leafed type of Boston Ivy that makes a good self-clinging plant for walls or up tree trunks. Its grape-shaped leaves are dark green in summer and brilliant reds in autumn.

P. t. **'Lowii'** This lovely smaller growing form has heavily cut foliage, which gives it an almost parsley-crested look. It has great autumn foliage and is probably the best form in restricted spaces or over low walls.

P. t. **'Veitchii'** This form also has smaller leaves than the type but larger than those of *P. t.* 'Beverley Brook' and very rich autumnal colour.

P. vitacea **syn.** ***P. inserta*** This American species is very like the true Virginia Creeper to look at, but climbs by using tendrils as opposed to the suction cups of its relative. Its leaves are also a darker shade of green with thicker leaflets. It also colours well but later.

× *Philageria veitchii*

A rare hybrid between *Lapageria rosea* and its relative *Philesia magellanica* that looks like a fine-leafed, small-growing form of the first parent. As my plant of this cross was done in Tasmania by Ken Gillanders using a red *Philesia* and a white *Lapageria* and it hasn't yet flowered, who knows what colour my clone will be! I'm betting on red. The original clone was produced by Veitches' Nursery in England, using two red parents in 1872.

Pileostegia viburnoides

A fabulous evergreen self-clinging climber that, in time, will grow to the size of its support. Originating from eastern Asia, I imported it from Christopher Lloyd's garden Great Dixter in England. It is related to the Hydrangeas and has long rich green leaves and heads of honey scented creamy-white flowers in late summer and early autumn. A light aspect with roots in moist shade suits best.

Rubus moluccanus (Himalayan Blackberry)

A lovely climbing plant that comes from South-East Asia, including Australia, with very large, handsome evergreen leaves (not unlike *Vitis coignetiae*). Sprays of small soft pink flowers followed by big black-red edible berries that taste better that the weedy blackberry. The stems are armed with fine bristle-like thorns.

Schizandra chinense

A vigorous deciduous climber from China with large light green leaves and white to pale pink scented flowers on slender drooping stalks in late spring.

Schizophragma hydrangeoides

A strong-growing self-clinging deciduous climber from Japan with rounded serrated leaves on red petioles and lacecaps of white flowers in summer. These differ from Hydrangeas, in that they have one-bracted, sterile flowers as opposed to four.

S. h. **'Moonlight'** This lovely form differs in that its leaves are grey-green with deep green veins. I imported this form only to find it was already here. Oh well, these things do happen!

S. integrifolium Large-growing deciduous climber from China with huge white lacecap type heads in summer to 30 cm across. This plant can take some years to flower but take my word for it, it is worth the wait. The large soft leaves will keep you entertained in the meantime. If you can't wait there is a photo in my second book.

S. i. **var.** ***fauriei*** I imported this form from America (although it is native to Taiwan), and so far don't know how it differs from the species other than that its leaves seem to be a bit smaller and a darker green, but it is nice to be able to offer it for the gardener who has everything!

Stauntonia hexaphylla (Staunton vine)

A quick-growing evergreen twining climber from Korea and Japan with bold foliage divided into five leaflets. It produces creamy bell-shaped flowers with purple markings that are fragrant and spring produced, followed by large edible purplish-pink fruit if you are lucky enough to get a female plant. Will grow in sun or semi-shade.

Trachelospermum asiaticum

A useful evergreen climber to 3 or 4 metres from South-East Asia that will grow equally well in sun or shade, with deep green foliage and small creamy-white, scented flowers in summer. In cold climates the foliage often turns burgundy in winter.

***T. a.* 'Theta'** I imported this unique form from Sean Hogan of Cistus Design Nursery in Oregon. It is named after his mother. (Isn't that cute!) It differs from the species in that it has very narrow leaves with a white vein down the centre. An altogether dainty elegant climber that I'm sure will be grown by the thousands once it becomes known here, damn it! Although, it may well stay obscure as it is a clone that doesn't flower.

***T. a.* 'Variegatum'** A lovely form with leaves edged with white that will turn burgundy with a pink edge in winter if it is cold enough. The small white-scented flowers are produced in summer.

T. jasminoides This species has larger leaves than *T. asiaticum* but is otherwise very similar.

***T. j.* 'Variegatum'** White variegated form of the above that will also turn burgundy and pink if the winter is cold enough.

T. yunnanensis This rare species (that may or may not be correctly named) has thinner, brighter green leaves than the better-known species with indented veins. If grown as a ground cover, which it is admirably suited to, its leaves stay quite small and it doesn't seem to flower. If used as a climber it produces the well-known, white-scented flowers of its relatives.

Tropaeolum ciliatum

A lovely summer-growing herbaceous perennial climber to 3 metres or so. It produces masses of red stained, yellow flowers throughout summer. It runs around underground and likes its roots in the shade and its top in the sun. All of the species are South American and in the same genus as the well-known Nasturtium although most people find this hard to believe.

T. pentaphyllum This winter-growing herbaceous species has trumpet-shaped deep pink flowers tipped with green in late winter and early spring then dies down to its potato-like tubers. Will grow to 3 metres and likes to stay as dry as possible in summer.

***T. speciosum* (Flame Creeper)** This is a stunning summer-growing herbaceous species that will grow to 4 metres or more. It produces its brilliant red flowers throughout summer and these are followed by blue berries. This plant needs a cool root run and can at times be a challenge to grow, however all good gardeners like a challenge, don't they!

T. tricolorum A quaint and unusual winter-growing herbaceous climber to 3 metres with tiny bright green leaves attached to very fine wiry stems. It produces its bizarre flowers in late winter and they look like bright red old-fashioned spinning tops, to make the similarity even stronger they have a black ring and a yellow-green tip. This plant is ideal in a pot and would look good growing through any deciduous shrub or climber. Keep this one dry in summer, and it features in my second book if you need to know more about it.

T. tuberosum A hardy summer-growing herbaceous perennial climber to 3 metres from South America. It produces attractive five-lobed fleshy grey-green leaves and the flowers that are produced in summer are bright orange and yellow with a long spur at the back. The large lumpy tubers are apparently edible though I can't give you any recipes.

Vitis coignetiae (Glory Vine)

Very vigorous deciduous climber from Japan and Korea that could grow to 25 metres or more, if space allows, with huge heavily veined grape-like leaves that turn brilliant crimson, orange, yellow, burgundy and scarlet in autumn. A sunny aspect over any large unsightly structure (like your house?) will suit.

***V. vinifera* 'Ganzin Glory' (Ornamental Grape)** A very hardy vigorous deciduous climber to 15 metres or so, grown for its brilliantly coloured autumn leaves. Ideal on pergolas or over large trees. Like its edible relatives it is a sun-loving and drought-tolerant plant.

***V. vinifera* 'Purpurea' (Purple Ornamental Grape)** Moderate-growing deciduous climber that has deep burgundy foliage from spring to autumn that turns almost black before shedding. Also has edible but bitter purple grapes. This form is the best if room is limited and it features in my second book so it must be good!

Wisteria brachybotrys 'Okayama' (Silky Wisteria)

This underused species from Japan has fat short drooping clusters of sweetly scented rich pink-mauve flowers and like the following cultivars it flowers quite early in spring. I also find they flower on very young plants so that you won't have to wait too long. They are also good bonsai subjects. All Wisterias are deciduous sun-loving hardy twiners. If you want to know everything there is to know about these plants then a copy of Peter Valder's book on them would be a good investment.

***W. b.* 'Shiro Kapitan'** A lovely form like the above but with white scented flowers with a yellow keel.

***W. b.* 'Showa Beni'** The mandatory soft pink flowered form of the above.

***W. floribunda* (Japanese Wisteria)** Fast-growing Japanese deciduous vine with very long fragrant spikes of pale mauve flowers in spring.

***W. f.* 'Caroline'** This selection (which could be a hybrid) has densely packed drooping spikes of slightly scented soft mauve flowers with slightly darker keels. This flowers a bit earlier than other forms.

***W. f.* 'Domino'** This selection has flowers from a young age and drooping racemes of soft mauve flowers. Like others that flower young this would make a good bonsai or pot specimen.

***W. f.* 'Hagoromo Nishiki'** This selection has flowers much the same as the species but the leaves are liberally spotted with yellow. This may not be to all tastes but is, I think, quite entertaining!

***W. f.* 'Honbeni'** This form has the deepest pink flowers of any Wisteria. Needs to be pruned properly to encourage good flowering.

***W. f.* 'Macrobotrys'** A lovely fragrant pale mauve flowered form with the longest racemes of all that can be up to 1 metre long. Remember to make sure that if you are going to put this one on a pergola to allow for the length of the flower spikes or you will have to duck whilst it is in bloom.

***W. f.* 'Royal Purple'** This form has long racemes of rich purple flowers which are about as dark as they come.

***W. f.* 'Shiro Noda'** A lovely pure white with long racemes. In some opinions it is the best white.

***W. f.* 'Violacea Plena'** An unusual double-flowered form with long racemes of usually dark mauve blooms. The colour is the darkest of all wisterias although in some conditions, it can flower paler than expected. This form usually doesn't flower at a young stage but don't be put off as it can be truly awesome.

***W. frutescens* (American Wisteria)** A rare North American species that flowers on the current season's wood in late spring and early summer. Although not as showy as its Asian cousins its drooping spikes of rich lilac blooms are lovely and produced well after the others. This species never makes the big heavy plant that the Asian species usually do, so may be useful on smaller structures or those built by the incompetent handyman!

***W. macrostachya* (Kentucky Wisteria)** This North American species has soft mauve flowers fairly late in the season and of all the species this one and its forms tolerate damp soils better than most.

***W. m.* 'Bayou Two O'Clock'** This selection has very attractive rich mauve-blue flowers and will, according to its introducer, grow in shallow water as well as growing perfectly happily in normal garden soil. I haven't tried it in water – perhaps you could!

***W. m.* 'Clara Mack'** This rare selection is a prolific white-flowered form worthy of a place in any garden.

***W. m.* 'Pondside Blue'** This form is a bit bluer than the species with longer racemes and is also supposed to grow well in very wet soil although it doesn't need it.

***W. sinensis* (Chinese Wisteria)** This is the most commonly planted species and is native to China. It has tight clusters of rich mauve scented flowers.

***W. s.* 'Alba'** A lovely white form of the above with slightly longer racemes.

***W. s.* 'Amethyst'** This form has very rich deep mauve flowers with a very strong perfume and bronze coloured new foliage.

***W. s.* 'Jako'** This white flowered selection has a particularly good perfume and flowers for me quite young.

Bamboos

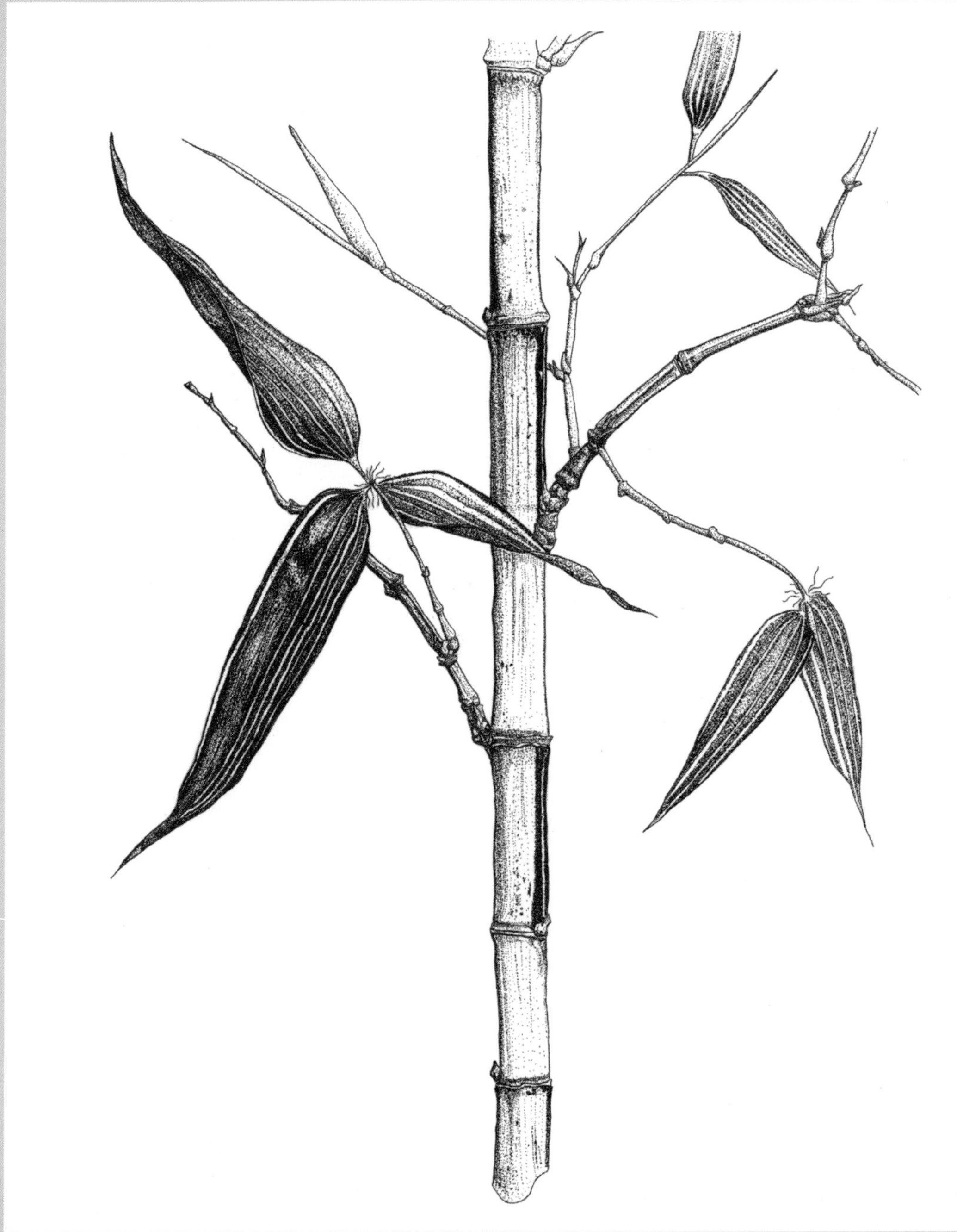

Phyllostachys bambosoides 'Castillonis'

Arundinaria dushanensis (Dushan Bamboo)
This running species from China can grow to 10 metres tall and the culms are about 2.5 cm in diameter and have quite long internodes. Its upright form makes it a good screen or grove bamboo. Tolerates temperatures down to –23°C.

A. gigantea ssp. _tecta_ (Switch Cane Bamboo) The only species of bamboo native in North America and in this form is an upright running bamboo to 2 metres or so that will be most useful if you need to whip your children or make them a fishing rod! This species is tolerant of poorly drained soils and temperatures down to –23°C.

Bambusa balcooa (Giant Timber Bamboo)
A giant clumping species from India that will grow to 25 metres, with culms to 15 cm in diameter. This species needs some room in which to grow as the culms arch outward taking up nearly as wide a space as they are tall. It can tolerate temperatures down to –5°C and possibly even lower temperatures if in a sheltered spot.

B. eutoldoides (Ox-eyed or Dai Ngan Bamboo) This clumping species from China has thick walled culms to 12 metres tall by 5 cm wide. It is often used in construction work and is useful in split weaving. Its dense habit makes it an attractive screen or specimen plant if you don't have any building aspirations at the moment! Tolerates down to –6°C.

B. multiplex 'Alphonse Karr' A large clumping bamboo up to 10 metres tall with bright yellow culms irregularly striped with green. This is a choice form that will grace the garden of anyone looking for good garden or container plant. Tolerates temperatures down to –11°C.

B. m. rivierorum (Chinese Goddess Bamboo) A dainty smallish-growing clumping bamboo to 2 metres or so with arching culms and very fine mid-green foliage. Ideal in small spaces. Tolerant of –11°C.

_B. m._ 'Silver Stripe' This tall clumping form can reach 7 metres and has some white stripes on both leaves and culms. It makes a good specimen or screening plant. Tolerant of –11°C.

_B. m._ 'Stripestem Fernleaf' This form of Hedge Bamboo has tall upright culms to 6 metres or more that are soft yellow with green stripes and an occasional bit of variegation in the foliage. Tolerant of –11°C.

B. oldhamii (Giant Timber Bamboo) This is a truly huge clumping bamboo from China to 17 metres or so with culms to 15 cm in diameter. The leaves are large and the whole will create that tropical, I-wonder-if-there-are-lost-Japanese-soldiers atmosphere! Think of all the building material you will eventually have. Tolerant of –7°C.

B. pervariabilis (Punting Pole Bamboo) This clumping species has straight culms to 10 metres tall and up to 5 cm or more in diameter. At the base of these the lowest internodes are striped with yellow. Tolerant of –7°C.

B. textilis 'Albo-stiata' This clumper from China grows to 11 metres tall with 5 cm wide culms that are yellowy-green with strong cream stripes. A good upright specimen plant. Tolerant of –11°C.

B. tuldoides (Verdant or Punting Pole Bamboo) This tightly clumping species from China grows to 14 metres tall and the dark green culms are 5 cm wide. It is a vigorous plant with an erect habit, and its tensile strength exceeds 40,000 psi if you care! Tolerant of –9°C.

B. ventricosa (Buddha's Belly Bamboo) This bizarre species of clumping bamboo will grow to 7 metres or more and has bright green culms that are often strangely swollen if the plant is kept slightly stressed. So make sure you call it stupid regularly! Tolerant of –9°C.

Chimonobambusa marmorea (Marbled Bamboo)
A running species from Japan which grows to 3 metres under ideal conditions with densely packed foliage and thin stems that are green and mottled with purple. Tolerant of –9°C.

***C. m.* 'Variegata'** This form has subtle white stripes in the leaves and, in the sun, will have bright red culms. This one wanders about just as much as the species. Tolerant of –9°C.

***C. quadrangularis* (Square Bamboo)** This running species from southern China grows to 8 metres or so and does indeed have square culms that have been used to make walking sticks, and the new shoots are considered to be quite succulent. It prefers a moist soil and a slightly shaded site, perhaps on the south side of the multi-storeyed town houses just built next door! Tolerant of –9°C.

Chusquea coronalis

A stunning and rare clumping Bamboo from Mexico with long arching culms that are solid (an unusual but ornamentally pointless feature). The foliage is tiny and clustered into balls along the stems. My partner has christened it the 'Dr Seuss Bamboo'. It likes a moist soil and a fairly sunny site and will in time produce culms to 7 metres long. Tolerant of –3°C.

C. culeou This is a rare clumping bamboo from Chile with deep green culms that can be 7 metres tall. The leaves are small and densely packed on the stems giving it a foxtail look. Of interest is the fact that unlike other bamboos the stems of plants in this genus aren't hollow and so this means that it is less likely to flag if cut for floral work. I imported this one at huge expense from Great Dixter and, if you have to ask where that is, you don't deserve one! Tolerant of –18°C.

Drepanostachyum falcatum (Himalayan Weeping Bamboo)

This shade-loving clumping species grows to about 4 metres and has arching culms with elegant fine foliage. Fairly rare and definitely desirable. Tolerant of –3°C.

D. khasianum This rare clumping species from the Himalayas will grow to 5 metres tall with upright green culms to about 1 cm in diameter. It likes a sheltered semi-shaded site to do its best. Tolerant of –6°C.

Fargesia nitida (Fountain Bamboo)

This western Chinese clumping bamboo has very attractive thin canes with a purplish colour and grows to about 4 metres tall. This species does best in light shade and like the following is a Panda food species and you never know when this information will come in handy! Tolerant of –29°C.

***F. spathacea* (Umbrella Bamboo)** This lovely clumping species from China is similar to the above but its culms are green turning yellowish with age and the leaves are smaller. Tolerant of –29°C.

× *Hibanobambusa tranquillans* 'Shiroshima'

This running Japanese Bamboo is supposed to be a hybrid and has thin culms to 2 metres tall and large heavily cream-striped leaves. One of the boldest variegated bamboos and very elegant to boot. Tolerant of –18°C.

Himalaycalamus falconeri

A lovely clumping Bamboo from Bhutan, Nepal and the northern parts of India, growing to 4 metres or so tall with arching elegant culms to 2 cm in width. The culms are bright green developing purple stains at the nodes and it does best in semi-shade and moist soil. Tolerant of –12°C.

***H. f.* 'Damarapa'** This distinctive and lovely form that has stripes of various widths of yellow up the culms that if exposed to enough light turn a rich cherry-red. Everything else is as for the species.

Indocalamus hamadae

This is a shade-loving bamboo from China with thin arching canes up to 2 metres long but the plant is rarely that tall as the weight they carry pulls them over. Its main attraction is its large impressive leaves that can be used in Chinese cooking or just left to look tropical. This is a running species but is not very fast or aggressive. Many authorities class this as but a form of the following species. Tolerant of –18°C.

I. tessellatus This form is a little shorter with slightly smaller leaves than the above.

Its smaller leaves could be used in weight-watchers Chinese food. Tolerant to –21°C.

***Otatea acuminata* ssp. *acuminata* (Smaller Mexican Weeping Bamboo)**
This rare and desirable species has thin arching dark culms to 5 metres with a whitish bloom and mass of very fine drooping leaves that exude elegance. It likes a sunny aspect and will tolerate dryish soil once established. Tolerant to –2°C.

***O. a.* spp. *aztecorum* (Mexican Weeping Bamboo)** This stunning and rare clumping species has long arching culms to 7 metres and is very like the above but obviously taller. Tolerant to –6°C.

***Phyllostachys aurea* 'Flavescens Inversa'**
This is a largish running bamboo to 7 metres tall or more with handsome green culms with light green internodal grooves alternating up the stems (sulcus). Tolerant to –18°C.

***P. a.* 'Koi'** This selection grows to about 7 metres and the culms are rich yellow with green sulcus (remember the sulcus!). The leaves will occasionally have white stripes. Tolerant to –18°C.

P. a.* forma *takemurai This form differs from the usual form in not having compressed internodes toward the bases of the culms and it grows a little taller to 10 metres. Not enough to stir the blood of the 'non-bamboo-aholic' but if it helps to sell it, it is much less common! Like its relatives it will take down to –18°C.

***P. aureosulcata* 'Aureocaulis'** This stunning running bamboo from China grows to 7 metres or so with culms that start out reddish and mature to a lovely yellow then reddish again as they age. The lower parts of the culm in all forms of this species often zigzag between the nodes, which can be quite entertaining. Tolerant all the way down to –26°C.

***P. a.* 'Spectabilis'** This form differs from the above in that its new culms are pinkish and at maturity they are yellow with green internodal grooves alternating up them making it a striking plant. Tolerant to –26°C.

***P. bambusoides* (Japanese Timber Bamboo)** A truly impressive running species to 20 metres tall or more with rich green culms to 15 cm in diameter. Older plants tend to be bare at the bottom and in this case a naked bottom is desirable as it shows off the stunning culms. Tolerant to –15°C.

***P. b.* 'Castillonis'** A striking running species with thick culms up to 9 metres tall. They are golden-yellow with a green strip alternating up either side of the culm between each node, in the sulcus again. Tolerant to –15°C.

***P. b.* 'Castillonis Inversa'** As the name would suggest this selection has green culms with alternating yellow stripes. Plant both and amaze your friends. Tolerant to –15°C.

***P. b.* 'Marliacea' (Wrinkled Bamboo)** This rare selection grows to 7 metres and is valued for its attractively wrinkled culms that create longitudinal grooves around the circumference. This form is prized in Japan for the creation of craft work such as vases and little flower pots (you could do it too!). Tolerant to –15°C.

***P. b.* 'White Crookstem'** This selection will grow to about 9 metres and has deep green culms that get a white bloom with age and are often crooked giving it a most unusual look that also makes it almost useless for garden stakes. Tolerant to –15°C.

***P. nigra* (Black Bamboo)** This well-known running species has tall elegant stems to 10 metres that turn jet black in their second year. This running species is usually quite restrained for a few years, then it's off and away. Tolerant to –18°C.

***P. n.* 'Boryana'** A very tall form to 15 metres in time with very thick green stems mottled and splashed with dark purple-brown. Also a runner that, if let go, could make a good forest in which you could get lost. This is probably the wild form of the above but is given a cultivar name as the 'Black Bamboo', was discovered first and wasn't really a wild species but a selected form. Tolerant to –18°C.

P. platyglossa A rare running species from China to 10 metres with dark green culms to 5 cm in diameter. It is used as a screen and windbreak and is well thought of for its edible shoots that start early in the season. Tolerant to –18°C.

P. rubromarginata This rarely seen running Bamboo grows to 14 metres or more but has slender culms for its size and long internodes giving it a comparatively dainty and graceful appearance. The culms are rich green later yellow-green with grey overtones. Its vertical habit makes it a good feature plant and is considered to have a future in paper pulp making. Tolerant to –21°C.

P. sulphurea A lovely running bamboo to 10 metres tall with strong vertical culms that start green and age to a soft yellow. It also has random green striping and, as it usually has little low branching, these are shown off well with little pruning needed.

P. violascens This running species grows to about 14 metres and its culms are green and striped yellow, brown, straw or even violet in a random fashion. Tolerant to –18°C.

Pleioblastus chino

A vigorous running bamboo to 4 metres with stiff upright green culms that hold their white sheaths and largish bright green foliage. If contained it makes an excellent screen or hedge. Tolerant to –15°C.

P. fortunei A small-growing running bamboo from Japan to 50 cm tall with fine stems and foliage heavily striped with white. Does need to be restrained but looks good in pots. Tolerant to –15°C.

P. lineatus An elegant slightly running bamboo to 3 metres or so with rigidly upright canes and narrow upward pointing soft green leaves. Tolerant to –15°C.

P. nagashima This vigorous running species will grow to 1.5 metres tall and has densely arranged upward-facing bright green foliage. This is a fine, tall ground cover and good for bank stabilisation. Not for the faint-hearted, but excellent in the right application. Tolerant to –18°C.

P. pygmaeus A tiny spreading bamboo from Japan to 25 cm tall with small mid-green leaves. Ideal ground cover for difficult banks and can also be pot grown. Like most of the smaller Pleioblastus species, it is a good idea to cut it to ground level at the end of winter to freshen it up. Tolerant to –15°C.

***P. simonii* (Medake)** This vigorous upright running species from Japan and China will grow to 5 metres or so and will make a good screen as well as fabulous garden stakes! The willowy leaves are born in congested clusters and the parchment-coloured sheaths persist. Tolerant to –18°C.

***P. s.* 'Variegatus'** This form differs in that it has a little fine variegation in the leaves. It isn't all that obvious so this plant should suit those that don't really like variegation! Tolerant to –18°C.

P. viridistriatus* syn. *P. auricomus A small running species to 1 metre with brilliant golden yellow foliage with some green strips. Cut it down in winter for best spring colour. This one is in my second book so look it up! Tolerant to –18°C.

P. v.* var. *chrysophyllus The same as the above except that it has no green stripes and its leaves tend to loose a bit of their gold colour later in the season. In spring it is, however, quite stunning. Tolerant to –18°C.

Pseudosasa japonica

This running species has rich green culms up to 4 metres or so with persistent parchment-coloured sheaths. Its foliage is rich green, moderately large and held slightly above horizontal. Tolerant to –21°C.

***P. j.* 'Tsutsumiana' (Spring Onion Bamboo)** This is as the above with a slight swelling at the nodes, although this isn't very obvious due to the persistent papery sheaths. Tolerant to –21°C.

Qiongzhuea tumidinoda syn. *Chimonobambusa tumidissinoda* (Chinese Walking Stick Bamboo)

A really rare and comparatively new species to Western horticulture; in fact, it only made it to England in 1987. It is a strongly running species with culms to 5 metres tall and its major claim to fame is the amazingly swollen nodes that have given it just the right look for walking-stick production in China and the reason it took a long time to find its way out from behind the 'Bamboo Curtain'. A highly entertaining species for those not scared of the Asian hoards! Tolerant to –12°C.

Sasa kurilensis

A very cold-tolerant slowing running Japanese species to 1 metre tall with congested, rich green foliage that has a slightly wavy edge. A good tall ground cover in sun or semi-shade. Obviously extremely cold-hardy as it comes from the Kuril Isles and the Russian island of Sakhalin, making it the most northerly occurring bamboo. Tolerant to –21°C.

S. palmata A very elegant but invasive bamboo to 2 metres or so tall with large rich green leaves usually clustered towards the top of its thin canes. Very worthwhile if it can be contained. Tolerant to –21°C.

S. p.* forma *nebulosa This form differs only in the fact that its slender culms have a marbled look of green and brown and the leaves are slightly heavier in texture. Just as invasive, so will need to be controlled unless you hate the neighbours! Tolerant to –21°C.

S. veitchii A charming running shade-loving small bamboo to 50 cm tall with quite large leaves. Its foliage dies around its edges during winter and this gives a pale straw-coloured variegated look. Cut down to ground level in early spring. This one features in my first book and is still one of my favourites. Tolerant to –18°C.

***Sasaelia masamuneana* 'Albostriata'**

This running species grows to 1.5 metres tall and has leaves striped with yellow that is most colourful in spring. It makes attractive, reasonably controllable drifts in sun or semi-shade. Tolerant to –18°C.

S. ramosa This is a running species from Japan with thin culms to 1 metre tall. The foliage is of a good size and narrow compared to many other bamboos of similar size. It is rich green and would make a good taller ground cover under trees or to control erosion on steep banks. Tolerant to –21°C.

***Shibataea kumasasa* (Lily Leafed Bamboo or Fortune Begetting Bamboo)**

This is a neat and lovely shade-loving bamboo to 1.5 metres tall with unique soft green stem-clasping foliage unlike any other. It is classed as a runner but is more like a walker and I have yet to have it live up to one of its common names, but live in hope. Tolerant to –21°C.

S. lancifolia This rare species makes a tidy slightly running plant to 1.5 metres. Its leaves are longer and narrower than the better-known species above. I hope that this species, which has no common name that I can find, may be fortune begetting as well. Tolerant to –21°C.

Sinobambusa rubroligula

This rare running species hails from southern China and grows to about 2 metres tall with slender but near solid and tender culms that as shoots are considered good eating! You could still use it for screening and as a windbreak if you don't want to eat it! Tolerant to –12°C.

***S. tootsik* 'Albostriata' (Chinese Temple Bamboo)** This rare running species grows to about 8 metres tall with slender culms and attractive white-striped foliage. Often planted around shrines and monasteries in China, perhaps our equivalent is the BBQ! Tolerant to –12°C.

Grasses, Reeds, Restios and Rushes

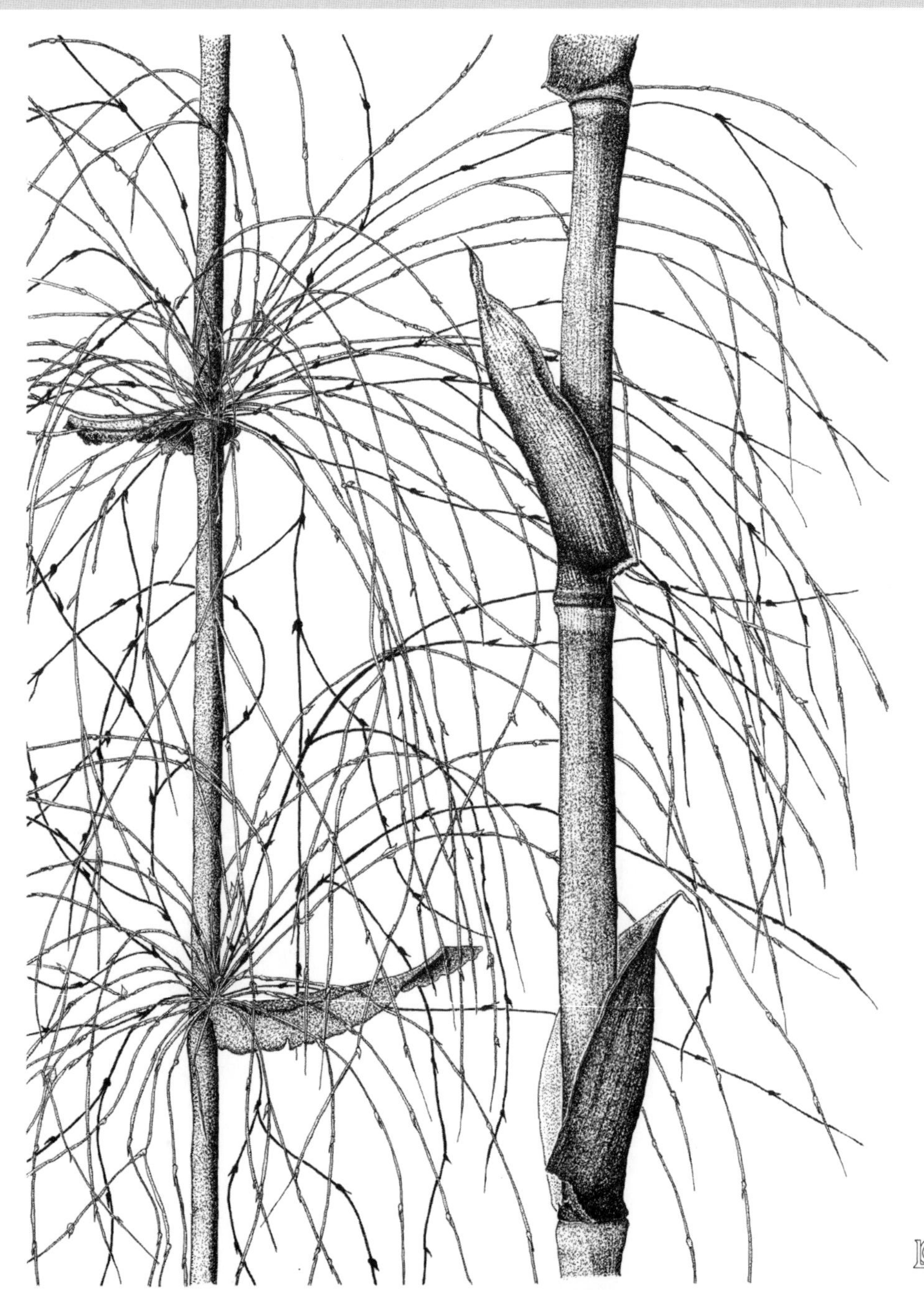

Elegia capensis

***Askidiosperma esterhuyseniae* (Thatching Rush)**
One of the large number of South African Restios that look a bit like the ancient Horse Tails. This species has rich green evergreen stems to 1 metre with golden-brown seed heads. It is lovely for picking and lasts well. These highly adaptable plants will grow well in wet soil that can then go dry for months on end and are thus very useful around lakes and dams.

***Calamagrostis × acutiflora* 'Karl Foerster'**
An elegant herbaceous grass to 1 metre or so tall with upright green foliage and very vertical buff-coloured flowers ideal to give strong accents in the herbaceous border that still pays for its space in winter when the whole plant is straw-coloured. Christopher Lloyd once suggested that it was his favourite grass. I bet he regretted that statement in due course!
***C. × a.* 'Overdam'** This form is similar to the above except that its leaves are silver variegated.

Carex comans
A densely-tufted grassy clump of soft grey-green foliage to 30 cm tall. This New Zealand native is a lovely plant for the rock garden or pool edge and does best in moist soil as do all this genus.
***C. elata* 'Bowle's Golden'** Attractive herbaceous clumping plant to 30 cm tall with bright golden foliage from spring till autumn. It likes a damp to wet site.
***C. hachijoensis* 'Evergold'** A very handsome evergreen rush to 30 cm produces golden variegated foliage and grows well in either sun or shade.
C. muskingumensis A lovely herbaceous sedge from North America to 40 cm tall with very bright green narrow foliage that turns buff coloured in autumn. It will grow in sun or shade as long as it has ample moisture.
C. secta A large clumping sedge to 2 metres tall from New Zealand. Its fine green leaves and arching seed heads create a lovely fountain effect.
***C. siderosticha* 'Variegata'** A clumping plant to 20 cm with quite broad, silver-striped foliage, which dies down in winter.

***Chasmanthium latifolium* (Northern Sea Oats)**
This herbaceous grass from North America grows to about 1 metre and has attractive bamboo like foliage that is rich green in summer turning copper in autumn. Its flower heads are drooping and consist of overlapping green scales that turn bronze in autumn and look like tiny flattened pine cones. They are good for cutting. A moist soil in sun or semi-shade will suit.

***Chondropetalum tectorum* (Thatch Rush)**
A lovely evergreen South African to 1.5 metres with rich green stems topped with brown flower heads. This is a traditional thatching material in its homeland, yet another cottage industry for someone enterprising. Also good for cut foliage. Grows best in a sunny site and likes winter wet and will tolerate some drying out in summer.

Cyperus albostiatus
A lovely evergreen dwarf relative of the Papyrus from South Africa that will grow well in moist to wet soils in sun or semi-shade. Its stems are about 30 cm tall topped with a cluster of bright green leaves arranged like the spokes of an umbrella surrounding its clusters of tiny copper flowers. Will grow well in sun or semi-shade and likes a moist to wet site.

Elegia capensis
One of the most spectacular South African Restios with stems to 2 metres tall with whorls of soft, drooping branchlets at regular intervals along the main branches supported by large brown bracts and topped with bronze flower heads. A sunny moist to damp site suits best and if you can't get a mental picture then turn to my book *More Exception Plants.*
E. grandis A smaller species with bright green stems with brown rings, up to 1 metre tall, it has fine golden-brown seed heads surrounded by handsome brown bracts.

***Hakonechloa macra* 'Aureola'**

A lovely little herbaceous grass with a neat clumping habit to 20 cm tall with rich yellow variegated bamboo-like foliage that often turns orange before dying. A moist spot in semi-shade suits best.

***Imperata cylindrica* 'Rubra' (Japanese Blood Grass)**

An upright slightly suckering grass to 30 cm with green-based bright red leaves. It looks as if it has been turned upside down and dipped in red paint. Prefers a moist soil and morning sun.

***Juncus effusus* 'Spiralis' (Corkscrew Rush)**

A moisture-loving evergreen clumping plant with cylindrical foliage that curls and twists in odd directions like a corkscrew stuck in an electrical socket! It grows to 30 cm each way and is a great novelty plant for a pool edge or decorative pot.

***Leymus arenarius* (Blue Dune Grass)**

A very hardy evergreen grass from Eurasia, to 45 cm or so tall, with intense blue-grey foliage. This is a very beautiful species but can be invasive so be warned or plant it in a pot. It likes a sunny aspect.

***Luzula nivea* (Wood Rush)**

A grassy evergreen clumping plant for moist semi-shade. It grows to 60 cm and produces fluffy white flowers in summer. Its green leaves have scattered white hairs.

***Milium effusum* 'Aureum' (Bowles Golden Grass)**

A lovely herbaceous clump forming grass to 60 cm with soft golden-green foliage topped by plumes of golden seed heads. It prefers a semi-shaded aspect and is likely to self-seed, but only lightly. It looks better in a drift anyway.

***Miscanthus* 'Giganteus'**

A truly impressive herbaceous grass to 3 metres with plumes of soft buff in late autumn. It will grow well in any sunny aspect. Often sold in Australia as *M. saccariflorus* or *M. floridulus*. This one should be cut down in winter as it doesn't die elegantly as so many others in this genus do, or strip the leaves and paint the canes as I do for a fun winter effect. You could then create the varieties 'Rubra', 'Aurea' or 'Violacea' depending on the spray paint you use!

M. sinensis An elegant clumping tall-growing grass species to 2 metres or so that is ideal for the back of borders or near water. It has bold green foliage and large plumes of bronze flowers in late summer. Even the dead foliage in winter is an attractive copper colour. It should be cut down to ground level in late winter.

***M. s.* 'Gracillimus'** A lower-growing form to 1.2 metres with finer foliage which turns lovely orange and gold colours in autumn. It also has lovely flower heads.

***M. s* 'Sarabande'** A lovely fine-foliaged form to 1.5 metres with soft pinkish flower heads produced rather late in the season

***M. s.* 'Variegatus'** A lovely form to 2 metres tall with silver-striped foliage and silvery flowers in summer.

***M. s.* 'Zebrinus' (Zebra Grass)** A form to 2 metres with bands of yellow across the leaf blade. This distinctive form has attractive flowers like the species.

M. transmorrisonensis A good clumping species from Taiwan to 1.2 metres that can be semi-evergreen although it often turns orange-red in autumn. Its flower heads are silvery.

***Oryzopsis lessoniana* (New Zealand Pheasant Grass)**

An evergreen species 60 cm tall by up to 1.5 metres across with fine arching foliage that turns orange in winter. It has arching flower heads of fluffy appearance and smoky colour in summer. A sunny moist aspect suits best and it will self-seed.

***Panicum virgatum* 'Rotstrahlbusch'**

A lovely fine-leafed herbaceous grass that grows to 1 metre with bright green leaves turning gold and copper in autumn. It has open panicles of tiny bronze flowers in summer that make a haze above the foliage like a cloud of tiny insects.

***Phalaris arundinacea* 'Feesey' (Variegated Gardeners Garters)**
A lovely semi-herbaceous grass to 1 metre tall with white-striped leaves with some pink staining especially early in the growing season. It gets upright, fluffy white flowers in autumn. It will make large clumps and may need some constraining by regular lifting and dividing.

***Rhynchospora colorata* (Star Grass)**
This moisture-loving plant related to the *Cyperus* grows to about 75 cm and has white foliar bracts in a star shape surrounding the tiny flowers at the top of the stems. This pretty plant is rarely grown here and is native to North America.

***Schoenoplectus lacustris* ssp. *tabernaemontani* 'Albescens'**
A water rush to 1.2 metres tall with cylindrical unbranched stems that are irregularly white striped along their length. Damp soil or shallow water for this plant with a name that goes on forever!
***S. l.* ssp. *t.* 'Zebrinus'** This form has stems ringed with broad bands of white and grows to the same height and likes the same conditions as the previous form.

***Setaria palmifolia* (Palm Grass)**
This evergreen plant from India and Africa is ideal for dry shade but is slightly frost tender. It grows to 1 metre tall and has very broad arching leaves up to 8 cm wide with a beautiful pleating along their length. It produces open heads of cream flowers in late summer.

***Stipa gigantea* (Giant Feather Grass)**
An evergreen species from Spain, Portugal and Morocco that, not surprisingly, likes an open sunny well-drained site. Its narrow arching grey-green leaves grow to 50 cm tall and its open feathery flower heads produced in summer can grow up to 2.4 metres.

***Thamnochortus insignis* (Thatching Rush)**
Another handsome evergreen South African plant to 2 metres tall with fine deep green stems topped with heads of bronze seed heads. Like most of its relatives, it quite likes damp spots but can cope with occasional drought conditions.

Uncinia rubra
A lovely New Zealand native clumping grass-like plant to 30 cm tall. Its fine arching leaves are a rich coppery-red intensifying to deep burgundy in winter. Ideal in a moist rock garden or pool margin. Don't weed around it with hairy arms as the seeds stick to the hairs and can only be removed if said hair goes with it!

Alpines and Perennials

Dicentra spectabilis

Acanthus caroli-alexandri

As the collection holder of this genus for the Ornamental Plants Conservation Association of Australia, I hope that you will also appreciate its charms. Who could hate such good foliage plants that are impossible to kill! This rare species has rich green, glossy, heavily cut leaves and flower spikes to 1 metre tall with the usual soft lavender flowers in late spring.

A. dioscoridis I imported this species from England in 2003. It has long, narrow, undivided grey-green leaves to 20 cm in length that look nothing like others in this genus. The flowers are rich pink and in spikes to 30 cm tall. This is supposed to be Martin Rix's selection so that those of you who know who this man is will obviously want one!

A. hirsutus A charming species from Turkey and some of the Mediterranean Islands that will grow to 30 cm tall and has bristly, heavily cut leaves and yellow flowers surrounded by bristly green bracts. I imported this one from the U.S.A. in 2005.

A. hungaricus No prizes for guessing where this species comes from. It has narrow serrated dull green leaves to 30 cm long and spikes of pale lavender flowers to 75 cm tall in summer. This is a winter dormant species.

***A. mollis* 'Hollard's Gold'** A truly spectacular perennial to 1.5 metres tall in flower. It has huge golden-green leaves and tall spikes of lavender flowers in summer. This form was discovered in New Zealand and has found its way to me via England. This one needs a fair bit of sun to colour up well but will still be a lovely light green if in shade.

***A. m.* 'Rue Ledan'** This form I imported from England (as did some other nursery people, damn it!) and it is very like the usual form but with white flowers and green bracts instead of the mauve tinge one usually expects and it is less likely to collapse in hot weather.

***A. m.*'Variegata'** A rare and beautiful form that is much less robust than the green-leafed plant. It grows to about 60 cm tall and its leaves are boldly edged and splashed with white and in fact, towards the end of the season, some leaves are pure white so no wonder it is a bit miffy! The flower stems' bracts and flowers are also white.

A. spinosus A hardy perennial from southern Europe to 1 metre tall in bloom. A stately plant with large spiny-looking dark green leaves and spikes of mauve-white flowers stained purple in summer. A wonderful accent plant.

***A. s.* Spinosissimus Group** This selection is smaller growing than the species with very finely cut leaves the tips of which have fearsome white spines. I imported this bizarre beauty from Beth Chattos' stunning nursery in England.

Aegopodium podograria 'Variegata' (Variegated Ground Elder)

The green form of this plant is a weed to be scared of, hard to eradicate and with no saving graces. The variegated form however makes spreading mats of cheery white-edged leaves from spring to autumn, which are useful in dryish shade and root-infested spots. Grows to about 12 cm tall and just be sure you want it where you are planting it as you can't change your mind.

Ajuga pyramidalis 'Metallica Crispa'

A strange but attractive clumping plant with crinkled and curled metallic deep green leaves and spikes of blue flowers on 8 cm stems in spring. Like all species in this genus, sun or part shade suits with a little moisture at the roots.

***A. reptans* 'Arctic Fox'** This selection has smaller than usual leaves that are edged in green with a large white and grey centre. The leaves are in fact much more white than green so it is a bit slower growing than most Ajugas (which may not be a bad thing). It has short spikes of blue flowers to 10 cm in spring.

***A. r.* 'Catlin's Giant'** A lovely ground cover with large bronze leaves and 15 cm spikes of rich blue flowers in spring.

Alchemilla mollis (Ladies Mantle)

A charming moisture loving perennial 25 cm tall from Europe for sun or semi-shade. It has soft grey-green hairy foliage that holds dew drops like quicksilver. It has heads of tiny green flowers in spring and summer.

Alstroemeria angustifolia

A beautiful dwarf perennial from South America to 25 cm tall. It produces exotic lily-like flowers of a rich pink with bronze markings and a bright orange patch on the lower three petals. A sunny spot in good soil suits most in this useful summer-flowering genus, and don't forget their use as cut flowers.

A. *hookeri* A dainty small species to 20 cm tall with fine grey leaves and heads of good-sized soft pink flowers finely spotted purple with soft yellow zones.

A. *presliana* ssp. *australis* This form is another bright pink and orange confection similar to *A. angustifolia* just a little taller with wider green foliage.

A. *psittacina* A species forming large clumps to 60 cm tall with clusters of attractive trumpet flowers which are deep red with white, green and brown markings. A very good cut flower and usually out for Christmas when its colours are most useful.

A. *p.* 'Royal Star' A lovely form with silver-edged leaves that make it, in my mind, drop dead gorgeous!

Anemone apennina

A clumping perennial from southern Europe with large soft blue flowers on 20 cm stems in spring.

A. *a.* var. *albiflora* Obviously a white form of the above.

A. *blanda* A low cormous plant from Europe to 7.5 cm, with deep blue flowers in early spring. This species and the following cultivars must be kept dry in summer and autumn or they are likely to rot.

A. *b.* 'Charmer' A soft mauve-pink flowered form.

A. *b.* 'White Spendour' A stunning large flowered white variety.

A. *flaccida* A lovely little wood anemone from China and Japan with leaves that are brown to start with later turning green with white markings. Its flowers are white with blue on the outside and it grows to 15 cm tall. Usually the first to appear in late winter.

A. × *fulgens* 'Alba' A stunning tuberous form to 20 cm tall with large white flowers with an almost black-stained centre. This one likes a sunny site that is dry in summer.

A. × *lipsiensis* A lovely pale primrose yellow hybrid wood anemone to 7 cm requiring the same conditions as *A. nemorosa* which is one of its parents.

A. *nemorosa* Small woodland plant with creeping underground stems and lovely soft mauve flowers in early spring on 7-cm stems. It can, like the following varieties, make extensive colonies under deciduous trees. All varieties, unless mentioned separately, grow to 7 cm and include:

A. *n.* 'Allenii' This is a robust form up to15 cm tall with quite large soft blue flowers.

A. *n.* 'Blue Bonnet' Single lavender blue.

A. *n.* 'Bracteata' Large semi-double white flowers surrounded by green bracts that also produces some single flowers.

A. *n.* 'Lychette' This selection has extra large single pure white flowers.

A. *n.* 'Pentre Pink' This variety is quite tall and robust to 15 cm with large white flowers aging to a rich deep pink.

A. *n.* 'Vestal' Late flowering pure white with a cluster of white petaloid stamens in the centre. My favourite.

A. *pavonina* This summer dormant species that comes from the summer dry hills of France and eastwards to Turkey grows to about 15 cm tall and has stunning brilliant red flowers with a white central zone and black stamens. All this happens in early spring then it dies down to its tubers and should be left dry.

A. *ranunculoides* A lovely companion for the *A. nemorosa* forms with bright yellow flowers on stems to 12 cm tall.

A. *sylvestris* (Snow Drop Windflower) A dainty looking but vigorous species to 30 cm tall from Europe with nodding white flowers from spring well into summer. If you want to know more or see a photo, look in my second book.

A. trifolia This dainty little clumping species is quite similar to the wood anemone, with tiny white flowers in spring but with less finely cut leaves, so it is more or less the Asian alternative and rarer, so we all have to have it!

Anemonella thalictroides

A charming little woodlander from eastern North America, which grows to 25 cm tall, has foliage rather like an Aquilegia and dainty little white flowers in spring. Moist soil in light shade suits best.

Angelica atropurpurea

A bold, short-lived perennial with large leaves divided into innumerable leaflets that start life as a rich coppery colour, later turning to green. It produces flat heads of green flowers in early summer on stems to 1 metre or more tall and like the rest of those I grow likes a sunny to semi-shaded aspect and the richer the soil the bigger it will get. Although all are short-lived I find that this genus usually self-seeds quite well.

A. gigas A stunning short-lived perennial, that will self-seed lightly, that hails from Korea. It has large serrated rich green leaves and flower stems that grow to about 1.5 metres topped with ball-shaped heads of black-purple flowers in summer.

A. pachycarpa (Glossy Angelica) A beautiful foliage plant with large compound leaves of rich dark green that are so glossy they look polished. It grows to about 1 metre tall and its lime green flowers erupt from green parcels of bracts in summer.

Anthriscus sylvestris 'Ravenswing' (Black Leafed Cow Parsley)

A beautiful ferny perennial with rich brown-black domes of foliage topped with sprays of white Queen Anne's lace-like flowers in spring on 1-metre stems. It holds its foliage through winter and makes a good cut flower. It will self-seed but make sure you cull any poorly coloured plants.

Aquilegia chrysantha

A tall species from New Mexico to 1 metre with very large long spurred lemon-yellow flowers and grey foliage. This is one of the species used to create the long spurred hybrids, none of which have its elegance.

A. skinneri A rare Mexican species to 1 metre with upward pointing orange spurs and bright apple-green petals. This is a late flowerer that often goes on well into summer so rarely consorts with other species. For a photo, turn to my second book.

A. shockleyi A very tall late flowering North American species to 1.2 metres with silvery foliage and dainty little orange and yellow flowers.

A. viridiflora A small growing species to 45 cm with very silver foliage and strange green-and-brown night-scented flowers.

Aralia continentalis

A truly impressive North American perennial to 2 metres or so in flower. It has huge compound leaves of a rich glossy green that get a little smaller as they go up the stout stems, till in late summer they are overtopped by showy balls of tiny white flowers in huge panicles. These are then followed by balls of equally showy black berries. Moist semi-shaded to sun aspects suit best and a rich soil will repay with extra growth.

Arisarum proboscoideum (Mouse Lily)

A quaint little shade-loving herbaceous ground cover with rich green leaves to 15 cm tall from Spain to Italy with strange brown-hooded flowers in late winter and early spring with a long curly tail that gives the appearance of mice disappearing under the foliage. A novelty loved by children of all ages.

A. vulgare (Monks Cowl) This species from the Mediterranean grows to about 25 cm tall and has white spotted spearhead-shaped leaves and brown-hooded flowers striped with white that look like a striking cobra. Ideal gift for those with a weak heart!

Armoracia rusticana 'Variegata' (Variegated Horseradish)

A large-leafed vigorous perennial to 1 metre tall which has paddle-shaped leaves that start out in spring creamy white with some green patches, sometimes they are even completely white, and they fade to straight green by summer. Its roots can be used to make the famous sauce which won't be variegated unfortunately! It isn't quite as invasive as the normal form but is equally hardy.

Arthropodium candidum purpureum

A fine grassy-leafed New Zealand native to 20 cm in flower. Its tiny white starry blooms are produced in open sprays during spring set off against its milk-chocolate-coloured leaves.

***A. cirratum* (New Zealand Rock Lily)** This is an altogether different looking plant to the above. With its broad strappy evergreen leaves to 60 cm, it makes bold clumps and is ideal in dry shade. It has large sprays of white flowers in spring and early summer. Watch out for slugs and snails as they have a taste for this one.

***A. c.* 'Joy Pink'** A newish form with pink flowers for the Barbara Cartlands amongst you!

Aruncus dioicus (Goats Beard)

An elegant tall perennial to 1.2 metres with large soft heads of tiny creamy-white flowers in late spring. For a moist aspect in semi-shade.

Asarum canadense

This is a lovely foliage plant for moist semi-shade as are all the following forms. They are collectively known as Wild Gingers, not to be confused with Ginger Lilies that are quite different. The roots of these plants smell of ginger and it doesn't do them or you any good if you keep pulling them up to check! This species is evergreen with rich green heart-shaped leaves under which hide the coppery brown starfish-like flowers. All the species that I grow rarely exceed 15 cm in height.

***A. caudatum* 'Album'** This evergreen species from western North America has large mid-green leaves that try to hide its long petalled green starfish flowers in spring.

A. caulescens This deciduous species from Japan has mid-green heart-shaped leaves and strange coppery-brown starfish flowers in spring with petals that turn straight back, so it's a starfish that has had a fright!

***A. delavayi* 'Sichuan Splendour'** I imported this Chinese species and assume this selection is from America and it has large glossy deep green evergreen foliage and strange deep brown flowers spotted with white spots and a white centre.

***A. europaeum* (Asarabacca)** As the species name suggests this is a European species and it has glossy deep green kidney-shaped evergreen foliage and small deep brown flowers hidden under the leaves.

A. lemmonii This is a deciduous North American species with mat green kidney-shaped leaves and small red-brown flowers (think more brown than red). This one seems to be more clump forming than running, and I imported this from Crug Farm in Wales in 2000.

A. magnificum This species has large slightly mottled leaves and black flowers with a white centre and it features in my second book.

***A. maximum* 'Green Panda'** This form I imported from North America and is an evergreen plant with large rich green spear-head-shaped leaves and large almost black flowers with a white throat hiding under the leafage.

A. splendens This stunning evergreen Asian species has large spearhead-shaped deep green leaves heavily marbled with white that would give even the best Cyclamen a run for its money. The flowers are deep grey-brown and would be looked down on by any self-respecting Cyclamen!

Aspidistra elatior 'Milky Way'

I imported this form some years ago from England and it varies from the norm by having smaller leaves to 30 cm tall that are liberally spotted white. Like others in this genus it will grow well in dry shade and will make a good indoor pot plant in a dark room.

Astelia banksii

A striking genus of foliage plants from New Zealand for moist sun to semi-shaded spots with rosettes of strappy leaves that in this case are 1.4 metres long and a metallic silvery-green. Like the following it could be a stunning feature plant in the ground or a pot.

A. chathamica **(Silver Spears)** This form comes from the Chatham Islands off the east coast of New Zealand and has broader leaves than the above to 1 metre tall that are really silvery. Possibly the crowning species in this lovely Genus and it features in my second book, naturally!

A. nervosa **'Westland'** This newish selection grows to about 60 cm tall with incredible metallic-bronze foliage.

Astrantia major 'Rubra'

A tufting perennial to 45 cm tall with dissected light green foliage and tiny flowers surrounded by a ruff of burgundy bracts in summer. A very long-lasting cut flower. This European likes a moist soil and morning sun.

Bergenia cordifolia 'Tubby Andrews'

Bergenias are fabulous hardy clump forming perennials usually to 35 cm or so with winter to early spring flowers and round paddle-like leaves. In this selection that I got from England we have the classic pink flowers of the species, but the foliage is liberally splashed yellow that stains with pink in cold in winter.

Beschorneria septentrionalis

This Central American evergreen perennial loves it hot and sunny. Its metre-long rich green leaves form in rosettes and from the middle, in time, an arching red flower stem with red bracts along it will erupt. From amongst the bracts at the top of the stem dangle red and green bell flowers.

B. yuccoides This evergreen rosetting plant has long strappy grey-green leaves like a Yucca that are about 1 metre long. It will produce tall arching flower spikes to 2 metres tall covered with big red-brown bracts, at the top of which come its pendant red and green flowers.

Blechnum penna-marina (Alpine Fish Bone Fern)

Tiny mat forming native fern that also comes from New Zealand with very dark green leaves to 7.5 cm tall that will spread to about 60 cm across. A good ground cover in moist sun or light shade.

Bomarea dulcis

A very rare upright perennial to 1 metre within a genus of plants that are usually climbers. This is native to the mountains of Peru and has stem-clasping, grey-green leaves and in my form deep pink waxy-drooping trumpets tipped green. A cool aspect in morning sun should suit for this Andean jewel. The rest of this genus will be found listed with the climbers.

× *Brigandia calliantha*

A rare inter-genetic hybrid that has a rosette of foliage very like an African Violet (not surprising as it is in that family) and it also grows to about the same size as said African Violet. It is a cool-climate plant, best in a pot or crevice between rocks in a shaded rock garden. It produces open sprays of buff cream trumpets veined with bronze-purple in the spring.

Caltha palustris var. *palustris* (Giant Marsh Marigold)

A wonderful evergreen creeping plant with huge glossy green waterlily-like leaves to 15 cm across and golden-yellow buttercups throughout late winter and spring. This plant is bog-loving and will even grow in shallow water. If you want to see more look in my second book.

Canna glauca (Water Canna)

A rare and beautiful Canna that grows to about 2 metres tall. It has comparatively narrow blue-grey foliage and soft butter-yellow flowers in summer. A sunny moist site or in a pot in a pond will work. I originally grew this from seed I got at Great Dixter garden and if you have to ask where that is you don't deserve one! If any Canna can be said to be dainty this has to be it.

C. musifolia A striking giant to 3 metres that has huge green leaves on blackish stems topped with comparatively small red flowers in autumn. It is for its foliage and stems that you would mainly grow it though compared with many plants its flowers are pretty showy just not up to usual Canna size.

***C.* 'Stuttgart'** An amazing variety to 2.5 metres tall with huge paddle-shaped leaves irregularly white slashed and sometimes more white than green. The flowers are smallish of a soft apricot and are pretty but not the main feature. Good light without direct sun for this one as the white will burn in direct sun.

Cardamine diphylla (Crinkle Root)

A dainty little creeping herbaceous perennial to 15 cm tall from North America with white-veined leaves, consisting of three leaflets, and clusters of small white flowers in spring. All the species I have grown seem to appreciate a moist, compost enriched soil in light shade.

***C. pentaphyllos* 'Alba'** This charming little European woodlander came my way via Beth Chatto's nursery in England. It grows to 15 cm tall and has bright green compound leaves slightly overtopped in spring with spikes of pure white flowers.

C. trifolia A charming clump-forming evergreen species from central and southern Europe to 15 cm tall with three dark green leaflets per leaf and clusters of tiny white flowers in spring.

Chamaepericlymenum canadensis syn. *Cornus canadensis* (Creeping Dogwood)

A mat-forming creeping Dogwood from North America to 15 cm tall. In summer it has pure white flowers often followed by red fruit. The stems are renewed from the creeping underground stems each year and the foliage often goes dark burgundy in winter.

Caulophyllum thalictroides (Blue Cohosh)

A strange and subtly attractive North American perennial to 60 cm tall with bluish stems and foliage that reminds one of Thalictrum, funnily enough. It produces small sprays of soft yellow flowers in spring followed by deep blue berries. Moist cool conditions suit best.

Chloranthus fortunei

This rare woodlander from Asia came my way via Crug Farm nursery in Wales. It grows clusters of 30 cm purplish stems with four deep green leaves with a purple reverse at the top. In spring, when the foliage matures from its centre, stands a spike of tiny white flowers. This plant isn't showy, but boy is it classy! Light shade and moist leafy soil or pot culture is what is needed.

Clematis heracleifolia

A slightly woody-based perennial to 1 metre with large handsome leaves and clusters of small deep blue-flared lanterns in summer. It comes from China and likes a moist soil in sun with a well-mulched soil as do most in this family.

C. integrifolia A lovely trailing species ideal for flopping over small shrubs with quite large blue-flared bells in summer. The stems will grow to about 60 cm long.

C. recta Herbaceous perennial from eastern Europe to 2 metres tall with masses of small white flowers in summer. It requires staking or allow it to grow through a shrub otherwise it is inclined to flop over.

***C. r.* 'Purpurea'** A lovely form of the above that has purple new growth that fades to green as the stems grow, leaving only a few dark leaves at the top.

C. stans This species grows to about 1.5 metres and produces clusters of small blue-white flared trumpets in summer. It is native to Japan.

Convallaria majalis (Lily-of-the-Valley)

The much-loved shade-loving perennial with usually two leaves per crown on either side of its spike of sweetly-scented white bells produced in late spring. A humus-rich moist soil is needed and some people seem to think a bit of luck as well!

C. m.* var. *rosea This form has slightly narrower leaves and soft pale pink flowers.

***C. m.* 'Variegata'** A rare form of this well-loved woodland perennial with the usual white highly-scented flowers in late spring. This form however has leaves with regular yellow stripes which will entertain well after the flowers are gone and brighten up a shady corner. It often goes green the first year but goes back to variegated after that, so don't lift and divide it too often.

Crambe cordifolia

A giant perennial from the Caucasus with huge rounded leaves loved by cabbage white butterflies (so be warned). Once it is well-established (which can take some time) it will produce 2 metre clouds of tiny frothy white flowers. A rich slightly alkaline soil suits best.

***C. maritima* (Seakale)** This charming European seaside plant has grey-green fleshy leaves with a fluted and wavy edge. It is worth growing for its foliage alone (which can be eaten if blanched), however it also has lovely white scented flowers on 60 cm stems in summer. For more information check out my second book.

Cryptotaenia japonica forma *atropurpurea*

This parsley relative from Japan, where it is also used as a garnish, has lovely coppery-brown leaves topped by open sprays of tiny pinkish flowers in summer. Scare your relatives and serve this in a salad or just enjoy it as a pretty 30 cm border plant. It will slightly self-seed if happy.

Dahlia 'Bishop of Llandaff'

A lovely old variety with dark plum-coloured leaves and brilliant scarlet single flowers with a yellow centre. Grows to about 1.5 metres and will grow well in any sunny well-drained aspect.

D. excelsa Another tree Dahlia differing from *D. imperialis* the more common species in its smaller leaves and more open daisy-shaped flowers of a richer magenta colour. It is easily grown and flowers earlier in autumn making it a good choice in frosty climates. Will reach up to 5 metres tall and features in my second book.

***D.* 'Stephen Ryan'** Yes, there is a plant named after me and I didn't do it, as I'm not that vain! This stunning form was named after me and obviously selected especially with me in mind. It is self-supporting, single, virginal white and slightly scented. What more can one say!

Dicentra 'Bacchanal'

A charming semi-shade loving colony-building perennial to 30 cm tall with soft grey-green ferny foliage and clusters of drooping magenta locket-shaped flowers from spring well into summer. All of these charming plants like semi-shade and some moisture to perform well.

D. cucullaria A tiny little spring-flowering perennial to 7.5 cm tall from North America, with fine ferny foliage and tiny white flowers with a yellow centre. This species has tubers that look like lemon pips and the whole thing dies down almost as soon as it flowers. Like most of the genus, a moist leafy soil in semi-shade suits best and as this one spends a lot of time underground just remember where you put it!

D. formosa A fast-growing herbaceous perennial from North America for moist sun or shade, to 30 cm tall. The ferny grey-green foliage is topped in spring and early summer with spikes of drooping pale pink lockets.

***D. f.* 'Alba'** White flowered form of the above with light green leaves.

***D.* 'Langtrees'** This hybrid form has silvery-ferny leaves and white lockets blushed faintest pink on 30 cm stems for months from midspring.

***D. spectabilis* (Bleeding Heart)** A beautiful spring-flowering perennial to 1 metre with soft green foliage and heart-shaped deep pink flowers with a small white tear-drop hanging from it. This native from Japan and Siberia likes morning sun and a rich vegetable garden-type soil.

***D. s.* 'Alba'** The rare pure white form of the above.

***D. s.* 'Gold Heart'** This comparatively recent introduction has the classic deep pink flowers but in this form they are set off against bright yellow leaves which stand out well in the semi-shaded aspects the species likes.

Dietes bicolor

A useful evergreen rush-like plant to 1.5 metres from South Africa. It is happy in sun or shade, moist or dry aspects. The soft lemon-yellow Iris-like flowers are blotched with brown and produced above the leaves throughout the warmer months.

D. iridioides Another evergreen South African species this time growing to about 60 cm. It is as hardy as the above but has flowers that are white with mauve and yellow markings.

D. robinsoniana A truly impressive large clumping plant, to 2 metres or more, from Lord Howe Island with broad bright green leaves and large flat Iris-like flowers in late spring and summer. These are white with soft yellow markings in the centre. Sun or semi-shade for this almost indestructible plant.

Diplarrena latifolia

Hardy Iris-like evergreen plant native to Australia. The attractive foliage is topped with white Iris-like flowers with inner segments marked deep mauve and yellow. It is slightly scented and grows to 60 cm.

Disporopsis arisanensis

This evergreen Asian perennial is closely related to Solomon's Seal and looks rather like one. The arching stems grow to 30 cm tall and under these it has small green, white and black bells. The leaves are a shiny mid-green. I imported this and the following from Heronswood Nursery in North America and I'm sure they will add greatly to the small range of evergreen woodland plants available here.

***D. pernyi* 'Bill Baker'** This plant is similar to the above but has longer deep glossy-green leaflets on arching stems to 45 cm tall under which hang the green and white bells.

Disporum cantoniensis

This Asian evergreen woodlander is like a Solomon's Seal on steroids with tall arching and branched stems supporting nodding pale yellow flowers in spring followed by small black berries. The plant can get to 2 metres tall and likes moist semi-shade as does its relatives.

***D. c.* 'Aureovariegata'** I doubt that this name is legitimate but it is all I have at this stage for a subtly different form imported from America. It would seem to grow to about 1 metre and has fairly rounded leaves that are bright green in the centre with a deeper green irregular edge. It shouldn't scare even the most hardened hater of multi-coloured leaves!

***D. c.* 'Green Giant'** This selection I purchased in North America and seems quite like the species but is supposed to grow to 3 metres tall (talk about steroid abuse!). This is another selection made by Dan Hinkley as is the following.

***D. c.* 'Night Heron'** This selection will grow to about 1.5 metres, and the new growth in spring is a lovely dark black-brown that goes green as it matures.

***D. sessile* 'Variegatum'** A lovely shade-loving perennial to 50 cm tall which looks something like a small Solomon's Seal. It has beautiful white variegated leaves, and green and white pendant bell flowers in spring. It will make lovely open drifts that can in time cover quite some ground that I for one never begrudge it.

D. uniflorum* syn. *D. flavens This herbaceous species from Korea and China grows to about 60 cm and has bright green foliage and nodding yellow bells that open in late spring. An elegant plant in a truly elegant genus.

Dryas octopetala (Mountain Avens)

A charming evergreen carpeting plant with bronze-coloured leaves in winter. It produces creamy white anemone-like flowers on 10 cm stems followed in summer by feathery, silver seed heads. It is native to northern alpine regions and the Arctic and likes a moist cool soil but reasonably sunny site.

Dymondia margaretae

An evergreen carpet plant from southern Africa with narrow grey-green leaves that curl slightly at the edge to reveal the white reverse. It has stemless yellow daisy flowers amongst the foliage off and on throughout the year. Ideal in sunny rock gardens or between pavers.

Eomecon chionanthum (Dawn Poppy)

A beautiful Chinese woodland perennial of suckering habit to 30 cm tall that has large grey-green kidney-shaped leaves and pure white Poppy-like flowers in spring. This lovely thug needs moist humus-rich soil and is in my second book.

Epimedium acuminatum

I recently imported this Chinese species from Aberconways Nursery in Wales and it has large heart-shaped leaflets with serrated edges that start out bronze and turn green. In spring it produces lovely dainty white flowers with long burgundy-spurred petals which give a charming two-tone effect. This genus all like semi-shade and leafy soil and are generally fairly drought tolerant once settled. Most species and forms that I grow rarely exceed 30 cm tall and many are shorter.

E. alpinum This ground cover plant comes from south-eastern Europe. Its heart-shaped leaves become burgundy in winter and should be cut down in late winter (as all the species should be) to expose the flowers, which in this case are cherry-red with a creamy yellow centre.

E. × cantabrigiense A hybrid found at St John's College Cambridge after the Second World War that has rounded bronze-tinged leaflets and small spurless claret flowers with a lemon centre.

E. diphyllum A dainty little Japanese species to 20 cm with usually two leaflets per. leaf that start out copper and turn green later. Its tiny white flowers are spurless.

E. dolichostemon Another lovely Chinese species I imported and this one has long serrated leaflets with mottled liver spotted foliage in spring (which is a lot nicer than it sounds!) and dainty little white flowers with rose-red petals.

E. ecalcaratum This species comes from China and has dainty, slightly serrated bronze leaves turning bright green, and neat little bright yellow cup-shaped flowers in spring.

E. epsteinii This rare species from China that was discovered in 1994 came back with me from Aberconways Nursery in Wales some time ago. It has lovely ruby new leaves and dainty white and burgundy spurred flowers.

***E. franchetii* 'Brimstone Butterfly'** Another I imported and in this case it has large serrated leaflets starting out soft copper, that show off the long spurred soft lemon and coppery flowers with long curved spurs to perfection.

***E. grandiflorum* 'Crimson Beauty'** A small growing selection with rounded leaflets and tiny dusty crimson spurred flowers in early spring.

***E. g.* 'Lilafee'** This tiny selection has lovely spurred purple petals with slightly darker sepals.

***E. g.* 'White Beauty'** A white flowered form of the above.

***E. g.* 'Shikinomai'** I imported this form from Wales and it seems to be a slightly smaller white variant than the above but otherwise similar.

E. leptorrhizum Another one I imported that originated in China with heavily serrated and veined leaflets that start out bronze spotted then turn a rich green. The long spurred flowers are a soft rose-pink. This species will make good-sized clumps.

E. membranaceum Another Chinese species that I imported with quite large, slightly serrated leaflets and soft yellow flowers with very long curved spurs.

E. ogisui Yet another I bought in – this time a newly discovered Chinese species with rounded leaflets and pure white flowers in spring.

***E.* 'Okuda's White'** A lovely short spurred white flowered plant that I got locally but can't find a reference to, even in the monograph on the genus. Any help would be appreciated!

E. pauciflorum A low-growing Chinese species with small rounded, heavily serrated bright green leaves and small white spurred flowers.

***E. × perralchicum* 'Frohnleiten'** This vigorous hybrid has large leaflets, bronze to start, with soft yellow spurless flowers in spring. This one will make a solid weed impervious clump and, like the following, good to plant in quantity to cover some ground.

E. pinnatum A good ground cover plant from the Caspian region for sun or shade with large leathery leaves. The foliage will often turn burgundy colours if exposed to frost. It produces masses of yellow spurless flowers with a tiny dark brown centre in early spring.

E. pubescens A lovely one I imported with leaflets that are liver-spotted burgundy when young setting off its sprays of tiny white spurless flowers in spring.

E. × rubrum A lovely hybrid of *E. alpinum* with larger spurless cerise flowers with a cream centre and beautifully bronze-marked leaves.

E. sempervirens A charming evergreen species from Japan with, in my form, long spurred white flowers.

***E. stellulatum* 'Wudang Star'** This selection has large leaves starting bronze and turning bright green. The flowers are open spurless stars of purest white on tall open sprays.

E. trifoliolatobinatum This impossible-to-say species from Japan has small roundish deciduous leaves and sprays of tiny white, straight spurred flowers in spring. (Amaze your friends and learn to say its name!)

***E. × versicolor* 'Neosulphureum'** This vigorous hybrid has large leaflets that start out bronze and soft lemon-yellow spurless flowers in obvious sprays. Another good 'quickish' filler.

E. × warleyense This form makes substantial suckering clumps and has large green heart-shaped leaflets and spikes of coppery-orange flowers in early spring. Another strong clumper and featured in my second book.

***E. × youngianum* 'Baby Doll Pink'** Naff name for a sweet little soft pink selection that I believe was made in America. Where else!

***E. × y.* 'Niveum'** A charming dwarf perennial for sun or shade with masses of tiny white flowers in spring. The foliage is heart-shaped, starting bronze and later soft green.

Eryngium pandanifolium 'Purple Form'

This imposing evergreen perennial from South America has long spine-edged, grey-green leaves to 2 metres long and 3 metre tall open spikes of tiny purple brown flowers in summer. It features in my second book and originally came to me from Great Dixter in England and was selected at the Chelsea Physic Garden, so it is obviously a superior form!

Euphorbia amygdaloides 'Purpurea'

A hardy perennial to 30 cm tall, with dark purple foliage during winter followed by heads of lime-green bracted flowers in spring.

E. a.* var. *robbiae A robust suckering plant to 45 cm from Asia Minor, with upright stems of dark green leaves and lime-green bracted flower heads in spring. Ideal tall ground cover for sun or shade, and so unlike the above that I hesitate to put it in as a form, but the pundits say it is!

E. characias A large evergreen shrubby Euphorbia to 1.5 metres with soft grey-green leaves and very large heads of lime-green bracted flowers in spring.

***E. c.* 'Portuguese Velvet'** This form has smaller heads of grey-green bracts with tiny almost black flowers. Any selected, named form should be kept away from lowly unnamed forms as they will consort and produce mixed forms.

***E. c.* ssp. *wulfenii* 'Jimmy Platt'** This selection has huge heads of lime-green bracts with tiny flowers in the same colour being well set off by the grey-green foliage.

E. cyparissias A dainty little suckering thug to 30 cm tall with fine needle-like grey-green foliage and small heads of lime-yellow flowers. Ideal to fill difficult spaces like the driveway!

***E. c.* 'Fens Ruby'** I imported this stunning form from Beth Chatto after seeing it in her world-renowned gravel garden. It is different from the above because its leaves start out a lovely burgundy that is particularly attractive with its limy flowers. Just as vigorous as the species!

***E. dulcis* 'Chameleon'** A lovely clumping perennial to 30 cm tall with deep bronze-purple foliage that turns rich pink before its dies down. Will lightly self-seed. This is in my second book.

***E. griffithii* 'Fire Glow'** A completely herbaceous plant with a suckering habit to about 45 cm tall. The pale green foliage is topped with bright orange flowers in late spring and early summer. Unlike many species this one does better with moist soil.

E. myrsinites An evergreen grey-leafed trailing plant with large heads of green-bracted flowers in spring. Ideal for a sunny well-drained rock garden, and a native of southern Europe.

E. rigida This species is like a giant form of *E. myrsinites* with very bold almost succulent-like grey foliage along the stems which are topped with heads of green flowers in spring. It grows to about 30 cm tall.

E. sikkimensis A herbaceous species to 1.2 metres with ruby-red new growth in winter fading to green later although keeping a burgundy central vein. The heads of lime green bracts are produced in summer on the tops of the stems. This one likes moist soil to do its best.

Fascicularia bicolor

A fabulous cold-hardy pineapple relative with large rosettes of grey-green toothed leaves to 60 cm long and, funnily enough, very like those of its more famous relative. When it flowers these are nestled down in the centre of the rosettes and are blue. However the showiest bit is the base of the leaves that turn brilliant red at flowering time. This indestructible beast comes from Chile.

Ferula communis (Giant Fennel)

A truly impressive herbaceous perennial from the Mediterranean with huge fluffy fennel-like leaves of a rich deep green up to 1 metre long that start growing in winter when other perennials are dormant. It sends up towering trunk-like flower stems in late spring to 4 metres tall and has clusters of tiny bright yellow flowers. It likes a moist soil in a sunny aspect. This fabulous thing features in my second book.

F. c.* ssp. *glauca This form differs from the above in having more grey-green foliage. Both will lightly self-seed.

F. tingitana This species has the same impressive bulk as those above but its shiny foliage is less finely cut though no less attractive.

Filipendula camtschatica (Giant Meadowsweet)

A statuesque herbaceous plant to 3 metres from Japan and Manchuria. It has large palmate leaves and fluffy masses of white flowers at the tip of the stems in late summer. It does best in damp to wet soil in a sunny aspect but is hardy enough for most areas.

Francoa racemosa (Bridal Veil)

A rosetting perennial with handsome evergreen foliage and spikes of tiny white-pink veined flowers in summer. Native of South America, it grows to 1 metre tall in bloom.

Furcraea bedinghausii

An amazing plant from Central America that looks like a grey-green giant-leafed Yucca with a short trunk to 1.5 metres tall. After quite some years it will send up a 7-metre flower spike that will have scented white bell flowers intermingled with small plantlets. At this time it will die and the plantlets will start the whole thing over again. It is drought tolerant and will grow in full sun or part shade.

Galax urceolata

An extremely rare North American evergreen ground cover with large round leaves to 12 cm tall that turn red in cold weather and spikes of tiny white flowers in spring. It likes a cool moist aspect and even then may not like you!

Gentiana acaulis (Swiss Gentian)

A spring flowering tufted alpine plant, to 7.5 cm in flower, with very large deep blue trumpet flowers. Probably only able to be grown in cool hill station gardens.

G. paradoxa A very rare summer flowering Gentian from Russia, which grows to about 30 cm with large royal-blue trumpets at the tips of the herbaceous stems. It has narrow almost pine-needle-like foliage.

***G. sino-ornata* (Chinese Ornate Gentian)** A lovely autumn flowering trailing species with large royal-blue flowers. This variety will die back to its crowns after blooming.

Gunnera cordata

An attractive evergreen carpet plant to 7.5 cm from Tasmania with deep green leaves and short spikes of red berries in autumn as long as you have a female form, which is, of course, just what I will sell you. It requires a damp to wet aspect in sun or semi-shade or a pot in a permanent saucer of water.

***G. manicata* (Giant Chilean Rhubarb)** A massive rhubarb-like plant from South America with leaves that can be over 2 metres across or more if you grow it well, as you should! Ideal waterside plant as it likes wet feet and rich soil. Not for the timid gardener.

G. perpense A rare herbaceous species from southern Africa with a suckering habit, that produces large kidney-shaped leaves to 30 cm across on 60 cm stems and tall open sprays of tiny coppery-red flowers. A lovely waterside foliage plant.

G. prorepens A dwarf, creeping evergreen ground cover plant from New Zealand with lovely bronze foliage and spikes of red berries in autumn. It grows well in constantly damp to boggy soil. This one featured in my second book.

G. tinctoria This species is often sold (by those that know no better) as *G. manicata* but, if one observes closely, it does have slightly smaller leaves that are more corrugated with pointier tips to the leaves. The differences are small but do matter to the pedants amongst us.

Haberlea rhodopensis

A very rare alpine in the African Violet family from Bulgaria and northern Greece. It makes a small rosette of evergreen leaves and produces clusters of lavender flowers in spring and early summer. It is happiest in a cool moist rock garden or a pot. It grows to 15 cm tall by about 25 cm across.

Hacquetia epipactis

A charming little woodland plant in the Carrot family, to 7 cm tall, with leaves that are rather like those of a Strawberry, and tiny flowers in clusters surrounded by quite large green petal-like bracts in spring.

***Hedychium coccineum* (Red Ginger Lily)**

A stunning sun-loving perennial to 3 metres with large bright green leaves topped by spikes of brilliant orange scentless flowers in late summer. A fertile moist soil suits best, but it is hard to kill! It's in my second book.

H. greenei A beautiful ornamental ginger to 1.5 metres tall with bronze-backed green leaves and spikes of soft orange flowers in autumn. Native to western Bhutan.

***Helianthus salicifolius* (Willow Leafed Sunflower)**

A striking perennial to 3 metres from America with very narrow green leaves all the way up the stems that for me are the main game. Its small yellow daisies with black middles are charming in autumn. A sunny moist aspect suits best.

Helichrysum argyrophyllum

An everlasting daisy from South Africa that is an ideal ground cover for the sunny rock garden. Its intense silver foliage is topped by bright yellow flowers in autumn and winter. It will quite quickly cover an area of at least 1 metre across.

Helleborus argutifolius* syn. *H. corsicus

Winter-flowering evergreen perennial with spiny-looking silver foliage and lime-green flowers on 60-cm stems during the winter. Ideal for shady spots but one species at least that will take full sun.

***H. a.* 'Pacific Frost'** A strangely attractive selection with leaves that are heavily marbled with white and green mottled flowers. This form comes fairly true from seed as long as you don't have it planted with the green-leafed forms of this species.

H. × ericsmithii This stunning rare hybrid includes *H. niger*, *H. lividus* and *H. argutifolius* and has lovely grey foliage and huge white flowers stained with rich coppery red. Is even better than it sounds!

H. foetidus A species with handsome dark green foliage and small nodding lime-green bells edged burgundy in winter. The form

I grow is an extra good compact form to 60 cm tall that a friend has rudely called 'Stephen's Squat'.

***H. f.* 'Gold Bullion'** This fairly new selection has stunning golden leaves and yellow-green flowers and comes fairly true from seed. Give this one a bit of sun to keep its leaves well coloured.

***H. f.* 'Red Silver'** A newish selection with fine deep grey-green serrated leaves and red-edged green bells in winter. Like all the other selections of this species, keep it away from other forms of the same species to keep it pure.

***H. f.* 'Wester Flisk'** This stunning form grows to about 1 metre and has nodding green flowers edged with burgundy-red stems and petioles and deep grey-green foliage.

H. lividus A lovely rare species from Majorca related to *H. argutifolius* but smaller. It has leaves stained purple-pink and creamy-green flowers stained purple-pink. Rarely exceeds 30 cm tall.

***H. niger* (Christmas Rose)** I stock large-flowered forms that start out white in winter and turn soft pink after pollination. (Don't we all!) Native to northern Italy.

H. × sternii A lovely hybrid between *H. argutifolius* and *H. lividus* that is usually between the two, with foliage more like the first and flowers with bronze on the outside.

Heloniopsis orientalis

A very rare clumping perennial, to 25 cm tall with narrow light green leaves, that in spring supports stems with nodding dusty pink bells. A leafy soil and a cool aspect are both a must.

Hepatica nobilis

A charming little evergreen clumping woodland plant to 10 cm tall, with three lobed leaves and soft blue anenome-like flowers in spring. This European native likes it cool and shady.

Impatiens omeiana

A lovely herbaceous perennial to 20 cm from China that in moist semi-shade will make good colonies. It has red stems and undersides of the leaves, the top of which are dark green with a white midrib. Throughout the summer it will produce soft apricot spurred flowers to entertain for months.

Iris foetidissima

An evergreen clumping plant to 60 cm that grows well in dry shade. It produces cream and fawn flowers in late spring and these are followed in winter by large green pods that split to expose masses of orange seeds which are, in fact, the main reason for growing this species.

***I. f.* 'Variegata'** This form has stunning white striped leaves that stand out well in shade but it doesn't however flower very often.

***I. pseudoacorus* 'Variegata'** A tall water-edge Iris to 1.5 metres with yellow spring flowers and boldly yellow-striped foliage. The leaf colour fades as the summer comes on so that in time they are green. Remove the seed heads as any self-sown ones will be green.

Jaborosa integrifolia

A ground covering perennial to 15 cm tall with large bright green leaves standing straight up, amongst which it produces large white night-scented trumpets at ground level. It hails from northern Argentina, Brazil and Uruguay and likes a sunny well-drained site.

Jeffersonia diphylla (Rheumatism Root)

A charming North American woodland perennial to 30 cm tall with small white flowers in spring and attractive leaves that are like two leaves next to each other. Slow-growing and with a short flowering period, but worth every effort.

Jovibarba allionii (Jove's Beard)

A genus of alpine succulents from the mountains of Europe. In this species one gets small rosettes of bright green with lots of little bronze pups that drop off and take root elsewhere (these are called rollers for obvious reasons).

J. allionii × hirta This is similar to the above with slightly larger bright green rosettes tipped with bronze.

J. arenaria I imported this one which has small green rosettes with red tipped leaves and lots of cute little red and green rollers. This one comes from the mountains of Austria and Italy.

***J. heuffelii* 'Be Mine'** I imported this form from the breeder in England. The *J. heuffelii* forms have large rosettes that split into new plants that actually have to be cut apart to make more plants. This one is darkest burgundy in winter with a bit of green in summer.

***J. h.* 'Bulgarium'** This form has large green rosettes with black tips to the foliage

***J. h.* 'Chocolato'** This form has extra large rosettes that are purple with a green centre in summer and deep brown in winter.

***J. h.* 'Greenland'** Another of my imports, this time with medium rosettes of green with some outer leaves flushed with orange.

***J. h.* 'Inferno'** This form has large rosettes that are a deep red-brown most of the time.

***J. h.* 'Mystique'** This new import has medium rosettes that are rich brownish-red with a green centre that darkens in winter.

***J. h.* 'Nanette'** I bought this one in as well and it has medium to large rosettes that are grey-green in summer turning greyish-purple in winter.

***J. h.* 'Purple Haze'** This selection has large brown-purple rosettes in winter turning grey-green flushed purple in summer.

J. hirta* ssp. *borealis This species has small burgundy-stained rollers and grey-green smallish rosettes with tips stained burgundy.

***J. hirta* 'Preissiana'** This form is similar to the above with small grey-green rosettes and deeper burgundy rollers.

J. sobolifera I imported this form from America but it comes from Bohemia and Poland. It is another species with small rosettes that produce rollers and in this case they are grey-green with slightly brown tips in winter.

Kirengeshoma palmata

A lovely if a somewhat fussy woodland perennial from Japan and Korea, to about 1 metre, with large, bright green maple-like leaves on dark stems topped in late summer with thick, petalled soft yellow flowers that look like drooping shuttlecocks. A shaded moist and sheltered site with rich organic soil is a must.

Kniphofia caulescens

A lovely South African Red Hot Poker to 1 metre tall in bloom. It has broad silvery-green leaves and its flowers, produced in autumn, are dusty orange in bud and soft yellow open. A sunny spot with good drainage is about all plants in this genus seem to need.

K. northii A truly spectacular species with very wide rich green leaves arranged like a giant pineapple top, to 1 metre. Its flowers are produced in summer on 1.5-metre stems and are in clusters nearly as wide as they are tall. In bud they are soft orange opening to a green-white.

Lamium orvala

A lovely clumping woodland perennial from Europe to 30 cm tall with rich green nettle-like leaves with whorls of dusky purple flowers in spring. Semi-shade to moist morning sun aspects should be just the ticket.

Leptinella pyrethrifolia ssp. *linearifolia*

A dainty little ground hugging plant from New Zealand that has fine ferny intensely silvered leaves over which hover its yellow button flowers on 10-cm stems in summer.

Libertia formosa

A handsome rich green reed-like foliage plant from Chile to 45 cm tall. It produces spikes of lovely white three-petalled flowers in spring.

L. ixioides A hardy evergreen rush-like New Zealand native that makes tight clumps of slightly bronze foliage to 30 cm tall. It produces stems of three-petalled white flowers followed by orange seed pods.

L. perigrinans A New Zealand alpine plant with a suckering habit making drifts to 30 cm tall with leaves striped bright orange. It produces small white flowers in spring followed by orange seed pods.

L. sessiliflora An attractive South American species to 60 cm with rich, dark evergreen reed-like foliage and spikes of small, pale, dusty, blue three-petalled flowers in spring.

Lithodora diffusa* syn. *Lithospermum diffusum

An attractive southern European ground cover with deep blue flowers mainly in spring for a moist aspect in morning sun. Ideal hanging over a low wall.

Lobelia aberdarica

A giant from Mt Kenya with 1-metre rosettes of bright green leaves. The plant in total may cover 3 metres or more across. It will eventually produce towering 3 metre spikes with green bracts and white flowers stained blue. A sunny, moist to damp aspect with good leafy soil is best.

L. tupa An impressive herbaceous perennial to about 2 metres tall, from Chile. It has large soft grey-green leaves topped with spikes of red tubular flowers in late summer and autumn. It's in the second book.

Luzuriaga radicans

This evergreen perennial comes from South America and creeps around in semi-shaded areas looking a bit like a dwarf unruly Solomon's Seal. It can be 20 cm or so tall and has small white starry flowers. A fernery or cool border will suit and it will grow well in a chunk of Tree Fern as well.

***Lysichiton americanus* (Skunk Cabbage)**

A truly amazing semi-shade loving bog plant that has huge yellow Arum-like flowers that erupt out of the mud in early spring followed by huge green paddle-shaped leaves to 2 metres long that will keep you entertained until autumn. If you don't have a bog then make one for this plant. Also look it up in book number two.

L. camtschatcensis This rare Asian form has slightly smaller pure white Arum-like flowers followed by half-sized, grey-green leaves, not quite as impressive as the above, except to those that are aware of its rarity!

***Macleaya microcarpa* (Plume Poppy)**

A spectacular, tall perennial from China, to about 3 metres tall. It has large sycamore-like, grey-green leaves topped with fluffy plumes of bronze flowers. Ideal background plant for a sunny border.

***M. m.* 'Spetchley Ruby'** This form has richer, redder fluffy flowers than the species.

***Maianthemum bifolium* (False Lily-of-the-Valley)**

A charming little woodland perennial to 10 cm native from England to Japan. It makes mats rather in the same way as Lily-of-the-Valley and has two heart-shaped leaves per. stem topped with a spike of dainty white star flowers in spring. These are sometimes followed by red berries.

***Matteuccia struthiopteris* (Shuttlecock Fern)**

A lovely herbaceous fern that will, in moist spots with good light but little direct sun, make colonies with 1 metre fronds that are delicate bright green as they come up in the spring turning mid-green in summer and russet before they die down. A lovely companion for Hosta and all those other desirable woodlanders.

Mukdenia rossii

A lovely woodland perennial to 60 cm from Japan with large, bright green maple-shaped leaves that turn brilliant colours in autumn. It produces spikes of white starry flowers in summer. Plant it in a very moist soil out of direct sun.

***Mysotidium hortense* (Chatham Island Forget-Me-Not)**

A magnificent and rare evergreen perennial for moist semi-shaded aspects. It has heavily pleated glossy rich green leaves, better than any Hosta. In spring it produces large clusters of brilliant blue flowers at least five times bigger than those of its common namesake and the whole plant can be almost 1 metre each way.

***Omphalodes verna* (Creeping Forget-Me-Not)**

A charming semi-shade loving ground cover perennial to 20 cm from southern Europe with light green spearhead-shaped leaves and masses of rich blue flowers during spring and early summer.

Oxalis magellanica

A tiny creeping evergreen plant to 3 cm tall, native to South America as well as the cool mountain ranges of southern Australia. It has bronze-tinged evergreen foliage and pure white flowers in spring. An ideal crevice plant in moist semi-shade.

***O. m.* 'Flore-pleno'** A rare full double form of the above with flowers like tiny waterlilies.

Pachyphragma macrophylla

A woodlander in the cabbage family from Turkey, that is a lot nicer than that sounds. In spring it produces spikes of pure white flowers to 25 cm tall, quickly followed by large round leaves that make for good summer ground cover. Light shade that isn't too dry will suit and if you are lucky it may even self-seed.

Pachysandra procumbens

An interesting clumping perennial to 15 cm tall from North America with spikes of tiny white flowers in spring and bronze foliage mottled with green that fades to a greener look as the season marches on. It likes a semi-shaded site with soil that doesn't dry right out.

P. terminalis A spreading evergreen ground cover with leathery olive-green foliage and terminal spikes of small green-white flowers. It is a native of Japan that grows to 15 cm tall and is ideal in dense shade amongst tree roots.

***P. t.* 'Green Carpet'** A smaller-leafed and tighter-growing form, ideal for restricted spaces.

***P. t.* 'Variegata'** An attractive silver variegated form ideal to light up a dark corner.

Paeonia mascula ssp. *russoi*

A very beautiful herbaceous plant from Corsica, Sardinia and Sicily. It grows to about 60 cm tall and produces its single, soft pink flowers in very early spring above its handsome burgundy-tinged foliage. Its seed heads open in autumn exposing the highly ornamental black seeds surrounded by red pulp. It's in book number two, so look it up for more entertaining information.

P. tenuifolium A lovely semi-dwarf species to 45 cm from south-eastern Europe with very fine ferny bright green foliage and small, bright red cup-shaped flowers in spring.

P. veitchii A rare and beautiful species to 45 cm from China with heavily cut bright green foliage and elegant single flowers in shades of pink from quite pale to almost cerise. Whatever the shade, take my word for it as someone who's not fully in love with the colour pink I still wouldn't like to live without this one.

Paris polyphylla

An extremely rare woodland plant to 1 metre tall. It has a cluster of green leaves at the top of the stem surrounding its green petalled flowers that have golden filaments and a purple-stained ovary. As we at this stage only have one clone it can't get pollinated, so no seed is set. The upside is that the flower stays fresh for what seems like months waiting for a friend! If it is all too hard to envisage, look it up in my second book.

Persicaria campanulata syn. *Polygonum campanulatum*

A vigorous shade-tolerant, moisture-loving perennial to 1 metre in bloom. It produces masses of tiny pink flowers that age to a deep burgundy-red throughout late summer and autumn. This Chinese plant also has large attractive leaves.

***P. microcephala* 'Red Dragon'** A fairly new import of great merit. It is a tall trailing plant to 1 metre tall by up to twice this in width. Its beetroot-red leaves have a silver cast over part of the leaf. It has tiny white flowers in clusters in autumn that are well set off by the leaves and like most in this family likes it moist.

P. virginiana A bold clumping perennial to 1 metre, with large green leaves and a central brown V-shaped pattern to each leaf. The flowers are tiny white and produced so late that in cold climates they may not even make it but this isn't any loss! It likes a moist soil and gives a tropical look to any planting. This one made it into my second book so it must be good!

***P. v.* 'Painters Palette'** This form has the same V-shaped pattern but the rest of the leaf is boldly blotched with yellow patches. For the gardener that likes to shun the subtle!

Petasites frigidus var. *palmatus*

A perennial to 45 cm tall for moist to damp soils that has clusters of white flowers in late winter before the leaves come up. When these do appear they look like large, bright green maple leaves. A Dicksonia Rare Plants import.

P. japonica* var. *gigantea A truly impressive herbaceous bog plant with heads of white flowers at ground level in late winter like little cauliflowers that are favoured in tempura whilst still in the bud stage. These are followed by huge kidney-shaped leaves that can be over 1 metre across on 1-metre stems. It has a suckering habit and will make large clumps that look stunning by a pond or lake.

***P. j.* 'Nishiki Buki'** This form has huge leaves splashed and splotched with yellow. Another plant for the in-your-face-gardener like me! It is a shame that it isn't more heavily variegated.

***P. j.* forma 'Purpurea'** This form has leaves about half the size of the above that are purple whilst young, later turning green with a purple reverse.

Phlomis russelliana

A hardy evergreen perennial from Turkey with large grey-green basal leaves. It produces spikes of pale lemon flowers in whirls up the 1 metre tall stems during summer. The dead flower stems can have great presence for months after.

Plantago major 'Rubra'

A handsome clumping perennial to 30 cm tall, with large pleated burgundy leaves and candles of tiny bronze-green flowers in summer. It will self-seed and often comes up in cracks between rocks or pavers where it looks very much at home. A moist soil in full sun suits best.

P. maxima This form from eastern Europe grows to about 30 cm and has large heavily-veined leaves and spikes of white stamens tipped pink on summer. This is a surprisingly attractive plant in a genus not renowned for its beauty. Like the above, it will seed around a bit so not for the nervous Nellies amongst you.

Podophyllum peltatum (May Apple)

A bold woodlander from North America with large lobed leaves to 30 cm across and usually two per stem. Between said leaves it produces nodding white flowers that tend to be lost in all that herbage. It produces edible yellow fruit in summer.

Polygonatum falcatum 'Variegatum' (Variegated Solomon's Seal)

A rare form that differs from the normal form that everyone knows by having a fine cream line around the edges of the leaves. It grows to about 30 cm tall and likes a cool aspect as do the others in the genus.

P. hirtum I imported this form which comes from Europe and it grows to 40 cm with comparatively large, shiny deep green leaflets on its arching stems. The flowers are the usual nodding green and white bells although they are biggish for this genus.

P. hookeri A truly bizarre species from Tibet and Sikkim that only grows to 2.5 cm tall with comparatively large upward-facing deep pink bells. This is probably one of the least representative species in this genus and is loved by slugs and snails, so you have been warned!

P. humile A tiny species to 15 cm tall with straight stems and green and white nodding bells.

***P. hybridum* (Solomon's Seal)** A charming shade-loving herbaceous perennial from Europe and Asia. The tall arching stems to 1 metre, hanging in clusters from the leaf axils, have bright green leaves and small white bells with green spots.

P. odoratum Basically identical to the classical Solomon's Seal but only grows to 30 cm tall.

So everyone will tell you that their Solomon's Seal is much bigger than yours!

P. oppositifolia A more or less evergreen species to 60 cm from the Himalayas with arching stems and leathery, deep green leaves, bronze tinged when young. Its small pendent flowers are greenish in colour and the effect is more elegant than showy.

P. verticillatum This rare species from Asia Minor has non-arching stems to 1 metre with narrow leaves in whorls from which small greenish bells droop.

Reineckea carnea

An evergreen ground cover for dry shade with strappy leaves to 15 cm long and small pale pink, slightly scented flowers a little like its relative the far more famous Lily-of-the-Valley. Unlike its relative it is an easygoing, rough-and-tumble-type plant.

Rheum alexandrae

A somewhat fussy Tibetan Rhubarb to 1 metre or so. It has large oblong leaves in a basal rosette that often turn red before dying down in autumn. The tiny flowers are produced on tall spikes and protected by large showy yellow-green bracts. It likes a sunny sheltered damp site for your best chance.

Rodgersia aesculifolia

A large-leafed herbaceous perennial from China for a damp shaded aspect. Tall spikes of tiny white flowers in summer. It grows to about 1 metre tall in flower and is ideal for the edge of a bog garden. This one found a spot in my second book.

***Romneya coulteri* (Californian Tree Poppy)**

One of the world's great flowers, which suckers magnificently, and will grow to 2 metres tall with handsome grey leaves up the stem, topped throughout summer with huge white crepe-paper poppies with a big boss of yellow stamens. As if this wasn't enough it is scented to boot! A sunny well-drained site is essential and it resents disturbance, as all aristocrats do.

R. c.* var. *trichocalyx I grow this form just to have both! It is just as nice and only differs in having slightly smaller, more crinkled flowers and the leaves are more heavily cut and both these and the stems have scattered bristles whilst those of the above are smooth.

Rubus pentalobus* syn. *R. calycinoides

A dense-growing ground cover ideal to cover banks. Attractive crinkled leaves that turn a burgundy-brown with frost, and small white flowers in spring.

Rudbeckia maxima

A sun-loving perennial to 1.2 metres from North America with upright stems clad in handsome grey paddle-shaped leaves and topped with bright yellow daisies with a black cone-like centre. These cones look good well into winter. A moist soil and fairly regular division seems to suit it.

***Rumex hydrolapathum* (Giant Water Dock)**

This water-loving plant has huge spearhead-shaped bright green leaves up to 1 metre long that turn orange and yellow before they die down. Its tiny bronze-brown flowers are produced on 2 metre tall spikes in late summer.

***R. sanguineus* (Red Veined Dock)** This species grows to about 45 cm tall and has bright green leaves veined with beetroot-red, topped by spikes of tiny burgundy flowers. A sunny moist aspect suits best.

***Sanguinaria canadensis* (Blood Root)**

A rare and choice woodland perennial from North America with short-lived pure white flowers in early spring rather like tiny poppies followed by serrated kidney-shaped grey-green leaves that disappear in late summer. A cool, moist aspect in humus-rich soil suits best. This is featured in book number two.

***S. c.* 'Multiplex'** This is the extremely rare double-flowered form that looks like tiny white waterlilies and they last several more days than the single form.

Saruma henryi

A lovely Chinese woodlander to 45 cm tall with heavily puckered heart-shaped leaves up the stems and amongst these it produces yellow three-petalled flowers that leave behind attractive green sepals. A moist semi-shaded aspect like its relative the Asarum. It only gives away its relationship when dug up, as the roots smell of ginger, although observant people will notice that its generic name is an anagram.

Scopolia carniolica

A pleasant if not showy spring-flowering perennial to 60 cm tall from Europe with light green foliage and nodding deep brown bell flowers that you may have to go looking for! Likes a sunny but not too dry spot.

Scrophularia auriculata 'Variegata'

A stunning perennial to 1.5 metres in flower with large leaves more white than green so it is obviously only for the lover of striking foliage. This is all topped by open spikes of tiny burgundy-red flowers that someone said looked like rats' eyes! This plant likes a cool aspect and moist to wet soil.

Sedum telephium ssp. *ruprechtii*

I imported this lovely succulent from Beth Chatto in England only to find I had been beaten to the punch. However, it is obvious that I wasn't the only one who liked it! It grows to 30 cm tall with rounded grey leaves on reddish stems and these are topped in autumn by clusters of the softest lemon flowers. Like its relatives a sunny spot with minimal summer watering will do.

Selinum wallichianum

Picture the foliage of a carrot, which is of course quite attractive, with flat heads of tiny white flowers also rather like that of a carrot and you have a picture of this light and lacy 60 cm tall perennial that will do well in sun or shade as long as the soil isn't too dry. Just don't expect carrots!

Semiaquilegia ecalcarata

A charming small perennial from western China closely related to Aquilegia but without spurs. The small dusty magenta blooms are produced in spring on stems to 30 cm tall.

Sempervivum 'Adelmoed' (House Leek)

This is part of my extensive collection of House Leeks that are cold-tolerant succulents from the mountains of Europe and northern Africa. They are good in pots or rock gardens and need little more than a well-drained sunny site. Many I have imported both from North America and England, as in this case from Fernwood Nursery in England, which holds the English National Collection. This form has smooth-leafed, medium-sized rosettes that are coppery-red in winter and grey flushed purple in summer.

S. 'Alchimist' This form has medium-sized green rosettes and the outer older leaves turn reddish in winter.

S. 'Amanda' This one has medium-sized rosettes with deep green leaves tipped with burgundy.

S. 'Angustifolium' I got this form locally and can't find a reference to it anywhere but it is a good thing, with medium-sized rosettes that have rich green leaves that are tipped rich brown and are slightly bristly. This one doesn't charge colour with cold.

***S. arachnoideum* (Cobweb House Leek)** This small rosetting species native to the Pyrenees and the Carpathians has green rosettes tipped with brown in winter and almost hidden by white cobweb-like hairs.

***S. a.* 'Hookeri'** This form has tiny rosettes of bright green with older leaves around the edge turning orange. It is so tiny that a well-grown clump looks more like moss than a succulent.

***S. a.* 'Stanfieldii'** This old form has rosettes slightly larger than the species with good cobwebbing.

S. 'Ashes of Roses' This selection has medium-sized furry rosettes that are green with bronze backs and white fur in summer and in winter has leaves that are half green-and-grey-brown.

S. atlanticum I imported this Moroccan species that has neat small mid-green rosettes with a faint copper tinge throughout the year.

S. 'Bascour Zilver' This form has small heavily cobwebbed rosettes that are green-leafed in summer and mahogany tipped green in winter.

S. 'Bernstein' This one has large yellow-green rosettes shaded with pink and red in winter.
S. 'Black Mini' This one has small rosettes of green shaded deep almost black-red especially in winter.
S. 'Black Mountain' A medium-sized rosette with narrow green leaves tipped with deep red to almost black, especially in winter.
S. 'Blue Boy' This has smooth medium-sized rosettes that are grey-green in summer with burgundy tips in winter.
S. 'Blue Time' Large rosettes of silvery-green with tiny bronze tips.
S. 'Bronco' Medium-sized rosettes with smooth and shiny leaves that are green with brown tips in summer and a dark red-black with a green centre in winter.
S. 'Bronze Pastel' Small rosettes with narrow leaves that are brown throughout the year.
S. 'Brown Owl' This one has medium to large brownish-red rosettes with a green centre.
S. 'Café' Large rosettes with smooth leaves that are olive-tipped with rich brown in summer and the tips turn near to black with milk coffee in winter.
S. calcareum This species from the French Alps (lucky thing!) Has smooth-leafed, medium-sized rosettes that are grey-green tipped with rich brown.
***S. c.* 'Atropurpureum'** This selection has smooth-leafed, medium-sized rosettes that are olive-green tipped burgundy in summer and almost completely purple-black in winter and is one of my first importations.
***S. c.* 'Grigg's Surprise'** This strange form has medium-sized rosettes of grey-green leaves tipped with brown but the leaves are round in cross section with hooked tips instead of the usual flat leaves.
***S. c.* 'Limelight'** I imported this form which has medium-sized rosettes with smooth leaves that are bright green in summer and tipped brown in winter.
***S. c.* 'Pink Pearl'** Large grey-green rosettes with tiny burgundy tips and pink tints in cold weather.
***S. c.* 'Sir William Lawrence'** This one has medium-sized rosettes with smooth grey-green leaves that are tipped with very deep brown and in winter the brown takes over half the leaf.
S. cantabricum* spp. *urbionense A species from Spain which has medium-sized rosettes with rough leaves that are bright green with a tiny brown tip in summer and turn grey-green tipped brown in winter.
S. 'Carmen' This form gets quite large rosettes that are green with a small brown tip and bronze tinged older leaves that stay much the same year round.
S. caucasicum Another of my imports that in this form has smooth-leafed, medium-sized rosettes that are green with brown tips year round.
S. 'Centennial' This form has large smooth-leafed rosettes that are purple with green tips in summer turning cherry-red with green tips in winter.
S. charadzeae This species from the Caucasus Mountains has very large rosettes of a bright yellowish-green.
S. 'Cherry Frost' Medium-sized furry rosettes that are grey-green in summer and cherry-red with green tips in winter.
S. 'Chocolate' This selection has large rosettes with smooth leaves that are a lovely deep brown year round.
S. ciliosum* var. *borisii A lovely species from Bulgaria which has small white furry rosettes with grey-green leaves with tiny brown tips in winter.
S. 'Climax' This one has smooth-leafed, medium-sized rosettes that are grey-green with a cherry-red flush in the centre in summer that turns to mottled deep red and green in winter.
S. 'Collage' Large smooth-leafed rosettes that have olive-green outer leaves with a mauve centre that in winter are mauve tipped with cherry-red.
S. 'Crispyn' One with smooth-leafed rosettes of medium size that are grey and mauve-pink in summer turning to plum in winter.
S. 'Dark Beauty' This form has medium-sized rosettes with smooth leaves that are green flushed and edged with burgundy in summer and almost black in winter.

S. 'Edge of Night' This one has smooth-leafed, medium-sized rosettes that are green with bronze tips in summer. The tips take up about a third of the leaf in winter.

S. 'Elene' This American raised form has large slightly furry rosettes that are bronze-grey tipped with burgundy year round.

S. 'Emmchen' A small rosetted type with furry grey-green leaves tipped with dark brown.

S. × *fauconnettii* This hybrid has small rosettes that green with good, white cobwebbing in summer, and then blush with bronze in winter.

S. 'Feugo' Very large smooth rosettes that are green tipped with burgundy that extends down the leaves in winter to take over at least half.

S. 'Flamingo' This form has large smooth rosettes that are grey-green flushed with mauve and pink in the centre that deepen in colour in winter.

S. 'Ford's Spring' This one has small rosettes that are green turning red in winter.

S. 'Fronika' A small rosetted variety with narrow dull green leaves turning brown in winter.

S. 'Gabrielle' This form has large smooth-leafed rosettes that are almost a black-red year round.

S. 'Georgette' This has small rosettes with narrow green leaves that turn orange with age.

S. giuseppii This species from northern Spain has small, neat, slightly furry rosettes of mid-green year round.

S. 'Grammens' This form has large smooth-leafed rosettes with broad leaves that are burgundy flushed with green in summer becoming brownish-green with fine burgundy edges.

S. 'Granby' This fine form has large rosettes with broad leaves that are deep beetroot red in winter with some green staining in summer.

S. 'Graupurpur' This one has large mauve-grey rosettes with purple tipped leaves and the colour is richer in winter.

S. 'Grey Lady' This form has large smooth-leafed rosettes that are grey in summer and edged with burgundy in winter.

S. 'Greyolla' This form has large rosettes with furry leaves that are grey flushed green with tiny brown tips in summer and winter.

S. 'Happy' Medium, slightly bristly rosettes that are bright green, with oldest leaves flushed red in summer that in winter have a burgundy centre and green part way-out, tipped with copper.

S. 'Hester' Soft velvety green leaves tipped with burgundy-red and a medium-sized rosette.

S. 'Icicle' A large rosetting form with bristly leaves that are ice-green with bronze flushing in summer, turning beetroot with white fur in winter.

S. 'Irazu' This one has medium-sized, smooth-leafed rosettes that are grey-green flushed with burgundy and orange in summer, turning beetroot with green edges in winter.

S. 'Jungle Fires' Large rosettes with burgundy-red leaves with a green base.

S. 'Justine's Choice' This form has smooth-leafed medium rosettes that multiply with gay abandon. They are mauve-green, tipped slightly with brown in summer, and in winter they are green in the centre with more than half the top of the leaf burgundy.

S. 'Kelly Jo' A smallish form with green, slightly furry narrow-leafed rosettes that are green in winter turning reddish in summer.

S. 'Koko Flanel' This one has smallish grey-green rosettes covered in white hairs that are most obvious in summer.

S. 'Korspelsegietje' This hard-to-say-or-spell form has medium-sized, smooth-leafed rosettes that are green tipped with burgundy in summer, turning to rich bronze-red greening towards the centre in winter.

S. 'Kramer's Spinrad' The largest of the cobweb House Leeks that I bought in some years back that has green foliage flushed with terracotta in summer deepening in winter.

S. 'Lavender and Old Lace' An extra large rosette with a lovely mauve colour to the leaves, which is strongest in winter.

S. 'Lavender Doll' This form has large rosettes with smooth foliage that is grey flushed plum in summer turning brown-green edged with burgundy in winter.

S. 'Lilac Time' Large rosettes with grey foliage flushed mauve in cold weather.

S. 'Little Darling' This form has small rosettes with smooth burgundy leaves edged with green year round.

S. 'Lively Bug' A form with smallish rosettes that are green and covered in fine white hairs.

S. macedonicum This species from the old Yugoslavia has small dull green rosettes with very narrow leaves.

S. 'Magic Spell' I imported this one which has large rosettes with narrow smooth leaves that are bright green flushed with copper in summer that in winter turn burgundy with a green edge.

S. 'Magnifica' This form has large rosettes with broad leaves that are mauve in summer and cherry-red in winter.

S. 'Mahogany' This one has medium-sized, smooth-leafed rosettes that are grey-green tipped tan in summer and a dark red-brown in winter.

S. marmoreum This lovely species from the Balkans has smooth-leafed, medium-sized rosettes that are green flushed plum in summer turning almost black in winter.

***S. m.* 'Brunneifolium'** This lovely smooth-leafed, large rosetting form has pinkish-bronze foliage throughout the year.

***S. montanum* spp. *carpaticum* 'Cmirals Yellow'** I am to blame for importing this form with the almost impossible name that is also a bit of a bugger to keep. It has small rosettes with narrow leaves that are green except in spring when they can be bright yellow.

S. 'More Honey' This form has very large rosettes with smooth leaves that are green flushed with copper in summer and deep bronze with green tips and bases in winter.

S. 'Mount Hood' A selection from America that I bought from a nursery there as I was looking at Mt Hood! This one has very large rosettes with smooth green leaves flared with beetroot red.

S. 'Mulberry Wine' I bought in this lovely form with medium rosettes of green flushed with burgundy that turns rich burgundy in winter with green central bands in the leaf.

S. nevadense This species comes from southern Spain and has small tight bright green rosettes with bronze tips.

S. octopodes* var. *apetalum This form of a Yugoslavian species (that is, the former Yugoslavia) has tiny rosettes of bright green with fine bronze tips. This form produces its pups on quite long stolons.

S. 'Oddity' This strange form has large rosettes of cylindrical leaves with a hollow end that are grey-green with bronze tips year round.

S. 'Old Rose' A form with medium-sized rosettes that are a rich burgundy stained with green.

S. 'Pacific Red Rose' This form has large rosettes that have smooth burgundy-red leaves year round that are probably richer in colour in winter.

S. 'Pastel' This slow to multiply form has medium-sized rosettes with narrow leaves that are a rich bronze year round.

S. 'Peacock' This form came home with me from America in 2003 and has large rosettes that are slightly fuzzy and are grey-green flushed pink and tipped burgundy year round.

S. 'Pekinese' This form has small rosettes and is bright green throughout the year.

S. 'Pink Puff' This one has narrow white furred leaves in medium-sized rosettes that are green-flushed burgundy in summer turning rich burgundy in winter.

S. 'Pink Surprise' If the name of this one is right then the surprise is that its large rosettes are grey-green tipped black, year round, without a sign of pink!

S. 'Pixie' This introduction has tiny rosettes that are bright green with tiny brown tips year round.

S. pumilum × ingwersinii This one has small rosettes of bright green leaves tipped with burgundy and is quite like the one above.

S. 'Purdy's' A large rosetting form with furry leaves, grey-mauve with beetroot edges that stay more or less the same all year.

S. 'Purple Haze' Medium rosettes that are grey-green flushed pink and tipped burgundy year round.

S. 'Quintessence' This American selection has large wide-leafed rosettes that are bright green with fabulous beetroot staining in the centre.

S. 'Raspberry Ice' This form has large furry rosettes that are green-flushed burgundy in summer and a dusty mauve-pink in winter.

S. 'Red Chief' This one has large rosettes with smooth broad leaves that are ruby-red year round.

S. 'Red King' This form has medium-sized rosettes that are green-flushed beetroot towards the centre in summer and dark beetroot-red in winter.

S. 'Reggy' This form has medium rosettes with bronze-green leaves with brown tips.

S. 'Reinhard' This very neat medium rosetted form has rich green leaves tipped black year round.

S. 'Reward' This form has medium-sized rosettes that are green flushed with beetroot that becomes beetroot with some green patches in winter.

S. 'Rita Jane' This selection has large greyish-green rosettes stained burgundy.

S. 'Rosie' This form I imported has medium-sized fuzzy rosettes that are green flushed with copper, that in winter go coppery-pink with a green centre.

S. 'Rotkopf' This one has large rosettes that are slightly furry and grey with bronze markings on the older leaves.

S. 'Rotund' As the name suggests this one has rounded leaves in rounded rosettes that are green, with bronze staining towards the tips.

S. 'Royal Ruby' This form has medium-sized rosettes that are blood-red-suffused green year round.

S. 'Rubrum Ray' This one has large mauve flushed grey rosettes that turn cherry-pink and grey in winter.

S. 'Saga' This form has large smooth rosettes that are grey-mauve in summer turning grey-tipped bronze in winter.

S. 'Sharon's Pencil' This one has large rosettes with long green leaves with burgundy tips.

S. 'Silver Thaw' This one has small, very hairy grey-green rosettes.

S. 'Skrocki's Beauty' This lovely form has medium-sized hairy and cobwebbed rosettes that are green with terracotta flushes and turn to burgundy in winter.

S. 'Slabber's Seedling' This one has medium, smooth rosettes that are grey-pink, turning rich burgundy-pink with darker tips in winter.

S. sosnowskyi A species from Armenia with very large emerald-green rosettes with bold burgundy tips.

S. 'Spangle' This one has medium rosettes with white cobwebbing that are green with some burgundy blotches year round.

S. tectorum This species from the European Alps has very large bright green rosettes with burgundy edges that are wider at the tips.

***S. t.* 'Atropurpureum'** This form has medium rosettes of smooth burgundy leaves flushed with green that in winter turn almost black.

S. t.* var. *boutignyanum This form from the Pyrenees has neat medium-sized, smooth rosettes that are green with dark tips that in winter becomes dark brown with green bases to the leaves

***S. t.* 'Sunset'** This lovely medium-sized form is a rich orange-brown with bright green leaf bases in winter and almost completely green in summer.

S. 'Thunder' This selection has furry grey rosettes of medium size with burgundy staining towards the tips that is stronger in winter.

S. 'Tiny Tim' This form has small bright green, white cobwebbed rosettes that develop a burgundy centre in winter.

S. 'Topaz' Smallish neat rosettes that are green flushed burgundy in summer turning dark red-brown in winter.

S. 'Tordeur's Memory' This one has narrow bright green leaves that can turn bright red, and smallish rosettes.

***S.* 'Tristesse'** This one has very neat medium-sized rosettes that are deep olive green with black tips.

S. velanovskyi This species has medium grey-green rosettes with fine white hairs.

***S.* 'Virginius'** A selection with medium slightly fuzzy mid-green rosettes in tight mounds.

***S.* 'Video'** This selection has large rosettes that are grey stained beetroot in the centre that turn almost all red with cold.

***S.* 'Weighton's Red'** This form has medium burgundy rosettes flushed with green that turn deep burgundy-red in winter.

***S.* 'Winter Beauty'** This form has medium slightly furry rosettes that are green flushed with bronze that become burgundy with green patches in winter.

***S.* 'Zaza'** This one has large smooth-leafed rosettes that are green tipped burgundy that turn rich burgundy with a green centre in winter.

Sinacalia tangutica

An elegant herbaceous plant from China to 1.2 metres that likes a moist aspect in semi-shade. It has large, pale green leaves with deeply cut lobes topped in late summer by pyramids of tiny yellow flowers. It has a suckering habit and may need to be restrained.

Sisyrinchium striatum

A hardy perennial to 60 cm with grey-green Iris-like leaves and narrow spikes of small, creamy yellow flowers produced during the warmer months.

***S. s.* 'Aunt May'** A very rare and desirable form with variegated foliage which is the same colour as the flowers.

Smilacina racemosa (False Solomon's Seal)

A lovely woodland perennial to 1 metre from North America, with arching stems topped with heads of fluffy white flowers in spring. followed by red berries. Like the Solomon's Seal, this genus likes a lightly shaded site in humus-enriched soils. In my second book.

S. stellata This species also from North America has more or less upright stems to 20 cm with clusters of small white stars at the tops in early summer.This plant wafts about, coming up here and there, but usually not making clumps.

Soldanella carpatica

A charming little evergreen alpine from eastern Europe to 12 cm tall in bloom. It has small, dark green kidney-shaped leaves and nodding purple bells with fringed petals like tiny tiffany lampshades in early spring. Likes a moist, humus-rich soil in a cool aspect.

Sonchus acaulis

An evergreen rosetting perennial from the Canary Islands to 1 metre across through which, in summer, erupt 1-metre-tall stems with large yellow daisies. Think dandelions on steroids! Its fabulous jagged foliage makes it a good feature plant and it will grow in a well-drained soil in sun or semi-shade. Other species in this genus are truly shrubby and are listed appropriately.

Stylophorum diphyllum (Celandine Poppy)

An attractive herbaceous woodland plant from North America to 30 cm tall. The silvery-green foliage is topped with yellow Poppy-like flowers in spring and summer. Semi-shade and not to dry and all will be well.

Symphytum 'Goldsmith' (Variegated Comfrey)

A very hardy colonising perennial 20 cm with large bristly leaves broadly edged with yellow. In spring it has nodding whitish bells stained blue in clusters just above the leaves. A sunny to semi-shaded spot is about all it needs.

***S.* × *uplandicum* 'Variegata'** A striking perennial to 1 metre in flower, with leaves broadly edged with white. The nodding flowers start pinkish and usually turn purple to blue as they age. Sunny aspect and deep soils suit best. Root cuttings will all come up with green leaves, so the plant has to be divided and any roots left in the ground poisoned, as they will come up green as well. Christopher Lloyd said it was one of the best variegated plants, which is saying a lot.

Tellima grandiflora

A shade-loving perennial from North America with attractive rounded leaves and spikes of greenish-white bell flowers in spring. It grows to about 30 cm tall and makes good-sized clumps.

Thalictrum aquilegifolium

A lovely upright plant from Europe to 1 metre with foliage very like that of an Aquilegia, hence the name. In summer it produces masses of fine fluffy mauve flowers. A sunny not too dry spot suits this one.

***T. delavayi* (Lavender Showers)** A lovely tall perennial to 3 metres from China with ferny foliage and sprays of tiny lavender flowers in summer. It is so tall that some non-obvious staking may be required, or let it lean into other surrounding plants. Sun or semi-shade and not completely dry soil as well as shelter from strong wind to get the best out of it.

***T. d.* 'Album'** A stunning white flowered form of the above.

T. fendleri This North American species grows to 1.5 metres tall has airy grey-green foliage are tiny white flowers in open sprays in summer.

T. flavum* ssp. *glaucum A dainty herbaceous plant to 2 metres or so from Spain and northern Africa. It has soft grey Aquilegia-like foliage and fluffy clusters of pale lemon flowers at the top of its stems in summer. It likes moist soil and a sunny site.

***T. f.* 'Illuminator'** This amazing form has golden new leaves that turn grey later and the usual soft yellow flowers.

T. javanicum This species from China through to India and Indonesia grows to 1.5 metres tall and has open sprays of white flowers often soft mauve within.

Trachystemon orientalis

A big bold herbaceous plant for moist shade from eastern Europe with bright blue Borage-like flowers in winter followed by large rough leaves to 60 cm long and as impressive as any Hosta but snail proof. It is in my second book.

Trillium albidum

One of the treasures of North America. This extremely slow-to-multiply woodlander has stems to 30 cm tall, topped with three marbled leaves in the centre of which it has three upward-pointing white petals often stained pink at the base. A humus rich soil and deep pockets are required to grow this one well!

T. chloropetalum This North American species to 30 cm has brown spotted foliage and handsome deep burgundy sessile flowers and is also so slow you have to start young or live a long time.

T. cuneatum This sessile species grows to 20 cm and has deepest liver-purple flowers and the foliage when young is attractively mottled white, later fading to almost straight green.

T. grandiflorum This species is extremely rare in Australia, but then, what Trillium isn't? It grows to 30 cm tall and has plain green leaves at the top of the stem. The flowers are on a short bent stem above the leaves so that they look outward. The petals are a lovely pure white.

T. kurabayashii This equally rare beauty has rich deep burgundy flowers with the same beautifully marked foliage and likes the same conditions, so if you can afford it buy all of them.

T. rivale This little beauty makes reasonable colonies of 7-cm stems topped with the usual three leaves that in this case are straight green and the cute-as-a-bug three-petalled flowers are very soft pink often with deep burgundy spots. This one won't break the bank but needs the same growing conditions.

Tulbaghia alliacea

Tough-as-guts South African relatives of the onion that will make bulb-less clumps of strappy leaves that in this case are 30 cm tall overtopped in summer with strange clusters of small olive-green flowers with an orange centre. Any sunny site will do for this hardy lot.

T. cepacea* var. *maritima This evergreen species has leaves to 30 cm overtopped all summer with heads of small deep mauve flowers.

T. cominsii This tiny species has fine grey leaves to 12 cm overtopped by tiny, softest pink almost white flowers all the warm months.

T. leucantha Another tiny little whitish one similar to the above but obviously necessary to round out the collection!

T. simmleri* syn. *T. fragrans This chunky species usually dies down in winter and has comparatively broad green leaves topped by clusters of slightly scented mauve flowers during the warmer months. I also grow a white flowered form.

Uvularia grandiflora (Merrybells)

A charming North American woodland plant to 30 cm tall, with soft green foliage on arching stems and pale orangy-yellow drooping bells in spring. Looks a little like its relative the Solomon's Seal and likes similar conditions to grow well, i.e. cool, moist soil with good levels of humus.

***U. sessilifolia* 'Cobblewood Gold'** This selection has smaller flowers than the above and its foliage starts out with a lovely yellow edge that fades as the summer sets in so that it looks non-variegated by this time.

Vancouveria hexandra

A North American woodland plant with evergreen leathery leaves of great quality, to 30 cm tall. In spring it produces spikes of tiny white flowers. It suckers and creates attractive drifts in any semi-shaded moist aspect.

Wachendorfia thyrsiflora

A bold clumping evergreen perennial from South Africa that likes a sunny aspect and will tolerate wet soils. The long pleated leaves grow to about 1 metre tall and are topped with spikes of yellow flowers in summer that, in a well-grown specimen, can be 2 metres tall or more.

Woodwardia radicans (Chain Fern)

A large hardy fern from China with fronds to 1.5 metres long, that will produce a baby plant at the tips of the fronds. Ideal for shady aspects and large hanging baskets. Fairly drought-tolerant for a fern, once established.

Bulbs

Fritillia pyrenaica

***Acis autumnalis* syn. *Leucojum autumnale* (Autumn Snowflake)**
A dainty little white autumn-flowering bulb to 15 cm, from Spain as well as several of the Mediterranean islands, that has recently been removed into this genus (like the following species). The only ones left in *Leucojum* are the taller green spotted ones. This easy little plant will grow well in sun or semi-shade and the flowers usually come up before the leaves.

A. longifolia* syn. *L. longifolium This rare species from Corsica grows to about 20 cm and flowers in spring. It usually has several white bells per stem.

A. nicaeensis* syn. *L. nicaeense A really rare little early-spring-flowered species to 15 cm from the south of France and Monaco with tiny nodding white bells and often curled, deep green leaves.

A. rosea* syn. *L. roseum Another tiny autumn flowerer to 10 cm that this time has tiny pale pink flowers and comes from Corsica and Sardinia.

A. tingitana* syn. *L. tingutanum This charming late winter-flowering species hails from Morocco and grows to 20 cm or so with quite showy white bells usually several per stem.

Allium amabile
A dainty little Onion to 10 cm tall with fine grassy foliage and dainty little, rich pink nodding flowers in summer. Native to south-western China. Like most of this tribe they like a sunny aspect with good drainage.

***A. ampeloprasum* (Giant Russian Garlic)** A tall-growing summer flowered species to 1.5 metres with large round heads of soft mauve flowers on often twisted or bent stems. It looks great in the border and is fabulous for picking.

A. caeruleum This stunning Onion from the Russian steppes and inland salt marshes grows to 60 cm tall and has smallish round heads of brilliant blue flowers in summer.

***A. carinatum* ssp. *pulchellum* (Keeled Garlic)** A lovely summer flowered Onion to 60 cm tall from Europe and Asia Minor has a fireworks display of soft mauve-pink flowers that are ideal for picking and drying or leaving in the garden if you don't like dust catchers. This one features in my second book.

***A. c.* ssp. *p.* 'Album'** A lovely white form of the above.

***A. cernuum* (Nodding Onion)** This lovely species comes from North America and grows to 45 cm tall with heads of mauve flowers on a stem that bends toward the ground just before the head.

A. christophii A truly spectacular species with large heads of metallic-mauve flowers to 16 cm across on 30-cm stems. It rarely multiplies by bulb division but seedlings will eventually flower if they aren't weeded out first! It comes from Iran and (the former) Soviet central Asia and will look at home in any border.

A. cyaneum A tiny Chinese species to 12 cm with rich blue flowers in late summer that needs to be in a pot or small rock garden so that it can be watched or it could be lost very easily.

A. cyathophorum* var. *farreri This dainty little Chinese Onion has narrow grey-green leaves and heads of mauve-pink flowers in summer. It grows to 12 cm tall.

A. dichlamydeum A charming little late-spring-flowering species from the U.S.A. with stems to 12 cm or so tall, topped by waxy rich pink starry flowers.

***A. falcifolium* (Scythe Leafed Onion)** A very small North America species with flower stems little more than 2.5 cm tall topped with deep pink flowers above its two curved leaves that give it its common name. Unlike many Onions its leaves stay fresh through flowering time.

***A. flavum* 'Nanum'** This small bulb is yellow-flowering and 12 cm tall and is ideal mixed with *A. cyaneum*, as they both flower together. Native of southern Europe.

A. karataviense A truly impressive Onion from Russia that, unlike most species, is probably more beautiful in leaf than in flower. In spring each bulb produces usually two big grey-purple leaves edged with red and heavily veined. Nestled into these and almost lost are 10 cm wide balls of soft mauve almost white flowers. Pretty enough but somehow a let-down after such promising leaves.

A. schubertii A truly impressive Russian Onion to 60 cm tall, with huge heads almost as wide, of tiny mauve flowers all at different lengths from the main stem but none-the-less making a King's Cross fountain-like effect. In the wild, the whole head breaks off when the seed ripens and will roll around like a tumbleweed.

Arisaema amurense (Cobra Lilies)

A strangely beautiful tuberous plant from northern Asia with solitary leaves composed of five leaflets on 30-cm-tall stems. Its weird hooded flowers are pale green, striped with deep green and produced in spring. This is one of the first in the genus to flower and like most, it likes a semi-shaded site.

A. candidissimum This stunning Chinese species has soft pink Cobras striped with white and is probably the least scary and prettiest of them all so growing this one won't have you lumped with axe-murderers! Its flowers usually precede its large glossy leaves consisting of three leaflets on 30-cm-tall stems.

A. concinnum This Asian species has leaves to 1 metre or so tall with leaflets like the spokes of an umbrella and hooded flowers below them that in the form I grow are apple-green throughout. It is in fact quite similar to the following species but lacks the leaf and flower filaments.

A. consanguineum This elegant Asian species can grow to 1 metre or more tall, with large leaves with leaflets spread out like an open umbrella. Each leaflet has a long filament dangling from its end and the lot is supported by a leopard-skin-patterned stem. Two-thirds of the way up this stem you will find the striking Cobra, which is in my form greenish towards the stem turning brown and also ending in a long drooping filament.

A. exappendiculatum This Asian species has, at least in the form I'm growing, a ghostly white stem with some brown streaking, topped with an umbrella-like set of about nine leaflets. Halfway up the stem it produces upright green flowers that never open right out and with a short point on that spathe.

A. flavum A quaint species from eastern Africa through to the Arabian peninsular with leaves to 30 cm or so tall divided into about 8 leaflets amongst which it produces its tiny chubby little yellow-green flowers that are hardly scary at all (not all that showy either but fun nevertheless).

A. franchetianum A lovely Asian species with huge leaves divided into three leaflets under which hides the large black and white striped flowers looking like a Humbug Cobra or maybe one in its pyjamas! The flower also has a long drooping filament at its tips.

A. jacquemontii A charming species to 45 cm tall with bright green leaves divided into three leaflets and cobra-shaped bright green flowers with a long upward-pointing spadix like a tongue testing the air.

A. ringens Another stunning Asian species with leopard skin stems and huge shiny leaves divided into three under which hide hooded green and white striped flowers with a big wavy black mouth. Hard to describe, so to get the full effect look it up in my second book.

A. tortuosum A truly impressive beast from India, Myanmar and western China that can grow to 1.8 metres tall with the leopard-skin stems with leaves that can have quite a number of leaflets. These sit just below the green, slightly hooded flowers that surround the base of a long sinuous black spadix that will scare the pants off the unsuspecting!

Arum apulum

A rare species from southern Italy with winter green foliage to 30 cm tall, amongst which in spring it has flowers that smell weakly of horse dung and urine. It has a green exterior with a purple interior and a dark purple spadix. I raised this one from English seed some time back and am pleased to offer this new plant to Australia.

A. 'Chameleon' I imported this stunner from England a few years back and am now happy to offer it for sale. It could be a form or hybrid of *A. italicum* and it is grown for its leaves with white and green swirling patterns. The flowers are apple-green throughout.

A. concinnatum This species from the eastern Mediterranean I have in two forms, one with plain foliage the other (raised as *A. nickelii)* has spotted leaves to 60 cm or more tall. The flowers smell of stale urine and the spathe is pale green, flushed purple on the edges externally, with the interior being pale green at the base, mid-purple above. The spadix is yellowish in some forms with some purple in others.

A. creticum This is probably the most striking of all species and comes from Crete, mainland Greece and several other islands in the region. The leaves are glossy deep green overtopped in spring by soft yellow spathes and a deep yellow spadix, all smelling unusually of Freesias and lemon. This species grows to about 60 cm tall and likes a sunny site.

A. cyrenaicum This lovely species comes from Libya and southern Crete and grows to about 45 cm tall. The leaves are mid-green and the horse-dung-scented flowers produced in spring are green on the outside and soft pink-purple inside with a brown spadix.

A. dioscoridis A lovely small Middle Eastern Aroid with winter-growing bright green spearhead-shaped leaves. The flowers which sit close to the ground, and smell of donkey dung and carrion, have a large buff-coloured spathe with large purple liver spots and the upright dark purple spadix that usually are found as the leaves die down. This sun loving species grows to all of 20 cm tall.

A. hygrophilum A rare species to 60 cm tall from Morocco and Cyprus, with classic-shaped leaves that pop up in the autumn. The flowers that open in spring have a nodded tip and are actually unscented. They are green with a fine purple edge and a purple spadix.

***A. italicum* (Lords and Ladies)** A quite common though no less desirable European species, with large rich green leaves marbled with white, that come up in autumn. The large flowers, that smell of a mixture of stale urine and occasionally a bit of pineapple and citrus, are green throughout and pop up in spring. These are followed by spikes of brilliant orange berries in summer.

A. i.* var. *albispathum This rarely seen form from the Crimea and the Caucasus has plain green leaves and a whitish spathe with a pale yellow spadix. As with the species it will produce spikes of red berries in summer.

***A. i.* 'Marmoratum'** The difference that this form exhibits is its extra well-marked leaves with veins of pure white in deep glossy green leaves.

***A. i.* 'White Winter'** This form has large leaves well-marbled with white veins and so far seems similar to the above on steroids! I imported it from the U.S.A. in 2005 so time will tell if it was worth the cost.

A. orientale This 60-cm species hails from western Turkey and extends into eastern Europe and has flowers in spring nestled in amongst the leaves that are green on the outside and purple within.

A. palaestinum This stunning species from the Middle East with large green leaves that are often growing down as its huge flowers open. They are green on the outside and rich velvet black inside. The spathe curls downward exposing its erect black spadix. The whole smells a bit like fermented fruit to some, more like dung or carrion to others.

A. pictum I imported this at huge expense from England and it was worth it! It comes from Italy and some of the Mediterranean islands and is the only autumn flowered *Arum* with its chubby purple black horse-dung-scented flowers standing proud and naked. These are followed by seriously glossy, rich green leaves that are edged with burgundy.

A. purpureospathum I raised this species that hails from Crete from seed some years ago and am I glad I did! It has rich green leaves and deep purple-black spathes with a short black spadix, the whole thing smelling slightly of horse dung.

Babiana ringens

A truly bizarre South African sun-loving, winter-growing, spring-flowering corm that has large narrow-petalled brilliant red flowers with a yellow centre that all sit near ground level. It produces a tall bronze stalk that is bare of leaves or flowers and acts as a perch for the birds to aid them in gathering nectar and thus pollinating the plant in the process. A sunny site that is dry in summer suits best.

Biarum davisii

This is a quaint group of *Arum* relatives from the Mediterranean that grow in sunbaked areas and flower at ground level to be followed in winter by the foliage. Unusually for this genus this one has small Pooh-Bear honey-pot-like flowers that are sweetly scented and white with pink spots inside.

B. carratracense This Spanish species is more in the usual mould with almost black smelly flowers followed by narrow wavy leaves to 12 cm tall.

B. dispar This is yet another little black and smelly Aroid to round out your collection and, in this case, with rather rounded leaves.

B. eximium This species from southern Turkey is similar to the above with a spathe that lies down on the ground when it opens.

B. ochridense Yet another black and smelly species with fairly narrow spathes that are slightly twisted and, like the following, needed by those that want the whole collection.

B. tenuifolium This Mediterranean species has black flowers as well that stink and are followed by narrow leaves with undulating margins.

Brimeura amethystina

A tiny spring-flowered European bulb to 10 cm, with pale blue bluebell-like flowers. This bulb is slow to multiply but most worthwhile and likes a semi-shaded aspect under a shrub or tree. Buy a few if you want a show!

Brodiaea californica

A charming sun-loving, early summer-flowering bulb to 20 cm tall that hails from California as the name would suggest and has rich mauve trumpet-shaped flowers in clusters at the top of the stem.

Calochortus uniflorus (Fairy Lanterns)

A dainty dwarf bulb to 15 cm from California and Oregon. The lovely pale mauve cup-shaped flowers have a darker blotch at the petal bases and are produced in late spring. It prefers a sunny well-drained aspect.

Cardiocrinum giganteum (Giant Lily)

A truly spectacular bulb from the Himalayas, growing up to 3 metres or more in size when flowering, with up to a dozen huge white scented trumpets at the top of the stem with purple stains in the throat. The handsome foliage requires protection from slugs and snails. Plant it in a cool aspect in soil enriched with cow manure and leaf mould by the truck-load!

Chionodoxa sardensis (Glory of the Snow)

Dwarf spring-flowering bulb from Turkey to 8 cm with intense blue flowers with a white centre. The bulbs like a cold winter and don't multiple vegetatively much but, where happy, will self-seed well. Plant under a deciduous shrub or tree to give it shade in summer.

C. siehei This lovely species from Turkey has star-shaped flowers very like the above that are slightly larger and at least in my stock can be rich blue with a white centre or pink or even pure white. A good doer in the same conditions.

Colchicum agrippinum

Autumn-flowering corm that has pale mauve-chequered flowers to 7 cm tall. The foliage comes up after the flowers, in winter. These are easy plants but the foliage can be gross if planted in the rock garden. All the species are best seen naturalised under deciduous shrubs or trees in light shade.

***C. autumnale* 'Album'** A form with white tulip-shaped flowers in autumn, to 10 cm tall.

***C. a.* 'Album Plena'** This form has full, double, pure white flowers with slightly raggedly-edged petals and is extremely rare.

C. cilicium This rare species has very narrow pink petals and its foliage is usually well up at flowering.

***C.* 'The Giant'** Large mauve-flowered form with a white centre, to 15 cm tall and 8 cm across.

***C.* 'Waterlily'** An amazing large double mauve form that outlasts all of the single forms in the garden and is also as rare as hens' teeth.

Corydalis diphylla

A dainty little tuber from the Himalayas, to 10 cm tall, with fine ferny grey-green foliage topped in early spring and dainty pinkish-spurred flowers with a dark purple lip. All the species like a cool spot, kept dry in summer.

***C. solida* 'George Baker'** A very choice small tuberous plant from Europe that flowers in late winter. It has grey-green maidenhair-fern-like foliage and spikes of rich pink-spurred flowers up to 10 cm tall.

C. wendelboi This choice little plant, to 8 cm from Turkey, has very fine grey foliage and tiny spurred flowers of pale smoky-blue in early spring.

Crocus banaticus

I sometimes have small stocks of this very rare Crocus. It blooms before its foliage in late summer and has rich blue-mauve flowers that look more like a tiny Iris. It likes some shade, never dry soil, and comes from Romania.

C. goulimyi A soft mauve autumn-flowering species, to 12 cm tall from Greece, that is rare in the wild but not too difficult in the garden.

C. malyi A rare little Balkan species to 10 cm, that has pure white flowers in late winter with prominent yellow stamens.

C. niveus Large pure white to palest mauve autumn-winter flowering species, from Greece, to 15 cm tall.

C. pulchellus Mauve autumn-flowering species from Greece to 10 cm, that flowers well before its leaves come up.

C. serotinus* ssp. *salzmann A strong-growing autumn-flowering Crocus from Spain with quite large clear mauve flowers, to 12 cm tall.

C. tommasinianus Very hardy variety from Dalmatia, to 10 cm, with pale mauve to purple flowers in early spring. The very best and easiest species to naturalise.

Cyclamen balearicum

A very small spring-flowered species from the Balearic Islands. It has nicely marked foliage and tiny white, sweetly scented flowers and, like most of the following, likes good light in winter and some shade in summer so all you need is a couple of acres of woodland or a deciduous shrub!

C. cilicium An elegant and rare species endemic to southern Turkey. Its kidney-shaped leaves usually have some silver markings and its pale pink flowers are produced in late autumn, early winter.

C. coum A tiny winter-flowering species in shades of white, pink and cerise and attractive round leaves often marbled white. This little charmer comes from the mountains of Bulgaria, Turkey and the Lebanon but won't miss its habitat in any Australian garden.

C. cyprium A very rare little autumn species from Cyprus with highly scented white flowers with pink noses and nicely marbled leaves.

C. graecum A rare species from Greece, Turkey and Cyprus with rich pink flowers in autumn and white marbled leaves with a burgundy reverse. This one should be planted deep and in a fairly sunny aspect preferably in amongst rocks.

C. hederifolium The most common but possibly the best garden plant in the genus, to 10 cm tall from Italy to Turkey, with pink or white flowers in autumn followed by rich green foliage marbled white, but different in every plant. This has to be the easiest to grow and the best to naturalise.

C. h* spp. *confusum This fairly newly described form has thicker more succulent glossy leaves usually unmarked and with flowers much like the species but a little later in opening.

C. intaminatum This is one of the tiniest species and comes from western Turkey. It has little round leaves and minute grey-white flowers in autumn. So small that it is only one for the collector!

C. libanoticum A truly beautiful species from the mountains of the Lebanon with large serrated grey-green mottled leaves with a burgundy reverse. Its large soft pink flowers are produced in spring and smell musky – not that it matters much, as they are held close to ground level.

C. mirabile A rare little autumn species with dainty pink flowers from Turkey with marked leaves with a plum reverse.

C. persicum This lovely spring-flowered species from the eastern Mediterranean is the one that the huge Mother's Day Cyclamen were bred from but don't hold this against them. They are dainty little plants to 20 cm with white or soft pink often fragrant flowers and beautifully marbled leaves.

C. purpurascens This species from the mountains of Italy, Yugoslavia and Czechoslovakia is more or less evergreen with deep pink, highly scented flowers mainly in summer. As it doesn't go dormant it needs summer moisture and constant light shade. One of the more difficult species but worth every effort.

C. repandum This dainty and rare species from France to Greece has silver marbled leaves and comparatively large, highly scented magenta flowers in late winter and spring. This one features in my second book.

***C. r.* 'Album'** A stunning white flowered form with the same scent and foliage.

C. r.* spp. *peloponnesiacum A rare form that differs from the species in that it has softer pink flowers and green leaves that are spotted white as if it has been visited by a flock of tiny birds!

Dactylorhiza elata

A lovely European ground Orchid that features in my second book. It grows to about 60 cm tall with spikes of small deep mauve flowers in summer. Grow it in well-drained but moist soil in morning sun.

***D. fuchsii* (Spotted Orchid)** Quite like the above but with paler flowers and brown spots on the leaves.

Dracunculus canariensis

A remarkable and attractive tuber from the Canary Islands, which grows to about 1 metre tall with leaves divided into several leaflets with a mottled stem. The large creamy-white, sweetly scented Arum-like flowers form in spring.

***D. vulgaris* (Dead Horse Lily)** This Mediterranean native grows to 1 metre or more tall and has stunning dissected leaves above its purple spotted white stems. The blooms produced in spring are like large fluted-edged, purple-black Arums with a black spadix and they stink to high heaven for a day or so, but it's worth it!

Eranthis hyemalis (Winter Aconite)

A charming little late winter woodlander from Europe that has bright yellow buttercup flowers surrounded by an Elizabethan ruff of greenery rarely more than 5 cm tall. It likes winter sun and summer shade and will, if happy, lightly self-seed.

Eremurus 'Emmy Ro' (Foxtail Lily)

These stunning plants have a starfish-like tuber just below ground that produces narrow leaves that are more or less dormant as the flowers open in early summer. The flowers are tiny and in tall spikes, in this case 1.2 metres tall, and bright orange. Plant this and the following forms in a well-drained sunny site and keep them dry from flowering time.

E. himalaicus A stunning form from the Himalayas with a rosette of narrow bright green leaves out of which erupts a tall narrow spike of tiny white flowers on stems up to 2 metres tall in late spring.

***E. × isabellinus* 'Cleopatra'** This form grows to 1.2 metres tall and has apricot-orange flowers.

***E. × i.* 'Pinokkio'** This one grows to 1.2 metres and has burnt-orange flowers.

***E.* 'Moneymaker'** This crudely named form grows to 2.2 metres tall and has soft lemon flowers so is a must-have!

***E.* 'Romance'** This 1.5 metre form has, as one would expect, soft pink flowers.

E. stenophyllus* spp. *stenophyllus This species features in my second book and has brilliant yellow flowers on 1.2 metre tall spikes.

Erythronium americanum

A dainty little Trout Lily with purple and green mottled leaves and small yellow flowers with bronze on the outside of the petals. All *Erythroniums* are spring-flowering although this one has a reputation for not flowering at all so there is a challenge for you!

E. californicum A stunning species to 15 cm tall with brown mottled leaves and creamy-white flowers with a slightly yellow centre with orange brown markings.

***E. c.* 'White Beauty'** Very much like the above but a little larger with usually more flowers per stem.

E. citrinum This species from California and Oregon is similar to the above but smaller and, if there is such a thing, a daintier plant. It is at least a rarer plant in Australia.

***E.* 'Citronella'** This lovely hybrid has soft lemon flowers and unspotted mid-green leaves.

***E. densi-canis* 'Charmer' (Dog's tooth Violet)** A lovely European species (the only one) with attractively marbled leaves and stunning mauve flowers with dark purple stamens.

E. helenae This rare species comes from California and like several other species is white with a yellow centre but it has a different poise that is obvious to those in the know.

E. hendersonii A charming Californian species to 15 cm tall with attractively marbled leaves and rich mauve flowers with a purple centre and purple stamens. It is one of my favourites but is, alas, slow to multiply.

***E.* 'Kondo'** This lovely hybrid has plain green leaves that are large and glossy and set off the pale lemon flowers beautifully.

E. multiscapoideum Another lovely white species with heavily marbled leaves that is very similar to many of the above except that it flowers earlier than the other whites, at least in the form that I grow.

E. oregonum Yet another North American white with a yellow centre and attractively marbled leaves. It sounds like so many others but once seen you will want an acre of this one to match the acre of all the others you already have!

E. o.* var. *leucandrum This form has white anthers! (Oh well, there isn't any such thing as a bad one it's just that some are quite similar.)

E. revolutum A showy species to 20 cm tall with large rose-pink flowers and yellow stamens. The foliage is pleasantly mottled. This one doesn't multiply much by bulb division but will self-seed well and is a featured plant in my second book.

E. tuolumnense A dainty bulbous plant from North America with bright green leaves and lemon-yellow nodding flowers on 20 cm stems in early spring. Usually one of the first species to flower and a good multiplier.

Eucomis zambesiaca (Dwarf Pineapple Lily)

A dainty little summer flowered bulb from East Africa with bright green leaves with a wavy edge that lie flat on the ground and spikes of white to greenish-white flowers to 15 cm tall topped with a cluster of small leaves. I regularly have people tell me that they grow better (bigger) ones than me not realising that it is a dwarf form. A sunny spot with some water in summer and it is easy, if slow, to multiply.

Freesia laxa syn. *Lapeirousia laxa, Anomatheca laxa*

A dainty little summer-flowering corm from Mozambique to 10 cm tall. The plant doesn't look all that much like the well-known Freesia which is possibly why it's had so many name changes. These are orange-red with cerise flairs on the lower three petals. Ideal for a sunny rock garden.

F. l.* var. *alba A lovely pure white form of the above.

F. viridis* syn *Anomatheca viridis This tiny little bulb from southern Namibia and western South Africa grows to about 20 cm tall and in spring produces scented green flowers with curled claw-like petals. Hardly showy but it makes me smile and it does well in a sunny rock garden or in a pot that can be held at eye level so you can see it!

Fritillaria acmopetala

A lovely Mediterranean bulb to 60 cm with narrow grey-green leaves and extremely elegant drooping bells of green with brown tips. I also have a dark flowered form that is more brown than green. A spot with ample winter-spring sun and some summer shade during dormancy suits most species.

F. affinis This lovely North American species grows to about 45 cm with bright green leaves in whorls and several green bells per stem that are heavily spotted with deep brown. I also have a form that only grows to 30 cm with rounder petalled bells that are more deep brown than green.

F. agrestis A dainty little species from California to 30 cm or so with smelly greenish-yellow bells that are usually up to five per stem.

F. alfredae* ssp. *glaucoviridis A lovely Turkish species to 30 cm tall with grey-green leaves and narrow-flared bells of a silvery-green. A subtle but elegant species that isn't too difficult.

***F. biflora* (Mission Bells)** This fairly easy North American species has bright green leaves mainly at ground level and grows to about 25 cm tall with up to six flowers per stem so don't believe its species name! The nodding open bells are purple brown with some green shading and are a bit smelly so tell your friends to take a good sniff!

***F. camschatcensis* (Black Sarana or Eskimo Potatoes)** This is the last species to flower and grows to about 40 cm with lots of bright green leaves topped in late October with several almost black and smelly open bells. Sounds a bit ordinary but is a lovely thing as long as you aren't looking for anything showy!

F. carica A dainty little Turkish species to 15 cm, with usually one nodding, soft yellow bell.

F. davisii This is a charming little species from southern Greece with quite large single bells of brown-chequered green on 16-cm stems.

F. eastwoodiae* syn. *F. phaeanthera This is probably a natural hybrid between two North American species, namely *F. micrantha* and *F. recurva*. It grows to about 30 cm tall and has several bells with re-curved petals per stem that are a lovely soft orange-spotted yellow. I have found this one easy so far, so now that I've said this I'll probably lose it!

F. elwesii Another Turkish species that in this case grows to about 30 cm tall and has one to three flowers per stem that have three outer petals that re-curve slightly and are mainly green and the inner three are mainly a dark purple-black. Elegant understatement!

F. grayana A North American species to 25 cm tall is a form of the diverse *F. biflora* but is different enough horticulturally to keep it separate. It has several nodding whitish bells per stem edged broadly with brown. The interior is all brown and it is also a little bit pongy! It is one of the easiest of the American species to grow.

F. latakiensis A lovely Turkish species to 40 cm tall with grey foliage and very narrow slightly flared, deep brown bells, green-stained. Slow to multiply but not too difficult.

***F. meleagris* (Snakes Head Fritillary)** A charming small bulb to 40 cm tall from Europe (including Britain). It produces dark purple nodding bells in early spring with paler chequering. Prefers semi-shade or morning sun and don't allow it to completely dry out. One of the best-known and easiest as well as one of the most beautiful.

F. m.* var. *alba This is a stunning pure white flowered form.

F. messanensis A charming species from northern Africa, Italy and Greece with narrow, sparse leaves and nodding chestnut brown bells with flared ends on 30-cm stems

F. michailovskyi A charming small species from Turkey with stems to 15 cm tall, topped with rich brown bells with bright yellow tips.

F. mutica This is really just another form of *F. affinis* but is different enough to want as a separate selection. It is a solid-looking plant to 45 cm tall with open glossy bells of black and cream checkers.

F. olivieri This small Iranian species grows to 30 cm and has a fairly large drooping bell of soft brown, with green stripes down the centre of each petal.

F. pallidiflora A truly superb species from (the former) Soviet central Asia, which grow to about 45 cm tall with lots of large grey-green leaves topped with several large drooping bells that are pale yellow, spotted inside with red. It seems fairly hardy and likes a sunny-ish site but keep the soil mulched (possibly with gravel) to keep the bulbs cool in summer. Slow to multiply.

F. pontica This one from southern Europe grows to 38 cm and has dainty nodding green bells tipped with bronze.

F. purdyi A rare and beautiful small species from California to 18 cm tall with several bells at the top of the stem that are thick and shiny with white petals heavily spotted with almost black. The leaves are grey-green and clustered at ground level.

F. pyrenaica This Spanish species grows to about 45 cm and usually has one slightly smelly brown chequered bell per stem with a yellowish colour inside.

F. recurva A very rare North American species and one of the gems of the genus. It grows to about 50 cm tall and has drooping bells with flared tips that are a rich orange with some yellow spotting. This is usually classed as difficult in books from the Northern Hemisphere, however, thus far at least, I haven't found it so!

F. stenanthera A very different-looking 'Frit' from Afghanistan, Uzbekistan and northern Iran with open outward-facing, grey-white flowers with obvious deep grey nectaries in late winter. It all looks a lot prettier than it sounds! This one likes it a bit cool and in its homeland grows in the snow melt.

F. stribrnyi This rare little Frit comes from Turkey and Bulgaria and grows to about 25 cm tall with small narrowly bell-shaped green flowers (at least in my form) with a fine purple edge to the petals.

F. thunbergii This dainty species grows to 60 cm and hails from Japan and China. It has several green bells per stem with fine brown veins, chequered brown inside. The leaves above the flowers curl, and are used to hold up the plant so that it is sort of a tiny climber!

F. uva-vulpis A charming little bulb from Iran to 30 cm with nodding bell-shaped flowers, brown in colour with lime-yellow tips. A subtle but easy species.

Galanthus 'Aitkinsii'

A rare spring Snowdrop to 12 cm tall with broad grey leaves and good-sized white flowers with green markings on the inner petals. All the forms I grow are in fact green and white so one may ask why so many? The answer is that they all have subtle differences that are very hard to convey in writing and at least I don't, as yet, have hundreds of forms as some Galanthaphiles have.

***G.* 'Brenda Troyle'** This lovely rare hybrid, probably originating from Ireland, has large flowers of good substance and with rounded petals.

G. × elcatus An early-flowering hybrid between *G. elwesii* and *G. plicatus* with good grey foliage and large green-marked white flowers to 15 cm tall.

G. elwesii A large-growing snowdrop from the Mediterranean area to 30 cm. It has large white, green spotted flowers in late winter and good silver foliage.

G. gracilis This species from Bulgaria, northern Greece, Romania and Turkey has slightly twisted leaves and classical white-green spotted flowers. It blooms in late winter and early spring and grows to 10 cm.

G. ikariae A rare species with broad arching, bright green foliage and good-sized flowers in late winter on 10-cm stems. I find this one slow to multiply.

G. lagodechianus This is a dainty little species with bright green glossy leaves and flowers in late winter. Grows to 12 cm tall and comes from the Caucasus.

***G.* 'Lavinia'** A superb hybrid Snowdrop to 15 cm. It is a double and the central bell has been converted into what looks like a small green, formal double Camellia. Hard to get but worth any price! This one usually sets single flowers in the first year after it is disturbed.

***G.* 'Magnet'** This lovely version has large flowers with big round petals of good substance on long fine arching flower stems that move in the slightest breeze and grows to 15 cm.

***G. nivalis* (English Snowdrop)** A dainty little white-flowering spring bulb, with green markings on the petals. It requires moist semi-shade and grows to about 10 cm. The classic English Snowdrop even though it isn't thought to be truly native to England and probably arrived there with the Romans.

***G. n.* 'Flore-plena'** This form grows in the same way as the species but instead of having a central bell it has a mass of ruffled green and white petals. A ragged but charming little urchin.

***G. n.* 'Scharlockii' Group** A rare variety that differs from the others by having two rabbit-ear-like green bracts behind the flowers. It will cost you a lot for the ears but it's worth it!

***G. n.* 'Viridiapicis'** This very rare form has green markings on the outer three petals as well as on the internal bell. This might not sound like it's much of a difference but Galanthophiles are into minutiae!

***G.* 'Ophelia'** Another of the lovely full double varieties that were bred by Mr Greaterex of Norwich and supposed to be his best double, but I find it hard to see any difference to G. 'Lavinia' – but then, I don't pretend to be a Galanthophile!

G. plicatus A hardy species to 17 cm tall from the Balkans with pleated grey-green leaves and good-sized white, green spotted flowers. I find this one a good doer in my garden.

G. reginae-olgae This very rare species from Greece looks very like the English Snowdrop but flowers in the autumn usually before the leaves start to emerge. Unlike most Snowdrops this one needs a dry summer dormancy and I find it slow to multiply and a little shy-flowering, but what a buzz when you have Snowdrops in autumn.

G. rizehensis A lovely tiny species from Turkey to 8 cm with well-proportioned white flowers above its deep green leaves.

***G.* 'S. Arnott'** This is a vigorous clone with large flowers that have rounded big white petals. Again, to those not in the know it is probably similar to many others, but well thought of to those that are!

Geissorhiza aspera

A tiny little South African bulb with tiny deep lavender-blue flowers in spring on stems to 10 cm tall. Like the following it likes a sunny well-drained site in the front of a border or rock garden. To the uninitiated this genus looks like some sort of Ixia.

G. inaequalis Another dainty little sun-loving bulb from South Africa that in early spring grows to 15 cm tall and has stems of rich mauve Ixia-like flowers. It multiplies well and you could do worse for a sunny rock garden or edge of border.

Gladiolus abbreviatus syn. *Homoglossum abbreviatum*

A strange spring-flowering species from South Africa to 45 cm tall with narrow tubular bronze-tinged red flowers and large coral-red bracts. This is a most un-gladiolus-like plant but pretty and like most other species needs little more than a well-drained sunny site with dry soil in summer to grow well. All the following are South African unless otherwise stated.

G. alatus A showy little Gladiolus to 15 cm tall with bright orange slightly nodding flowers marked with greenish-yellow on the lower petals. The court jester of the genus!

G. angustus This dainty species grows to 45 cm tall and produces cream narrow-petalled flowers with deep red flares on the lower petals.

G. aureus An extremely rare, almost extinct in the wild species from the southern Cape Peninsula. At last count only a handful were found! It flowers in early spring and grows to 30 cm tall with bright yellow flowers with an even shape that makes it look more like an Ixia than a Gladiolus.

G. brevifolius A delicate little autumn flowered species with tiny candy pink flowers on 30 cm stems that open before the leaves come up.

G. carmineus A very attractive small species to 30 cm tall that flowers in autumn before its grey-green leaves. Its large blooms are rich deep pink with white flares on the lower three petals.

G. communis* ssp. *byzantinus A fast-growing tallish species from Spain and Sicily with stems to 90 cm that produce rich magenta flowers with white pencil-line markings on the lower petals in late spring.

G. involutus An unusual-looking spring flowered species to 30 cm or so, with narrow arched petals that are white with yellow and plum markings on the lower three petals.

G. lewisiae This plant grows to 40 cm and has open-faced cream flowers with burgundy central flares on the upper three petals in spring.

G. odoratus A beautiful winter flowered species to 30 cm tall with scented purple flowers with white markings and frilled petals. This one made it into my second book, probably mainly due to the fact that I had a good photo of it! Not that it isn't a good thing, it is!

G. orchidiflorus A dainty sweetly scented species to 20 cm or so that flowers in very early spring. The base colour, cream, is heavily overlayed with brown. The top petal is long and erect and the lower three are yellow marked with bronze or green.

G. palustris This central European species is very like *G. communis* ssp. *byzantinus* and differs in its softer magenta flowers that are smaller and on stems only to 50 cm. It obviously hasn't been taking the drugs!

G. priorii This dainty winter species was once included in the now defunct genus *Homoglossum* and grows to about 50 cm tall. Its flowers have a long curved tube and the whole flower is a strong scarlet with a little yellow in the throat.

G. pritzelii This fine stemmed little gem grows to about 30 cm tall and supports slightly bell-shaped creamy yellow flowers with red-brown internal markings and a lovely scent.

G. quadrangulus A tiny dainty little thing, once thought to be an *Ixia*, that grows to 20 cm and flowers in late winter and early spring. These are rounded-looking (hence the trouble in identification) and the softest of pinks veined with purple

G. stefaniae This rare autumn flowered species grows in the mountains near Montagu in South Africa and gets to 40 cm tall. It has one to three quite large cerise-red flowers per stem marked on the lower petals with white.

G. tenellus This fine dainty species has rush-like leaves, grows to 20 cm tall and has open starry yellow flowers in late winter through to spring

G. uysiae This bizarre little species comes from south-western South Africa. Its flowers are a veined brownish-purple with greenish lower petals. The whole thing looking more like an Orchid than a Gladdie!

Helicodiceros muscivorus syn. *Dracunculus muscivorus* (Dragons Mouth)

A truly bizarre tuberous plant from the Balearic Islands and Corsica and Sardinia that has handsome leaves attached to purple spotted white stems that in turn support flowers that are white with purple spots outside and pinkish with lots of hairs inside and smelling of rancid meat. It is trying to convince blowflies that it is a dead something! If you don't think my description will sell it to you, look it up in my second book.

Hermodactylus tuberosus (Widow Iris)

A strange but beautiful relative of the Iris (that will probably be put back into *Iris* soon if it hasn't already) from Europe, the Middle East and northern Africa that grows to 40 cm tall. Its narrow grey-green leaves come up in winter and its sombre flowers are produced in spring. The falls are rich velvety black and the standards are bronze-green. Although not really showy, it has a sweet perfume and, as many good plants do, it makes an appearance in my second book.

Hesperantha cucullata syn. _H. baurii_
A charming, spring-flowering South African bulb to 30 cm tall for the sunny well-drained rock garden or border. The lovely Freesia-like white flowers have deep pink on the back of the petals and close during the day to open again at night. You will find a picture under its synonym in my second book.

Ipheion 'Rolf Fiedler' (Spring Star Flower)
A lovely unusual form of the very common Star Flower that has its late winter, early spring flowers that are a clearer shade of sky blue. It comes from South America and grows well almost anywhere and to about 5 inches tall.

Iris cristata (Crested Iris)
A tiny little woodlander from the U.S.A. with surface-dwelling, creeping rhizomes. It flowers in midspring and these are a good mid-mauve-blue marked white on 8-cm stems. An easy plant that will make good colonies but watch out for slugs and snails.

I. histrioides 'Major' A lovely bulbous dwarf iris to 15 cm tall from Turkey with large rich dark purple-blue flowers in late winter with white and yellow markings on the falls. Keep dry in summer.

_I._ 'Katharine Hodgkin' A lovely hybrid dwarf bulb to 15 cm with surprisingly large flowers in late winter. It has cream falls with a yellow blaze, spotted and streaked throughout with purple. The standards are white with fine purple veins. Almost impossible to visualise so needs to be seen to be believed!

I. reticulata 'Cantab' A dainty little pale blue bulbous Iris with small yellow blotches on the falls that all up struggles to top 15 cm. All the reticulated forms like a sunny aspect and kept dry in summer.

_I. r._ 'Harmony' Similar to the above but with slightly larger royal blue flowers marked with yellow on the falls.

_I. r._ 'J. S. Dijt' This form also has very deep blue flowers with yellow on the falls.

_I. r._ 'Pauline' This form has flowers of darkest royal purple with white and yellow on the falls.

Ixia flexuosa
A dainty little corm that, like all species, likes an open, sunny, well-drained aspect and comes from South Africa. This one grows to about 30 cm and has soft mauve, slightly nodding flowers in spring.

I. latifolia This one will multiply with speed into very satisfying drifts. In the case of this species it has soft clear mauve flowers on 20 cm stems in spring.

I. paniculata A striking apricot to cream form to 60 cm with tubular flowers clustered at the top of the stem. This one featured in my second book.

I. rouxii A dainty little plant to 25 cm that, in spring, has starry white flowers with a black centre. Its fine foliage usually curls at the tips.

Ledebouria cooperi
A quaint little eastern African bulb to 10 cm tall with clusters of tiny deep pink flowers in spring just as the leaves are coming up. The leaves stay up till autumn and are very attractive as they are bright green with parallel dark brown stripes. As a summer grower it will need some water whilst actively growing.

Lilium candidum (Madonna Lily)
A tall, late spring flowered *Lilium*, that comes from Greece and the Lebanon, with large white, highly scented flared flowers on 1.5 to 2-metre stems. It produces a rosette of foliage at ground level in autumn so has a very short dormancy and this is why it is rarely offered for sale as it can't be sold by mail in a dormant state as other species can. Unlike most, this species likes a sunny site and does well in an alkaline soil.

L. lancifolium var. _flaviflorum_ (Yellow Tiger Lily) This beautiful form has daffodil-yellow flared flowers that are spotted black on dark stems that can reach 2 metres or more tall. It produces lots of black bulblets up these stems that are useful in creating more plants.

L. martagon A stunning species to 1 metre tall with whorls of leaves up the stems that are topped with several mauve-pink flowers in the classic Turk's-cap-style in summer. This species has a huge range from France to Siberia.

L. m.* var. *album The rarely seen and truly desirable white form.

L. wardii A very rare species from China, to 1.5 metres tall. It is stoloniferous and produces its perfumed, nodding Turk's-cap flowers in summer. The colour is a soft plum-pink with darker spots. This one found its way into my second book.

Merendera montana

A dainty little autumn flowered bulb from Spain that looks like a tiny Colchicum. It differs in having narrow petals that aren't joined into a tube. They are soft mauve-pink and they bloom before the leaves. Grows to 8 cm tall in bloom and likes a sunny spot and if you can stop it raining whilst it flowers it could be a good idea as this tends to flatten the flowers!

Moraea tripetala

A lovely lavender-blue, Iris-like plant to 40 cm tall with spoon-shaped petals marked white towards the centre. Like many other South African bulbs this one likes a sunny well-drained site that is dry in summer.

Muscari armeniacum 'Argaei Album'

A lovely pure white form of the traditional blue grape hyacinth that will stain blue as the flowers finish. Slightly smaller plant, and not quite so prolific as its coloured form.

Narcissus 'Angel's Breath'

A lovely dwarf *N. triandrus* hybrid raised in Tasmania. It has three blooms per stem and grows to 15 cm tall. The flowers have cup-shaped trumpets with reflexed petals, are lemon-yellow throughout and sweetly scented.

N. assoanus* syn. *N. requienii A charming tiny Jonquil from France and Spain with fine reedy foliage and heads of short trumpet golden-yellow flowers on 10-cm stems with a strong perfume. It likes a sunny aspect like most daffodils and multiplies well.

N. asturiensis A tiny little spring flowered trumpet daffodil from Spain and Portugal. It only grows to 6 cm or so tall and the flower stems grow on an angle. The colour is clear yellow throughout.

***N.* 'Barlow'** An American hybrid of *N. cyclamineus*. Bright yellow throughout, with a long trumpet and well-reflexed petals. This is a good doer retaining some of the grace of its famous parent and grows to 20 cm tall.

N. bulbicodium* var. *graellsii This lovely Hoop Petticoat daffodil from Spain grows to about 12 cm with quite good-sized flowers of lemon in early spring.

N. b.* var. *tenuifolius Bright yellow flowers in early spring to 10 cm tall. This form has an all round daintier and smaller look than classic forms of Hoop Petticoat Daffodils.

***N.* 'Candlepower'** This is a truly stunning tiny trumpet daffodil to 10 cm tall that starts off pale lemon and fades to pure white. Every one loves this and will fortunately pay almost any amount to get one!

N. cantabricus A creamy-white, late autumn to winter flowering form of Hoop Petticoat daffodil from Morocco and Algeria. It likes a sunny site that is quite dry in summer and will grow to 15 cm.

N. cyclamineus A very choice little species for woodland conditions that hails from Portugal and Spain where it was thought to be extinct for some time and grows in damp meadows and beside streams. It grows to 15 cm tall with bright yellow flowers with a long trumpet and fully-reflexed petals like donkeys' ears. This one featured in my second book.

***N.* 'Eye Spy'** This is a lovely pure white Hoop Petticoat daffodil with flattish trumpets that are formed from early winter. This hybrid was produced at Glenbrook Bulb Farm in Tasmania, the source of many good dwarfs, including the owner!

***N.* 'Fenben'** A lovely little Jonquil with usually 3 flowers per stem although it can have more. This scented charmer is another great hybrid from Rod Barwick at Glenbrook Bulb Farm in Tasmania.

N. fernandesii A dwarf Jonquilla-type with fine grassy leaves and small bright yellow scented blooms, normally two to a stem. It comes from Portugal and Spain and grows to about 20 cm.

N. 'Flomay' A charming little white flowered Jonquilla-type daffodil with a short cup and a lovely scent. It will grow to 15 cm tall and was bred in England in 1946.

N. 'Fyno' A Tasmanian raising Hoop Petticoat daffodil with lovely white flowers from late autumn through winter. It grows to about 15 cm tall and is a good multiplier.

N. 'Glenbrook Ta-Julia' A lovely Tasmanian-raised hybrid winter-flowering Hoop Petticoat with widely flared lemon flowers on short stems to 10 cm tall.

N. 'Hawera' A dainty little hybrid of *Narcissus triandrus* raised in New Zealand in 1938 with drooping pale yellow flowers generally produced in pairs on stems to about 20 cm tall in spring.

N. hedraeanthus A diminutive species of trumpet daffodil from Spain with tiny pale yellow flowers on stems that actually lie flat on the ground at a convenient height for slugs and snails. Probably only a collector's piece although clients often coo over it as they would over a puppy!

N. jonquilla A dainty little spring flowered species from Spain and Portugal to 20 cm tall with three or so tiny, bright yellow, sweetly scented flowers per stem.

N. 'Kholmes' This Tasmanian-raised hybrid Hoop Petticoat has creamy-yellow flowers and is a good doer.

N. 'Nylon' A lovely creamy-white, winter-flowering Hoop Petticoat-type to 12 cm, bred in England in 1949. A good doer and fairly reliable flowerer.

N. obesus A form of Hoop Petticoat daffodil that is often listed as a *N. bulbocodium* form and may well end up there. It has extra large golden yellow flowers on 12-cm stems in high spring.

***N. odorus* var. *rugulosus* (Campernelle)** A tall-growing species with golden-yellow, short trumpeted flowers, usually three or four to a stem. It grows to over 60 cm tall and is highly scented. It is a good species for naturalising in rough grass.

N. romieuxii One of the loveliest winter flowered hoop petticoat Daffodils with widely flared soft lemon-yellow flowers. It comes from northern Africa and grows to 10 cm tall.

N. r.* ssp.*albidus* var. *zaianicus A lovely Hoop Petticoat from the Zaian Mountains (look them up for yourself!) with soft palest of yellow flowers in winter, on stems to 10 cm tall. It is a shame that the name will probably put most people off; I know I hate writing out the labels.

***N. r.* 'Julia Jane'** An exceedingly rare form with almost flat trumpets of soft lemon with a fluted edge. I usually only have a couple for sale each year as it is very slow to multiply so will charge appropriately.

N. r.* ssp. *mesatlanticus Yet another lovely form with soft yellow flowers and a name one hates to put on labels!

N. viridiflorus A bizarre autumn flowered species from Spain and Morocco with one or two tiny highly scented dull green flowers per stem to 15 cm tall. Not overly showy but a fascinating collector's item.

Nectaroscordum siculum

A lovely summer flowered bulb once included in the Onions with tall stems to 1 metre or so with tall and floppy leaves that are often almost gone by blooming time. It has a cluster of drooping green and dusty-pink bells at the tip. It comes from Europe and likes a sunny well-drained aspect and looks good erupting up through shorter plants. It also makes a fabulous cut flower if you can bear to pick it.

Nerine filifolia (Grass Leafed Nerine)

A dwarf autumn-flowering South African bulb to 20 cm with grassy leaves and narrow, crinkled bright pink flowers. For a sunny aspect.

N. masoniorum Probably the smallest *Nerine* species only growing to about 15 cm tall, with small heads of pale pink crinkle-petalled flowers are produced in early autumn.

N. pudica A very rare species to 20 cm, with more funnel-like flowers than is normal to this genus, that are pure white with a fine pink line down the centre outside of each petal.

***N. sarniensis* forma *fothergillii* (Gold Dust Nerine)** This well-known species is usually sold as *N. fothergilli* 'Major' but the new name should be applied I guess! It flowers in early autumn and has 30-cm-tall flower stems with brilliant scarlet flowers that seem to glisten with gold dust in the light. Easy in sun or light shade and like most of the larger species likes to build up into tight clumps to flower well.

Notholirion thomsonianum

A lovely bulb from the western Himalayas, to 1 metre tall. It is related to the Liliums but differs mainly in its monocarpic bulbs (they flower once and die but produce ample baby bulbs). It flowers in spring and has up to 15 or more pale pink scented trumpet-shaped flowers. A sunny well-drained site with humus-enriched soil is best. This will be found in my second book.

Ornithogalum nutans

A late winter, early spring-flowering bulb from Greece and Turkey to 20 cm tall with spikes of nodding icy-green flowers that are good for picking.

O. sigmoideum A charming little South African bulb with a rosette of fine grey foliage that sits almost flat. Its flowers are green and white and sit like a little posy in the centre of the leaves in late winter. Hardy and sun loving.

Oxalis bowiei

One of my largest species growing to 25 cm tall, with very large, bright green clover-shaped leaves and big bright pink flowers in late autumn and early winter. It, like all the following, hails from South Africa (unless specified). All the cool-season species I grow like a sunny spot, and aren't pernicious weeds but stunning garden flowers and are happy with completely dry summer conditions. Most have a 2 to 3-month flowering period, which is better than most bulbs.

O. depressa* syn. *O. inops A charming summer growing plant with three-leafed clover leaves and small soft mauve flowers in summer. This one will make small drifts in time and rarely exceeds 5 cm in height.

O. fabifolia* syn *O. namaquana A lovely autumn flowered species with huge primrose-yellow flowers and grey-green foliage with two leaflets like a pair of donkey's ears to 8 cm tall.

O. flava A very handsome yellow flowered species with red edges to the outside of the petals so that when closed they look like strange-coloured barber's poles. It has light green palmate foliage that grows to 8 cm tall. I also have this species in several forms that all look different and I can't find varietal names for and, in fact, some may well turn out to be different species altogether. They include a white-flowered form with red outside edges and long narrow leaflets, a similar form with lavender pink flowers, and one with almost thick succulent browny-green leaves with yellow flowers without different-coloured edges.

O. furcillata A dainty little species with leafy stems up to 8 cm tall. The leaves have three narrowish leaflets, and it has pure white flowers in late winter, spotted and streaked with dark purple on the backs of the petals.

O. glabra A lovely winter flowered species with fine-notched leaflets and bright cerise flowers with a yellow centre. It grows to 10 cm tall and makes goodly patches in time.

O. hirta A well-known clumping bulb with masses of mauve flowers in autumn and early winter on 15-cm stems. The leaves consist of three narrow sessile leaflets. All the forms of this species have attractive colour in the foliage as it dies down in midspring.

***O. h.* 'Compacta'** A dwarf form to 8 cm with good-sized deep cerise pink flowers.

***O. h.* 'Salmon Form'** A lovely salmon-pink flowered form that flowers rather later than the other forms and has narrower leaflets.

***O. h.* 'Rosea'** A deep cerise pink flowered form.

O. lobata A tiny Chilean species with clover-shaped leaves to 6 cm tall and bright golden flowers in autumn. This is usually the first cool weather species to flower for me, and the first flowers usually come up before the leaves.

O. massoniana A charming slightly trailing Oxalis that makes neat clumps, to 7 cm tall. It produces masses of apricot-orange flowers with yellow centres in autumn and early winter. The Oxalis even all Oxalis-haters will love!

O. melanosticta A ground-hugging slightly spreading species to 3 cm tall with soft, furry grey clover-shaped leaves and bright yellow flowers in autumn.

O. obtusa A beautiful ground-hugging species to 3 cm tall with tiny grey leaves and surprisingly large salmon-pink flowers with a yellow centre in late winter and early spring.

***O. obtusa* M. V. 7087** This selection that I grow under its collector's number has green instead of grey leaves, and its flowers are a more apricot-pink.

O. palmifrons A stunning foliage plant to 3 cm with ground hugging rosettes of grey hand-shaped leaves. It has large, pale lavender flowers but is a bit shy to bloom, especially in pots. This shouldn't deter you from planting it, as its leaves are more than enough reason to have it.

O. polyphylla This is a most un-oxalis-like plant with stems up to 10 cm tall supporting fine bright green pine-needle-like foliage. It gives the game away when it produces its classic mauve flowers in autumn.

O. p.* var. *heptaphylla This lovely form has narrow almost ground hugging foliage and soft pink flowers edged on the back of the petals with burgundy. A stunner!

O. tetraphylla* syn. *O. deppei A summer-growing species from Mexico to 20 cm tall with large Four-Leafed Clover leaves with bronze V-shaped bands one-third of the way from the centre. The deep salmon-pink flowers produced all summer are produced in clusters at the top of the flower stem.

***O. t.* 'Iron Cross'** In this form the flowers and size of the plant haven't changed but the leaves have the inner third completely burgundy. A great foliage form.

O. triangularis This Brazilian summer-growing species to 15 cm has flowers that are soft pink and its leaves are like giant clover with very triangular leaflets that are deep plum, centrally marked with mauve. A knockout! This and the following are fairly shade-loving and, as summer growers, will obviously need a little watering.

O. t.* ssp. *papillionacea* syn *O. regnellii A rare summer-growing and flowering species from Argentina, Brazil and Peru with pure white flowers up to 15 cm tall, from December to April, just clear of its large, bright green leaves that consist of three triangular leaflets.

O. truncatula This lovely species 5 cm tall produces large deep mauve flowers in autumn just as its leaves are coming up. The foliage is grey and furry to start with, and later large, green and clover-shaped.

***O. versicolor* (Barbers Pole Oxalis)** A lovely late winter, early spring-flowering form to 6 cm that has white flowers when open, and pink and white striped buds. A real must for the rock garden.

O. zeekoevleyensis This cute little species with a seriously difficult name has small clover-shaped leaves to 6 cm and soft mauve-pink flowers in early winter.

Pancratium maritimum

A bulb with grey-green upright leaves to 30 cm and clusters of highly perfumed white flowers in summer that look a little like frilled Daffodils. It likes a very sunny well-drained site and grows naturally in southern Europe along the Mediterranean.

Pinellia cordata

A charming shade-loving, summer-growing arum relative from Japan, with spearhead-shaped leaves that sit almost on the ground and are dark green with cream marbling, almost like a Cyclamen, the underside is burgundy. It produces little bulbils where the leaf joins the stem. The flowers, which are sweetly scented, are small and green veined with purple and the spadix is curved and sticks out like a snake's tongue.

P. pedatisecta This species is an altogether bigger thing from China with bright green divided leaves to 30 cm tall throughout summer, amongst which erupt its narrow green spathes encircling its erect spadixes. Like the following species this gives a good effect in the ground or as a pot specimen.

P. tripartita Similar to the above, from southern Japan but with broader wavy-edged leaflets of bright green, and more flared spathes with long sinuous spadixes. This one also grows to 30 cm and will quickly build into a good clump.

***P. t.* 'Purple Face' syn. *P. t.* 'Atropurpurea'** This form has spathes that are rich dark purple inside and green outside.

Puschkinia scilloides

A dainty little woodland bulb to 8 cm tall from the Middle East. White scilla-like flowers are banded with blue down the centre of each petal. Watch out for slugs and snails with this plant, as they love it, but so will you!

Ranunculus ficaria 'Brambling' (Lesser Celandine)

A lovely little tuber with spearhead-shaped leaves of chocolate-brown marbled with silver during winter and early spring in mounds to 8 cm tall. This is a lovely foil for its bright yellow buttercups. All the forms like plenty of winter moisture and light, with some summer shade, and don't mind drying out.

***R. f.* 'Brazen Hussy'** A lovely form discovered by Christopher Lloyd in a Sussex wood. It comes up with ground-hugging brown-black foliage in late winter and the usual golden-yellow buttercup flowers that together really make it live up to its name. This one featured in my second book.

R. f. 'Cupreus' This form has glossy apricot-orange flowers and green leaves that are marbled with silver and have a brown central stripe. It all sounds rather hectic but it works well.

R. f. flore-pleno This form has rich slightly marbled green leaves and full double glossy yellow flowers.

Romulea atrandra

These are lovely sun-loving, mainly South African corms that all have fine, tough, reedy leaves that in this case grow to about 8 cm tall with good-sized, rich pink Crocus-like flowers in late winter. All like a sunny well-drained site dry in summer.

R. citrina This species grows to 8 cm tall and has golden-yellow Crocus-like flowers in early spring.

R. clusiana A charming dwarf corm to 5 cm tall with quite large soft mauve Crocus-like flowers in spring.

R. columnae* ssp. *grandiscapa A Mediterranean species to 6 cm tall with lovely, deep mauve Crocus-like blooms in early spring.

R. hirta This species to 8 cm has soft yellow flowers, with brown markings where the petals separate, and a richer yellow throat.

R. montana A very large yellow flowered species that rarely exceeds 5 cm, with dark streaks in the throat.

R. sabulosa A truly spectacular species to 15 cm tall, with huge satiny red flowers with almost black central blotches edged in yellow.

R. tetragona A lovely small species to 6 cm, with unusually veined and slightly furry leaves and chubby little brilliant pink flowers with a dark centre.

Roscoea cautleoides

A strangely beautiful ginger relative from China, with yellow or purple orchid-like flowers that erupt from its pleated leaves in summer, and grows to 15 cm or so. Light shade and summer moisture is needed for all species in this desirable genus.

R. humeana This stocky large-flowered species from China to 20 cm has rich mauve flowers with a large lower petal, and the whole looking as if it was made of crushed silk.

R. purpurea A strong-growing species, to 30 cm or more tall from Nepal and northern India, with rich deep mauve to purple flowers.

Sauromattum venosum (Voodoo Lily)
A strange Aroid from northern India and Tibet, it flowers in spring before its leaves come up. It has a long buff-coloured spathe like an un-ironed tie covered in purple liver spots (perhaps gravy stains!). The spadix is bronze-coloured and the whole flower smells like rotting meat. Once that is over, it sends up stunning palmately lobed leaves up to 45 cm across on 60 cm brown spotted stems. It likes a semi-shaded site and makes a good garden plant or pot specimen. (Just don't take it indoors whilst in flower!)

Scilla autumnalis
A tiny, dainty little bulb from Turkey all the way to England. It produces spikes of tiny blue flowers in late summer and autumn even before its leaves start. So small, it isn't very showy but its flowering time makes it a useful addition to the rock garden or a pot. Wants a sunny, well-drained site.

S. bifolia A dainty little spring-flowering bulb to 8 cm with showy, blue, star flowers. It comes from the mountains of Asia Minor and Europe and would be a good addition to the rock garden or semi-shaded spots under shrubs.

***S. b.* 'Alba'** A lovely, pure white form of the above.

S. bithynica This lovely little bulb from Bulgaria and north-west Turkey grows to 8 cm tall, has brilliant blue star flowers in spring and will self-seed with gay abandon, so will be good to naturalise in sun or semi-shade.

S. greilhuberi A lovely Middle Eastern Bluebell to 15 cm tall. Its flowers are rich blue and are outward-facing open cups with reflexing petals.

S. litardierei A lovely Slavic species to 20 cm tall with starry blue flowers in spring, and long leaves that tend to lie along the ground.

S. melaina This charming species is similar to *S. siberica* but is slightly taller and a softer blue. The snails don't seem as keen on it, but you should be!

S. mischtschenkoana* syn. *S. tubergeniana This Bluebell with the unpronounceable name comes from northern Iran and the Caucasus and has quite large palest-of-blue star flowers with a deeper blue stripe down each petal. The flowers are slightly scented, but as it only grows to 6 cm you may not be able to get down low enough to check this out! Semi-shade in a pot or front of a rock garden will suit, but watch out for snails.

S. monophyllos A tiny little bulb to 6 cm from Spain and northern Africa. Each bulb produces only one leaf and a spike of tiny, soft, lavender blue flowers in early spring.

S. morrisii This Cyprian species was only described in 1975 and it grows to 15 cm with bell-shaped, pale pinkish-mauve flowers in spring.

S. siberica A stunning spring flowered bulb to 13 cm tall with rich, brilliant blue, nodding bell-shaped flowers. Loved by gardeners as well as slugs and snails. Somewhat slow to multiply and preferring a semi-shaded site.

S. verna A dainty little European species with tiny blue stars in small rounded heads, in high spring after many other species are finished, so it isn't splashy but is a good plant in a semi-shaded rock garden or in a pot on an outdoor table where you can appreciate it without bending low.

Serapia lingua
A dainty little Mediterranean ground orchid to 30 cm tall with spikes of one-lipped flowers that can be dusty light purple or buff-coloured. It flowers in spring and is easy to grow as long as you keep it away from slugs and snails.

Tecophilaea cyanocrocus (Chilean Blue Crocus)
An extremely rare bulb long thought to be extinct in the wild although it has recently been re-discovered. It is spring-flowering and grows to about 6 cm tall with the most intense blue Crocus-like flowers you will ever see. I only ever have a couple to sell each year, so expect to be disappointed. *Tecophilaea* likes good light but not hot sun and a cool not dead dry dormancy.

T. c.* var. *leichtlinii This equally rare form has brilliant sky-blue flowers with a white centre and is just as desirable and expensive, so you have been warned.
T. c.* var. *violacea As for the above in everything except that the flowers are rich purple. It's just as rare and beautiful but I have to say the blue forms sell faster.
T. violiflora This species, also from Chile, is the only other species in the genus so I have them all now. This one has very small purple flowers at least I think so as it can be lilac or white in the wild and at the time of writing this manual I haven't flowered it.

Tulipa clusiana (Ladies Tulip)

An elegant small tulip to 20 cm tall with fine grey leaves and narrow buds that are white with a broad pink band up the outside. When it opens it is pure white inside with a small purple centre and dark purple stamens. One of the loveliest, and naturally in my second book. A sunny site suits most wild tulips and, if happy, they can be left to naturalise.
T. cretica This tiny little Cretan species, to 10 cm, with small soft pink to almost white flowers.
T. greigii A very striking Tulip to 18 cm tall with large grey-green leaves, heavily blotched and streaked with purple. Its huge wide-cupped flowers are on short stems and brilliant red.
T. humilis A stunning little thing to 15 cm tall, with grey leaves and in my form rich red flowers with a tiny dark centre. This one and its forms come from the Middle East and adjacent parts of Russia.
T. h.* var. *pulchella Just like the above but with deep purple flowers.
T. kurdica This dainty little thing from Iraq has lovely little red flowers with a greenish-black central blotch on stems to 15 cm tall.
T. linifolia A beautiful little Tulip to 10 cm tall with grey foliage and dainty, brilliant red flowers with dark purple eye. Native to Soviet Central Asia.
***T. l.* Batalinii Group** A charming dwarf Tulip to 15 cm tall with soft apricot-yellow flowers almost triangular in bud and grey foliage.
***T. l.* Batalinii Group 'Red Jewel'** A lovely red form with a serious name problem.
T. neustruevae A tiny little Tulip to 5 cm tall with brilliant yellow starry flowers with a green back to the petals. Native to (the former) Soviet central Asia.
T. saxatilis A quick-growing species Tulip from Crete that will drift around in any sunny site due to the stolons it produces in quantity. It has large pinkish-mauve flowers, which have a yellow centre, with usually several to each 25-cm-tall stem, my record is 12!
***T. s.* Bakeri Group 'Lilac Wonder'** Something of a confused name for what is a slightly smaller, heavy blooming form that doesn't run around as *T. saxatilis* does.
T. vvedenskyi A species from (the former) Soviet central Asia, to 12 cm tall with wavy-edged leaves and comparatively large orange-red flowers with a small yellow centre.

Urginea maritima (Sea Squill)

A tall bulb from the Mediterranean, with huge bulbs that sit with their necks well out of the ground. It has large grey-green leaves in winter and sends up from the dormant bulbs metre-tall spikes of tiny white flowers in summer. These flowers look very like *Eremurus* (Foxtail Lily), but this bulb is much easier to grow, requiring nothing more than a sunny site. This plant features in my second book.

Wachendorfia panicula

A charming South African plant to 60 cm tall with bright red tubers, attractive pleated leaves through winter, and open panicles of apricot-yellow flowers with a dark brown basal blotch in spring. A sunny well-drained site suits best.